The Journey of Our Love

The Letters of
Saint Gianna Beretta and Pietro Molla

Edited by Elio Guerriero

auline
BOOKS & MEDIA

Boston

Library of Congress Cataloging-in-Publication Data

Beretta Molla, Gianna, Saint, 1922-1962.
  [Lettere. English]
  The journey of our love : the letters of Saint Gianna Beretta and Pietro Molla / Gianna
Beretta and Pietro Molla ; edited by Elio Guerriero.
       pages cm
  ISBN 978-0-8198-4565-8 -- ISBN 0-8198-4565-5
   1. Beretta Molla, Gianna, Saint, 1922-1962--Correspondence. 2. Christian saints--Italy-
-Correspondence. 3. Molla, Pietro, 1912---Correspondence. I. Molla, Pietro, 1912- II.
Guerriero, Elio, editor of compilation. III. Title.
  BX4700.B42A4 2014
  282.092--dc23
  [B]
                          2013029412

Originally published by Edizioni San Paolo Milan in Italian as *Lettere: A cura di Elio Guerriero* copyright © by Edizioni San Paolo s.r.l.—Cinisello Balsamo (MI). Editor: Elio Guerriero. Authors: Gianna Beretta Molla and Pietro Molla.

Translated by Ann Brown

Many manufacturers and sellers distinguish their products through the use of trademarks. Any trademarked designations that appear in this book are used in good faith but are not authorized by, associated with, or sponsored by the trademark owners.

Unless otherwise noted the scripture quotations contained herein are from the *New Revised Standard Version Bible: Catholic Edition,* copyright © 1989, 1993, Division of Christian Education of the National Council of the Churches of Christ in the United States of America. Used by permission. All rights reserved.

Excerpts from the Encyclical Letter of the Supreme Pontiff Benedict XVI *Charity in Truth, Caritas in Veritate* copyright © 2009 by Libreria Editrice Vaticana. All rights reserved. Used with permission.

Cover design by Rosana Usselmann

Cover photo: Archives of Pietro Molla

Photos: Archives of Pietro Molla

Published by Pauline Books & Media, 50 Saint Pauls Avenue, Boston, MA 02130-3491

Printed in the U.S.A.

www.pauline.org

Pauline Books & Media is the publishing house of the Daughters of St. Paul, an international congregation of women religious serving the Church with the communications media.

2 3 4 5 6 7 8 9   22 21 20 19 18

Contents

Presentation

By Cardinal Angelo Scola

The letters exchanged between Saint Gianna and her husband, Pietro Molla, stand as evidence of a family life developed with original spiritual intensity in the fertile soil of the Ambrosian Church.[1] Since childhood the future spouses had participated in Catholic Action. Between the two wars, while they were still relatively young, they had been members of FUCI, the Italian Catholic Federation of University Students. In the postwar reconstruction years, this group remained a guiding light to both of them. The members were involved in politics as leaders in the Catholic party, and as such they helped lead their homeland into a new future.

Around the time Gianna and Pietro got to know each other and then married in 1955, Giovanni Battista Montini was appointed the new archbishop of Milan. Once he arrived in Milan, Montini, a pastor with great diplomatic and political experience, energetically began his episcopal ministry in the large diocese. He preached on

---

1. This is a reference to the Ambrosian or Milanese Rite of the Catholic Church, so named for Saint Ambrose, fourth-century archbishop of Milan. — Ed.

feast days, promoted liturgical education, and cared for Catholic associations. Very quickly, however, he saw how the developing industrial situation eluded these concerns. He launched the famous "Milan Mission," a renewed effort to proclaim the Christian message—something that today we would call an effort to bring the new evangelization to the workplace. In the following years, as a new pope was elected and the start of the Second Vatican Council was announced, he tried to prepare his diocese adequately for this great ecclesial event.

Gianna and Pietro responded enthusiastically to the pleas of their archbishop. Saint Gianna, a pediatrician by profession, put into practice the charity she had been taught in her family and had learned through her active participation in the life of the Church. Mr. Molla, an engineer, was already an industrial manager by the time the new archbishop arrived, and at the time of his marriage was a competent leader in technological advancements. His deep concern for charity and justice caused Pietro to seek ways to create new jobs to replace those lost to the accelerated methods of production. With conviction both husband and wife participated in the life of the Church, especially in the liturgy. Gianna was also committed to Catholic Action as the president of the women. From this foundation both of them practiced great charity. A testimony to this was their friendship with Father Olinto Marella, whom the prominent journalist Montanelli called the "vagrant priest." Father Marella would come to Magenta from Bologna, in an old truck, to pick up from Pietro's factory anything that could be useful for his orphanages. Another testimony is the family life revealed by these letters. One can sense their great love for one another, their limitless dedication to their children, and, as the basis for all this, an intense prayer life.

The letters of Gianna and of her husband were published in the year marking the fiftieth anniversary of her death and of the opening of Vatican II. The link between the two events comes from the fact that the Council called by John XXIII and finished by Paul VI favored a new vision of relations between men and women and of marriage in Christ, of which there is an anticipatory trace in these letters. That same year, the Seventh World Meeting of Families took place in Milan. Its theme of "Family Work and Celebration" is another reason to read these letters and to imbibe their spirit. This collection is a precious witness of the strength-giving power of that human fullness which can thrive in a marriage lived through faith.

ANGELO CARDINAL SCOLA
Archbishop of Milan

Foreword

By Cardinal Angelo Comastri

The ancient people of the covenant were used to being called "espoused," "virgin," "my bride," "my joy." This unique people knew well the vocabulary of the love of God who often spoke of himself as the "bridegroom" and had solemnly declared:

> And I will take you for my wife forever; I will take you for my wife in righteousness and in justice, in steadfast love, and in mercy. (Hos 2:19)

> Do not fear, for you will not be ashamed. . . .
> For your Maker is your husband,
> the LORD of hosts is his name;
> the Holy One of Israel is your Redeemer,
> the God of the whole earth he is called. (Is 54:4–5)

> For as a young man marries a young woman,
> so shall your builder marry you,
> and as the bridegroom rejoices over the bride,
> so shall your God rejoice over you. (Is 62:5)

The people of the covenant knew this language that had been continually used by the prophets to describe the relationship between God and Israel. However, in the case of a love poem like the Song of Songs, this people found it difficult to recognize an incarnation of the word of God: the difficulty in accepting this book is an important lesson to us and a great motive for reflection.

Here are the facts. In the year A.D. 90, when Palestine was occupied by Roman forces, the Jews gathered at Jamnia on the Mediterranean coast. Being unable to reconstruct the holy city, they took refuge in the word of God and proceeded to gather together the canon of the Bible, establishing the books in which the word of God itself was manifested.

There was some perplexity regarding the Song of Songs, because the language of this book seemed so carnal and sensual that it offended the ears of some pious Israelites. Then Rabbi Akiba, a great rabbinic teacher, presented the most beautiful defense of the Song of Songs: "No one in Israel ever doubted that the Song of Songs could dirty his hands. No one has ever thought about this. The whole world is worth less than the day the Song was given to the People of Israel. All the Bible's books are holy, but the Song is the Holy of Holies." And because of this passionate defense by Rabbi Akiba, the Song of Songs was placed in the Hebrew canon.

A nuptial song or a mystical song? Certainly the Song of Songs draws from the nuptial songs of the week-long weddings in Palestine, but none of this should cause any difficulty, because the word of God is truly incarnate in human history. Certainly the Song of Songs maintains the language of human love, which is looked upon with wonder and awe, much like the Creator who, when he created the first human couple, "saw" them with wonder and awe:

> Then God said, "Let us make humankind in our image,
> according to our likeness . . ."
> So God created humankind in his image,
> in the image of God he created them;
> male and female he created them.

God saw everything that he had made, and indeed,
it was very good. (Gn 1:26, 27, 31)

Certainly the Song of Songs cannot be read through the prism
of the logical Western mentality. It is a love letter. It is the highest
poetry, a free explosion of the noblest feelings that are understand-
able only in the "senseless logic" of those in love. All this is true,
beautiful, and human. But the question still remains: is the Song of
Songs a human love poem or a mystical poem?

The answer is simple: the Song of Songs is a canticle of two
people in love, a song which God makes his own in order to reveal
his love for humanity.

Thus, in every true love song of engaged or married couples one
can catch a glimpse of God's Love Song, and this glimpse leaves the
seer fascinated.

This is the experience one has on reading the letters of Gianna
and Pietro, which are a golden thread of beautiful, pure, and authentic thoughts and feelings. These letters can relight the yearnings and
hopes of our hearts to see reflowering in the world a time of love
worthy of the name.

Saint Gianna, wife and mother, intercede that this dream might
become a reality. And to this prayer, may the prayers of your beloved
Pietro be joined.

ANGELO CARDINAL COMASTRI
Archpriest of the Papal Basilica of Saint Peter (the Vatican)

Preface to My Wife's Letters

By Pietro Molla[1]

The letters that Gianna wrote to me during our engagement were beautiful waves bearing enthusiasm and joy, of tenderness and love, a stirring and providential invitation to enjoy the beauty of life and the wonders of creation, to live my faith with joy and trust in Providence.

In her first letter (February 21, 1955), Gianna went straight to the heart of my ideal and my will to do the same when she declared, "I really want to make you happy and be what you desire: good, understanding, and ready for the sacrifices that life will require of us . . ." and, "I intend to give myself to form a truly Christian family. . . ."

In her other letters, Gianna's references to God, to his help and his blessing, to her trust in him, and to our duty to be grateful to

---

1. We reproduce here the preface that originally appeared in: *Gianna Beretta Molla, Il tuo grande amore mi aiuterà a essere forte. Lettere al marito*, ed. Elio Guerriero (Cinisello Balsamo: Edizioni San Paolo, 1999) published in English as: *Love Letters to My Husband: Blessed Gianna Beretta Molla* (Boston: Pauline Books & Media, 2002).

him, confirmed to me how rooted the faith was in her and how profound was her spirit of prayer.

In her letter of April 9 of that same year [1955], Gianna, in her humility, wrote to me, ". . . Pietro, I want to be that strong woman of the Gospel! Instead, I think and feel myself weak. . . ."

In reality, she was a strong woman from the beginning. When I asked her to move to a little villa on the property of the company of which I was the manager, she said yes at once. Even during the prolonged and very burdensome strikes from 1956–1958 when she shared my worries and disappointments, she never asked to move; she knew that living there would make it easier for me to fulfill my tasks and responsibilities.

With her invitation, which I immediately agreed with, to celebrate our official engagement with a Holy Mass and Communion and, above all, with her invitation to me in her letter of September 3, 1955 to prepare ourselves to receive the *sacrament of love* with a triduum of Holy Masses and Communions, Gianna truly edified me.

In our communion of life and love of our family, that the births of our children made fuller and more demanding, Gianna always felt fully gratified. Her letters confirm this, and I like to remember her that way.

Now, I kneel before her, a marvelous and strong woman, fiancée, wife, and mother, who, in her love for life and for the child in her womb, knew how to scale the heights of the greatest love which Jesus showed us.

PIETRO MOLLA

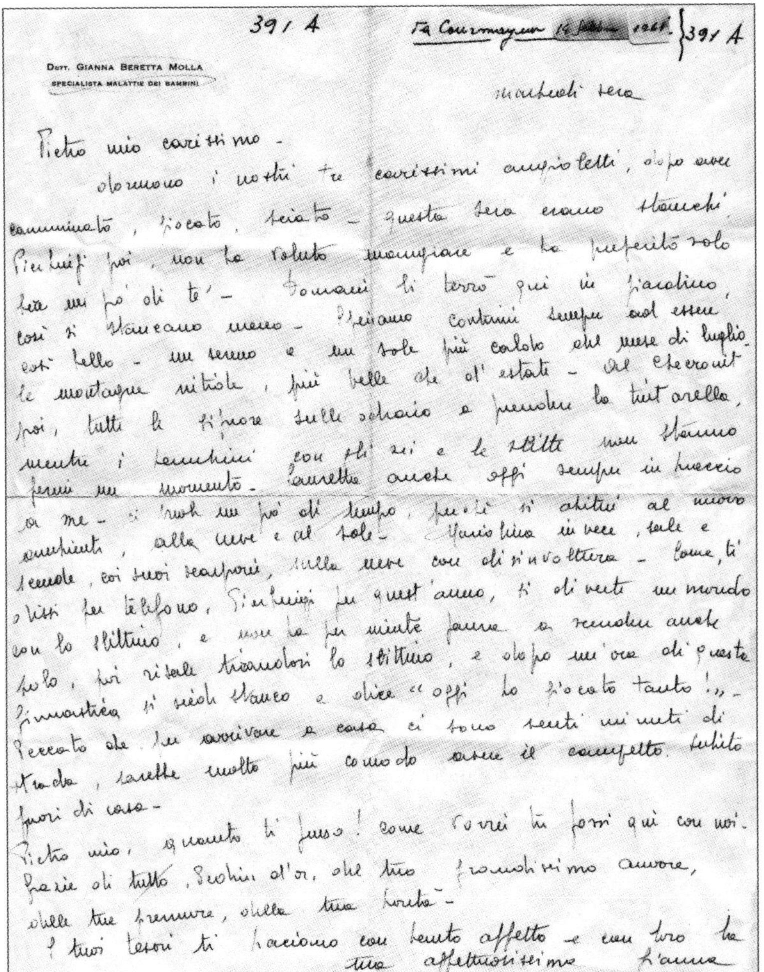

391 A

Da Courmayeur 14 febbraio 1961. } 391 A

DOTT. GIANNA BERETTA MOLLA
SPECIALISTA MALATTIE DEI BAMBINI

martedì sera

Pietro mio carissimo -

dormono i nostri tre carissimi angioletti, dopo aver camminato, giocato, sciato - questa sera erano stanchi. Pierluigi poi, non ha voluto mangiare e ha preferito solo fare un po' di tè - Domani li terrò qui in giardino, così si stancano meno - Speriamo continui sempre ad essere così bello - un sereno e un sole più caldo che mese di luglio. le montagne nitide, più belle che d'estate - Al Checrouit poi, tutte le signore sulle sdraio a prendere la tintarella, mentre i bambini con gli sci e le slitte non stanno fermi un momento - Lauretta anche oggi sempre in braccio a me - ci vuole un po' di tempo, perché si abitui al nuovo ambiente, alla neve e al sole - Mariolina invece, sale e scende, coi suoi scarponi, sulla neve con disinvoltura - Come, ti dissi per telefono, Pierluigi per quest'anno, si diverte un mondo con lo slittino, e non ha per niente paura a scendere anche solo, poi risale trascinandosi lo slittino, e dopo un'ora di questa ginnastica si sente stanco e dice «oggi ho giocato tanto!» - Peccato che per arrivare a casa ci sono venti minuti di strada, sarebbe molto più comodo avere il campetto subito fuori di casa -

Pietro mio, quanto ti penso! come vorrei tu fossi qui con noi. Grazie di tutto, Pietro d'oro, del tuo grandissimo amore, delle tue premure, della tua bontà -

I tuoi tesori ti baciano con tanto affetto e con loro la

tua affettuosissima Gianna

Letter dated February 14, 1961 from Gianna to Pietro.

Magenta, 22.2.55.

422

3

Mia carissima Gianna,

ho letto più volte la tua lettera e l'ho baciata.

Incomincia per me una nuova vita: la vita del tuo grande e desiderato affetto e della tua luminosa bontà. Giorno inizio alla vita del nostro affetto.

Ti voglio bene, mia carissima Gianna.

[...]

Con tutto l'affetto,

Pietro

Letter dated February 22, 1955 from Pietro to Gianna.

Preface
to My Father's Letters

By Gianna Emanuela Molla

Dearest Papa *d'oro*,[1]
I know well and feel that now you are watching over me from Paradise, together with Mamma and Mariolina. You are the three guardian angels who protect, help, and guide my steps. Together with you, permit me to share with the readers of this book the intense and moving experience I lived during these last few months to transcribe, read, and re-read, in their completeness, all your magnificent letters to Mamma.

In doing this I had another confirmation—though I didn't need one—that you really were a husband and papa *d'oro,* the most worthy spouse of my saintly mother.

It's a little past four o'clock in the afternoon on Tuesday, September 20, 2011, and I've just finished gathering together in the

---

1. "*D'oro*" is a title of endearment (literally "of gold"). —Ed.

ring binder all the letters, cards, and notes you wrote Mamma with boundless love. Tomorrow I will give them all to Dr. Guerriero for publication.

The moment has finally arrived to make your letters known as well—the moment many have hoped and waited for, especially those who already knew of and appreciated all the letters that Mamma wrote you with equal love.

Cardinal Carlo Maria Martini, who was then archbishop of Milan [and who died on August 31, 2012], and who wrote the beautiful foreword to the book of Mamma's letters to you, also hoped that yours would be published. "Aside from the frequency, Gianna and Pietro's written rapport is an extraordinary example of communication. It permits us to glimpse a few luminous flashes of that 'life lived according to the Gospel'—into that 'spirituality'—which characterized Gianna's experience, and, with her, that of her husband, Pietro, whose letters also (judging from a few comments in his wife's letters), could contribute to outline a more complete picture of the spirituality of this couple and this Christian family." [2]

I remember so well, though, how you, being the very reserved person you were, always preferred to put off their publication until after the Lord had called you to himself, and, quite rightly, we respected your wish.

It was October 1, 2010—just a few months after that Holy Saturday, April 3, when you flew to Paradise to embrace again and forever your most beloved Gianna and your Mariolina, leaving a gap that cannot be filled—when Dr. Guerriero approached me again with the suggestion of Edizioni San Paolo to publish your letters to Mamma, and I immediately told Laura and Pierluigi.

Knowing well your extreme reserve, I remember that I was in doubt at first. I asked myself whether it would be right. I almost

---

2. Guerriero, *Love Letters to My Husband*, viii–ix.

feared violating your soul that was so noble and pure, so God-fearing, and the deepest feelings you had in your heart—in your great, your very great heart.

Afterward, however, I became convinced that your letters, which continually reveal your deep faith and your trust in the Lord and our Heavenly Mother, by whose light you have always lived your boundless and very tender love for Mamma and for us children, for your family and your neighbor, could do a lot of good. I became convinced that you throughout your long life did nothing but good for others, and have always been a great example to us until your last breath. I thought you would certainly be pleased to be able to continue doing good from Paradise as well.

And so, in agreement with Laura and Pierluigi, I began with all my good will and care to transcribe, one by one, your seventy-three letters, thirty-nine cards, eleven notes—all written with a fountain pen and green ink—and your telegrams to Mamma. Because complex handwriting is not easy to read, I checked my transcriptions word for word, over and over, with your originals, so that each word would be faithful to your original. What a long, meticulous task it was, but necessary; I was more than happy, honored, and profoundly edified to do it.

Especially when reading your early letters, but also other later ones, many of them written late at night when you were already very tired, I couldn't hold back my tears. On the one hand I reflected on how deeply you and Mamma loved each other and us children, and your immense joy to embrace each other again in Paradise after forty-eight years; on the other hand, I missed and suffered the loss of your visible presence and your boundless affection more than ever.

Slowly, as I transcribed your letters, I understood more and more how great was the grace that you and Mamma had received from the Lord and our Heavenly Mother: the grace of meeting each other, of becoming "one heart and soul," with all of Heaven's blessings; I understood completely that your love was so great, could be so great, profound, and true because the Lord and our Heavenly Mother were always present. They were an integral part of this love, just as they were already an integral part of your whole lives.

And in your letters there is a continual thanksgiving to the Lord and our Lady for all the graces and blessings you had received; there is a continual, devout, and intense prayer for your most beloved Gianna, your most beloved children, and your family—always, and even more when your work, which was of great concern and responsibility, also took you far, very far away, and for long periods of time.

"The prayer of my flights" is truly magnificent, so much so that Mamma wrote back to you, "You really are the dearest and most affectionate little husband, a saintly papa, not of gold but of diamond, the biggest and most precious one there is on earth!"

More than once during these months I remembered vividly how, when I read some of your letters together with you, I told you, with all my heart and with joy, "O Papa, you're a poet!" and you smiled at me, so very happy to see my joy.

And then I would add, "Papa, you were certainly inspired by Heaven when you wrote Mamma these letters," and in your profound humility, you did not hesitate to confirm my thought.

While you were alive, I knelt before you and asked your blessing. Now that you are in Heaven, with Mamma forever, I really don't know how to thank the Lord for the immense gift he gave me, together with the gift of life: two holy parents. And I pray to him every day, as best I can, to make me worthy of you both, so that I may join you and embrace you again one day and forever.

Your most affectionate,

Gianna Emanuela

Introduction:
Love Is Stronger Than Death

By Elio Guerriero

I first met Mr. Pietro Molla the day after the beatification of his wife, Gianna Beretta, in 1994. We met for a book-length interview which has been very successful in Italy and around the world.[1] At the time, he mentioned his wife's letters, especially those from the time of their engagement, as "one of the most touching relics I keep of my wife." Right away I asked him whether we could publish the letters, but he wisely preferred to wait a while. Nevertheless he promised me he would let me know when the time had come. Gentleman that he was, he kept his word, and when his wife's

---

1. The volume by P. Molla *Gianna: La beata Gianna Beretta Molla nel ricordo del marito,* ed. E. Guerriero (Cinisello Balsamo: Edizioni San Paolo, 1995) was reprinted several times in Italy and was translated into five foreign languages. From here on we will refer to the second edition of 2005, entitled *Santa Gianna Beretta Molla.* The citation is found on page 44 of that edition.

canonization was coming up in 2004, he phoned me to ask whether I was still interested in overseeing the publication of Gianna's letters. Of course I responded in the affirmative. At the same time, I told him that the letters would be more readable and complete if his letters were published as well. Pietro did not immediately refuse; he asked for time to think about it, but in the end he answered me as I had expected: his reserve prevailed.

After his death, I called Gianna Emanuela, his daughter who was such a tremendous help to him in his last years, and who today is the soul of the Saint Gianna Beretta Molla Foundation. She told me that her father had discussed my request with her and that now we could publish his letters along with those of his wife. Truly he was a man of his word.

The exchange of letters between Saint Gianna and her husband Pietro introduces a new and significant chapter in Christian spirituality. Better than a theological treatise, these letters are a convincing proof that the way of holiness does not necessarily pass through religious life or the priestly ministry, but can unfold in the midst of the world, living one's own vocation as a Christian called to holiness with Christ in married life. This ancient truth (as we can see in the Acts of the Apostles, *saints* is synonymous with *Christians*) was hidden in oblivion during certain centuries which passed over in suspicious silence anything that had to do with the body and sexuality. Among the different types of saints (martyrs, confessors, doctors, virgins), there seemed to be no room for the many Christians who had embraced married life and had viewed it as a mission given them by God, as the field in which to bring their talents to fruition. More often than not, the few married persons (Rita, Nicholas of Flue, Frances of Rome, Jane de Chantal, Louise de Marillac) whom the Church proclaimed as saints had more or less renounced their marriages. Gianna and Pietro, however, died in the married state, and their letters testify to the joy of life lived together in a Christ-centered marriage, and to the strength and tenderness of their love for their children. In fact, lifting the veil on their private life, they show us that love centered in Christ takes away nothing of the beauty of being in love, of attraction toward and passion for the beloved, of loving transports and dedication to the children. On the contrary, in these letters of husband and wife, these sentiments are set before us, fresh, pure, and joyful, ever renewed by participation in the Church's liturgy and by communion in prayer which kept the two united during their separations, the birth of new babies, and the demands of their professions.

At the beginning of his *Meditation on the Church,* Cardinal Henri de Lubac drew attention to the sufferings of many Christians constrained to speak of the mystery of the Church "which they would prefer simply to adore." [2] In spite of this, he believed the moment had come to speak of the Church, to lay the foundations for a solid ecclesiology in opposition to the misunderstandings of the period between the two wars, misunderstandings of the concept of a community founded by Jesus Christ. I think today it is necessary to apply the cardinal's thinking to married life. Right now when the Christian concept of matrimony is misunderstood and mocked on all sides, the time has come to put aside reserve in order to propose to the world the beauty of common life between husband and wife, above all in answer to the many detracting voices. It is urgent to show by example rather than words that Christian marriage is eminently livable, that it is a rational and humanly gratifying way to spend one's life.

---

2. H. de Lubac, *Meditazione sulla Chiesa* (Milan: Jaca Book, 1979), 8.

The fact that the correspondence between Saint Gianna and her husband Pietro is being published the same year that the Seventh World Meeting of Families is being held in Milan on the theme of celebration and work is an even greater reason to see the publication as fitting. To Pietro, Gianna was a woman of celebration, the wife who infused everyday life with an atmosphere of joy. Pietro was a working man whose excessive dedication to his profession was tempered and balanced after he married. Being at the same time an upright and devout man, he and his wife created a communion of life and prayer that was the origin of their marriage's serenity and joy, and their openness to children who were welcomed and cared for with love and dedication. This volume is, therefore, an invitation to Christian spouses to take these letters in hand, read them attentively, and discover in them the concrete possibility of living Christian marriage with love, whether during their engagement, the joy of the first years of marriage and parenthood, or the years of keeping the sacrament alive each day and caring for the children's education. Even the fatigue of work—both of them had demanding jobs—can draw us into this harmonious picture, harmonious by a love which, as Benedict XVI has said more than once, is not born solely of the first attraction but must be cultivated each day.[3]

To facilitate reading these letters I will first offer two points: some information on the husband and wife, and then some information about the letters themselves. I will conclude with some theological considerations.

---

3. See Benedict XVI, *L'amore si apprende* (Cinisello Balsamo: Edizioni San Paolo, 2012).

THE PROTAGONISTS

Gianna[4]

Gianna's parents, Maria de Micheli (1887–1942) and Alberto Beretta (1881–1942), were solidly planted in the Lombard Catholic tradition, more attentive to doing than to doctrinal elaborations. From the social point of view, the Berettas were rather well off, but they did not flaunt their standing, and their help to the neediest was never lacking. The family was noted for its care in forming the children. The parents had thirteen children, of whom five died young: three of the Spanish flu and two because of the common medical conditions of the time. The other eight had the opportunity to study and each one earned a professional degree. This was truly exceptional at the time.

Saint Gianna was the tenth child, the seventh sibling to live beyond childhood. She was born in Magenta on October 4, 1922, the feast of Saint Francis. Out of devotion toward the *Poverello* [poor one] of Assisi, the parents, who were both Franciscan tertiaries, added the name of Francesca to her first name, Gianna. A week after her birth she was baptized by her paternal uncle, Father Giuseppe, in the Basilica of Saint Martin. The family then returned to Milan, to Risorgimento Square, where Gianna passed her first years surrounded by the love of brothers and sisters, already breathing in the profoundly Christian atmosphere reigning in her family.

In 1925 the family moved to the upper part of Bergamo, but the family's lifestyle did not change. Prepared by her mother and her older sister Amalia, who was nicknamed Iucci, Gianna received

---

4. For biographical information on Gianna and her family, see *Posizione sulle virtù della beata Gianna Beretta Molla,* Pro manuscripto, Rome 1999 (the biography is by Monsignor Antonio Rimoldi). Also see P. Molla-E. Guerriero, *Santa Gianna Beretta Molla,* cited previously.

her first Communion on April 4, 1928, at the age of five and a half. From that day on she assisted at Mass daily with her mother. That same year she began her schooling at the Beltrame di Colle Aperto elementary school in Bergamo. According to her younger sister, Mother Virginia, "Gianna was very serene, transparent, sincere, and active." [5] She was not brilliant in school, but her family atmosphere helped and motivated her to study harder. In 1930 she was confirmed in Bergamo's cathedral, and that year she attended school taught by the French Daughters of Wisdom. During the following years, however, on account of her mother's illness, she attended, together with her brother Giuseppe and her sister Virginia, a school taught by the Canossian Sisters. In 1933 she began her gymnasium years [grammar school] at the Paolo Sarpi public school.

The first documents we have about Gianna are from these years. They are letters she wrote to her siblings and parents in which she reveals a deep attachment to her family and also a dislike for school. In 1936 she failed her Latin and Italian exams and was held back in those subjects. During the summer she had to stay behind in Bergamo, where she wrote to her parents vacationing on Lake Maggiore in Viggiona, "Here I am, dear Mamma; unfortunately, today I'm alone and I wanted to write you so I could spend some time with you. I went to catechism class at Saint Vigilio and after that I spent some time studying. . . ." [6]

Having with difficulty passed the exams in September, Gianna then attended her fourth year of gymnasium at the Paolo Sarpi Institute in Bergamo.

The following year, the family moved to Genoa where the girl acquired a more decisive personality and, above all, deepened her Christian life. She continued her studies at the Dorothean Institute

5. In *Posizione sulle virtù,* op cit., 113.
6. September 6, 1936.

at Quinto al Mare where, in the spring of 1938, she took part in a course of spiritual exercises given by Father Michele Avedano, S.J. From this retreat, which was a significant event in the life of the fifteen-year-old, we have a notebook entitled *Ricordi e Preghiere*. Gianna wrote a summary of each of Father Avedano's sermons, her resolutions, and some prayers to recite during the day.

Her studies improved so much that at the end of that year, she was promoted with good grades. Her health, however, was a cause of worry to the point that, at the beginning of the new school year, her parents decided to keep her home to strengthen her delicate constitution. Gianna accepted her parents' decision with good will and occupied her free time with activities that testify to the delicacy of her spirit: under the guidance of her mother she progressed in her piano studies, did some oil paintings which gave vent to her love for nature, and helped out at home. Most importantly, she enrolled in Catholic Action, in which she served for many years and where she developed her leadership skills. Another gift of this year was meeting Monsignor Mario Righetti (1882–1975), one of the founders of the liturgical movement in Italy, who gave the young woman a love for the Church's public prayer.

After this year of rest, Gianna resumed her studies at the classical school of the Dorothean Sisters at Genoa Albaro, earning consistently good grades. She graduated in June 1942, right in the middle of World War II. The year 1942 was a difficult year in other ways as well. Because of their mother's worsening illness and the constant bombings in Genoa, the Beretta family decided to return to Bergamo. The two youngest sisters remained behind in the Ligurian capital city since they still had to finish their studies. In April, their mother, Maria, died suddenly, and in September of the same year, their father, Alberto, also died.

Gianna sorely missed her parents, but she continued resolutely on with her studies and her Church-related activities. The family, meanwhile, led by the oldest brother Francesco, definitively returned to Magenta from which Gianna could easily reach Milan for her university studies. She had chosen to study medicine following the example of her brothers Ferdinando and Enrico, the future Father Alberto, but above all to fulfill her desire to help her neighbor and to bring joy and serenity to the suffering. During the tragic war years, years of internal struggles in Italy and the fall of Fascism, Gianna traveled to Milan to be trained as a physician. But when the war situation worsened at the beginning of the fourth year (1945–1946), the young woman switched to the University of Pavia.

On emerging from the war, Italy turned toward Republicanism and reconstruction. Like many young people of that time, Gianna worked hard to help her country recover. Her niche was Catholic Action. At first she was the delegate for the youngest members with the responsibility of guiding their education and spiritual growth. From 1946 to 1949 she was the president of the young women. With the help of her sisters and of Sister Marianna Meregalli, a Canossian sister who had become her friend and spiritual guide, she undertook many initiatives: conferences, pilgrimages, games, and recreations; frequently she had recourse to the family bank account to help the neediest young girls.

Numerous testimonies speak of her educational method, which was based not on her speaking ability but on charity and the ability to listen. One of her girls declared: "In her apostolate she aimed for charity above all, given individually; she took an interest in every interior or family problem, wherever she thought it useful to help out with a word of encouragement, counsel or comfort." [7]

The year 1948 was decisive as Italy found her place in the international scene. Like most Catholics, Gianna worked for the political

---

7. Testimony of Enrica Parmigiani, reported by Fernando da Riese, *Un sì alla vita: Gianna Beretta Molla* (Rome: Edizioni Paoline, 1980), 45.

campaign of the Christian Democrats. Her numerous activities, however, did no harm to her studies. On November 30, 1949, she earned her long-desired diploma in medicine, and the following year, the new doctor opened a medical office in Mesero, 5 km from Magenta. Beginning her professional life required a change in the way her life was organized, but not in her desire to give. It was a significant time in her medical profession, [she wrote]:

> Unfortunately, today even our work is superficial. We take care of bodies, but often incompetently.
> 1. We must do our part well. Study hard. Today everyone is after money.
> 2. Let us be honest. Be faith-filled doctors.
> 3. Care [for our patients] affectionately; remember that they are our brothers. Be delicate.
> 4. Do not forget the soul of the sick person. [8]

Faithful to this plan, the young doctor wanted to continue her studies, so she enrolled in a pediatric specialization course in Milan. Her decision was influenced by her great love for children and their mothers. At the same time, she dreamed of joining her brother, Father Alberto, who was a missionary in Brazil. Father Alberto, with the help of their brother Francesco who was an engineer, was building a modern hospital in Grajaú in the Maranhão region. To this end, Gianna studied at the Mangiagalli Obstetrical Clinic and studied Portuguese as she prepared to leave.

She wrote to her brother, "Dearest Father Alberto, I am so happy to be coming, and I really think this is my vocation. I too have prayed about this. At the end of the month I'm going on retreat to see whether the Lord will say yes or no." [9]

---

8. This text is classified as document 27–31 and recorded in A. Rimoldi, *Gianna Beretta Molla: Una vita per la vita (1922–1962),* Pro manuscripto (1978), 131.

9. Letter to Father Alberto, September 12, 1952.

When Francesco returned from Brazil, he told his siblings about the illnesses that could attack someone who was not in robust health. The family was alarmed. They knew that Gianna, like her mother, was very sensitive to heat, and they begged her to change her plans. Her spiritual director and the bishop of Bergamo[10] were also concerned. Bishop Bernareggi said, "From my experience with priests and bishops I have learned that when the Lord calls a soul to the missionary ideal, in addition to a great faith and an outstanding spirituality, he also gives them physical strength to help them deal with difficulties and situations we can't even imagine over here."[11]

Gianna listened to these authoritative opinions and was particularly impressed by the story of her mother. In her youth, Mrs. Beretta had also wanted to be a missionary, but instead, had become an extraordinary mother. In spite of the momentary disappointment, Gianna turned her attention to family life.

Pietro[12]

Pietro Molla was born in Mesero, a little town west of Milan along the road to Turin, on July 1, 1912. His parents were Maria Salmoiraghi (1885–1978) and Luigi Molla (1884–1956), two people of great faith and profoundly Christian values. His three older siblings all died before their first birthdays. After him were born Rosetta, Adelaide, Luigia, and Teresina. His father, Luigi, a

---

10. Archbishop Adriano Bernareggi (1884–1953) was the Bishop of Bergamo from 1936 until 1953.

11. This is related by her brother, Father Giuseppe Beretta, in *Terra Ambrosiana*, 1 (1994), 36.

12. Some of these facts about Pietro Molla come from what he told me himself in the book-interview P. Molla-E. Guerriero, *Santa Gianna Beretta Molla*, cited above. Others come from his daughter, Gianna Emanuela, who was a great help to me.

shoemaker who taught his trade to many in Mesero, placed his hopes in Pietro for whom he desired a better professional future than his own. With deep earnestness he sustained many sacrifices so that his son could study, and encouraged him in difficult moments. Pietro, on his part, was a diligent boy who was much loved. In 1919, according to the practice introduced ten years earlier by Pope Pius X, he was confirmed and received his first Communion at age seven. He earned good grades at the local school. The first difficulty he encountered had to do with finishing elementary school. In Mesero they only had the first four grades, and to go on to the fifth grade, one had to pass an exam. With the help of the parish priest, Pietro's father turned to the Sisters of the Precious Blood who had recently settled in town, and whose superior, Mother Giovanna Colloni, personally took charge of preparing the boy for this exam. He took and passed the exam at the elementary school run by the Canossian Sisters in Magenta.

At this time, Fascism was gaining strength and consolidating its recently acquired power. In 1923, Pietro had to leave Mesero to continue his studies. His father chose for him the Collegio Villoresi San Giuseppe in Monza, a boarding school run at the time by the Barnabite Fathers. From west of Milan, the boy moved east of the principal Lombardian city, toward Venice.

Discipline at the boarding school was severe, but Pietro studied hard, partly to please his father who had placed so much confidence in him. One gets the impression that the suffering caused by this early separation from his family formed a strong character but also made him a bit reserved. This reserve only dissipated slowly with the years, as he recovered his spontaneity and joy in relationships with others.

At Saint Joseph's his teachers were good priests who taught, along with Latin, a respect for others, but the discipline was rigid. The education, which was given with an excessive insistence on strict rules of work and study, was not well suited to the younger pupils. However, Pietro did not seem to resent these difficulties and advanced quickly in his studies, happy to please his father, a man of great rectitude, whom the pastor relied on to restore the administration of Catholic hospital care, while the city appointed him Justice of the Peace.

In 1928, having finished the gymnasium years, Pietro remained at Saint Joseph's as a resident and also served as a prefect in charge of discipline for a group of younger boys. He pursued his classical studies at the Bartolomeo Zucchi State School in Monza. From his decisions it is not hard to see the young man's desire not to be a financial burden to his family. We should emphasize the choice of school for his classical studies. Pietro, although he later pursued scientific studies, always had a love for his classical heritage and a taste for scriptural research.

Finally, in 1931, when he had graduated, the young man could finally leave Monza and move back in with his family in Mesero. His father, Luigi, and his mother, Maria, were proud of this son who won honors in his studies. They were confident when Pietro decided to go on to study engineering. This still required sacrifices on their part, but these were made willingly in view of a better financial situation for the whole family.

The trip by bicycle from Mesero to Magenta and by train from Magenta to Milan was nothing to Pietro who had many expectations to meet. There was the head of the regional Fascist party who wanted to put him in charge of the local chapter, and the pastor who wanted him to work in Catholic Action. Grateful for the trust placed in him, Pietro accepted both responsibilities without pay. In his political work, Pietro put an end to waste and mismanagement. He came up with a plan for distributing government aid based on an accurate method of determining need; he straightened out the birth and marriage benefits and the procedures for determining which children could attend summer camps. On Sunday afternoons he taught catechism to adults. In spite of all this extra work, which often meant late nights for him, in 1936, at age twenty-four he graduated from Milan's Polytechnic with a degree in mechanical engineering.

The swift succession of milestones during the second half of 1936 is mind-boggling. He graduated on November 7. In November and December he studied for and passed his state engineering exams, which qualified him to practice his profession. On December 9 he was hired by the SAFFA Company. At the time, young graduates had no trouble finding work; however, it is apparent that the young Mr. Molla was a very talented person. He had also looked into the Franco Tose di Legnano Company, but he chose the job at SAFFA, which stands for *Società per Azioni Fabbriche Fiammiferi ed Affini,* a large company which produced wooden matches, with headquarters in Ponte Nuovo di Magenta, not far from home. He took on the position of technical secretary to the plant's manager in Ponte Nuovo, but by 1938 he had already been promoted to vice manager of that plant and was also in charge of the other plants and their machinery in Asti, Fucecchio, Este, Jesi, Naples, Moncalieri, and Perugia. At a very young age he was entrusted with heavy responsibilities and had to give orders to persons much older than himself, people who had already spent a lifetime working at SAFFA. The young manager was noted for his great dedication to his work and his interest in differentiating his company's production, always attentive to new developments in technology.

Fifty years later, he declared in an interview: "Compared to Gianna, I did very little in the strictly ecclesiastical sphere. I worked hard, though; my whole life I tried to create new jobs. That was my life." [13] But it was his commitment to Catholic Action that ultimately

---

13. P. Molla-E. Guerriero, *Santa Gianna Beretta Molla,* op. cit., 26.

saved him from the implications of being involved in Fascism. Until 1939, the disputes between Pius XI and Mussolini over Catholic Action, which had frequently jeopardized their 1929 agreement, had no consequences in Mesero. However, once the war broke out everything changed. In December 1940 the young engineer received three orders. He was advised that he was no longer to hold office in the party; that he was relieved of his responsibilities in the Balilla National Operation; and he had to give back his university's militia uniform. "All this because I was involved in Catholic Action. How could I miss this sign of Providence?" [14]

Momentarily taken aback, the young SAFFA manager simply immersed himself deeper in his work, trying to develop his factory as much as possible and putting into practice that respect for others which he had been taught by his family and by the Barnabite Fathers at Saint Joseph College—respect which he believed saved his life on more than one occasion. On March 7, 1944, when the war was already coming to an end, Pietro was arrested for the first time, along with three of his workers—the Communist Pietro Grassi and the Socialists Armando Armi and Giuseppe Martini. They were arrested by two militant Fascists from the notorious Muti gang. Transferred at gunpoint to Magenta, they were already being loaded into a van to be handed over to the Germans when, notified by the other SAFFA workers, Umberto Parmigiani, the head of the local Fascist group, ran to the rescue. This gentleman, after a long discussion during which he put his own life on the line, managed to obtain the release of young Molla and the other three.

A year later, just a few days before Mussolini's execution and the shameful exposing of his body in Loreto, Pietro was arrested again under more dramatic circumstances, once again by the Muti gang.

---

14. Ibid., 26.

This time, Pietro, along with SAFFA's manager, Francesco Bordone, was already on a truck destined for a German concentration camp when Mr. Parmigiani again arrived on the scene. Again there was a long discussion that led to the prisoners' release.

The end of the war brought some dramatic aftershocks. Two days after Milan's liberation, on the bridge over the Ticino River near SAFFA, the Germans attacked, irritable and angry because their defeat was inevitable. The Americans arrived from Milan with a line of military trucks headed toward Novara, and they immediately wanted to fight. However, there were the workers, the civilians, and the factories to consider. This time it was Mr. Molla himself who intervened. Thanks to the providential presence at the factory of a worker, Giuseppe Megler, who spoke excellent German and English, Pietro invited the two opposing captains into his office and sent his chauffeur to the city of Como so that the German official could ask his commander, General Wolff,[15] for permission to surrender. With his patience and good sense, the conflict came to a happy ending. The Germans surrendered, no blood was shed, and the factory was saved and swiftly resumed operations.

Certainly, this is a minor story compared to the whole picture of the war, but if SAFFA was able to immediately resume full operations during the reconstruction years, it was due to the calmness and nerves of steel of its vice manager. On his part, Pietro did not rest contented with these results but quickly saw that manufacturing wooden matches would not be enough and sought other products to manufacture. He traveled widely in Italy and abroad, visiting factories, especially in Sweden and the United States. His star rose swiftly

---

15. General Karl Friedrich Otto Wolff (1900–1984) in February 1944 was sent to Italy where he remained as acting governor and supreme commander of the S.S. and the North Italian Police until the liberation.

in the company. In 1950 he was named central director of the plant in Ponte Nuovo.

With all this unceasing activity, Pietro had no time for feelings or diversion, but during this very same year, a funeral forced him to stop and reflect on the fragility of human life. His sister Teresina, the youngest of his siblings, fell seriously ill. As a child she had had nephritis that had not been adequately diagnosed or taken care of, and now the illness overcame the twenty-three-year-old. Pietro, who had met Gianna the first time in September 1949 in Magenta at her brother Ferdinando's clinic, saw her a second time on April 16, 1950, at the hospital in Magenta where she had just finished giving Teresina a blood transfusion. Teresina died a few days later. However, the moment had not yet struck for the two to become better acquainted.

Engagement and Marriage

Gianna and Pietro lived and worked just a few miles apart. After a few casual encounters, they became friends at the end of 1954. At the celebration following the first Mass of Father Lino Garavaglia, future bishop of Cesena, the two young people ended up seated across from each other at table. Each took a liking to the other, which quickly led to a friendship born of mutual esteem. The shy glances of the first meetings became more intense and affectionate. Suddenly it seemed as if a veil had fallen and each discovered the wonder and beauty of the other, the harmony of their ideals (love of family, of children, of those around them) that had been culti-vated yet hidden from indiscreet eyes. Gianna was a beautiful woman, and Pietro quickly fell in love. She fascinated Pietro to the extent that she was able to draw him out of the isolation and worka-holism that threatened to engulf him. On his part, Pietro gave a sense of security to the young woman who had already lost her parents some years before.

Their first meetings were followed by others, and soon they began to talk of engagement and marriage. Pietro wrote in a memoir addressed to his children: "Beginning in February 1955 we met more and more frequently; we confided our hopes and dreams to one other, and we came to understand each other even more." [16]

By the end of February Pietro proposed, and Gianna accepted with joy. Some of the most beautiful letters in this book date from this period. Gianna and Pietro were by no means adolescents, but the exchange of letters shows that their love was fresh and young, tender and heartfelt. Gianna wrote, "I really want to make you happy and be what you desire: good, understanding, and ready for the sacrifices that life will require of us." [17] Pietro answered: "I've read your letter over and over, and kissed it. A new life is beginning for me: the life of your great (and greatly desired) affection and of your radiant goodness. We are starting the journey of our love." [18]

The official engagement took place on April 11, with promises of fidelity; wedding preparations then began in earnest. During this time Gianna was both joyful and anxious, cultivating thoughts of self-donation and openness to sacrifice, both of which, as she well knew, are part of love. In her letters she often referred to chapter 31 of the Book of Proverbs: "A capable wife who can find? She is far more precious than jewels. The heart of her husband trusts in her, and he will have no lack of gain. She does him good, and not harm, all the days of her life" (verses 10–12). The biblical author praises an affectionate and faithful woman, persevering and practical, a model toward which Gianna continually aspired. She prepared herself spiritually, but she also enjoyed the practical aspects of

---

16. From *Posizione sulle virtù*, 452.
17. Letter of February 21, 1955.
18. Letter of February 22, 1955.

preparation: she chose furniture, bought sheets and towels, and had a seamstress make her wedding dress.

The wedding date was set for September 24. A few days beforehand, Gianna wrote to Pietro: "In only twenty days, I'll be . . . Gianna Molla! What would you say about our making a triduum to prepare spiritually to receive this Sacrament? Holy Mass and Holy Communion on the twenty-first, twenty-second, and twenty-third, you at Ponte Nuovo, I at the Shrine of the Assumption. The Blessed Mother will unite our prayers and, because strength is found in unity, Jesus can't help but listen to us and answer our prayers." [19]

On September 24, the bride and groom witnessed to their love before Christ and the Christian community. When Gianna entered Saint Martin's Basilica in Magenta on the arm of her brother Francesco, spontaneous applause broke out. This showed the gratitude of those present for Gianna's generosity, an acknowledgment of how committed the two young people were, and the welcome extended to them as the newest among the community's married couples. Pietro, too, was being congratulated and thanked for all his work and efforts that had resulted in many new jobs for his fellow citizens. The celebrant was Father Giuseppe, Gianna's priest-brother. Immediately after the wedding, the couple left on their honeymoon.

On their return, the couple settled in Ponte Nuovo di Magenta, in a little house SAFFA provided for its manager. Gianna resumed her medical work and continued her involvement in Catholic Action. Having been president of the young women, she was now elected president of the Catholic Action women in Ponte Nuovo—a post she held until her death.

---

19. Letter of September 3, 1955.

Here we must emphasize something. After her marriage, Gianna did not neglect her family of origin. She wrote frequently to her distant siblings, and often visited the nearer ones and invited them over. Her brother Ferdinando, with whom she had shared a medical office in Magenta for a time, had a daughter named Iucci. She was her Aunt Gianna's favorite, and during Pietro's frequent absences, Gianna had her come to spend the night.

Gianna seemed to have a special love for motherhood, and her own maternity was not long in coming. In the spring of 1956 she realized she was pregnant and was delighted, as was Pietro. We have no particular details of this pregnancy, except that she went a few days beyond her due date. Their first child, Pierluigi, was born on November 19, 1956, and Gianna's joy was great. Once again, the words of Jesus came true: "When a woman is in labor, she has pain, because her hour has come. But when her child is born, she no longer remembers the anguish because of the joy of having brought a human being into the world" (Jn 16:21). The baby was baptized in the little church at Ponte Nuovo by his uncle, Father Giuseppe, and immediately afterward, as would be the case with each child in the family, he was consecrated to Our Lady of Good Counsel.

Outwardly the couple's life did not change: Gianna continued her medical work and Pietro continued guiding his factory toward diversification and new goals, but the baby's presence gave new impetus to their conjugal affection and created new bonds of love. Of course, they were not without the normal worries and problems: Pierluigi, who was nicknamed Gigetto, suffered from a dislocated hip, Gianna had heartburn, and Pietro was overwhelmed with work.

Toward the end of spring 1957, Gianna became pregnant again. A few months later, Gianna went to the village of Courmayeur and rented a house where she spent the summer with Gigetto and her relatives. Pietro, however, visited mostly on the weekends. In

September the parents changed places: Pietro stayed up in the mountains with Gigetto, and Gianna returned to her medical practice in Magenta. On December 11, ten days past the due date, their second child was born: a girl named Maria Zita, whom they nicknamed Mariolina.[20]

The beginning of 1958 was particularly difficult for husband and wife. In February Pietro had to go to San Remo to take a break. Gianna had to take care of two small children, one of whom, Gigetto, had stomach problems, while the other, Mariolina, hardly slept at night. These are difficulties every family faces, but Gianna knew how to live them in her love of Christ, and this is really the core of her sanctity. Cardinal Martini wrote: "Gianna's holiness is within reach of each one of us: she experienced our problems, she suffered as we do, and she had the same difficulties we have in everyday life, in our professional lives. She attended to her family, welcomed guests, and patiently bore the vicissitudes of everyday life." [21]

In the summer of 1958, Gianna with her two children returned to Courmayeur on vacation. In the mountains, the children grew tanned and healthy. With joy and pride, Gianna described them to her brother, Father Alberto: "Pierluigi and Mariolina are well. Fifteen days ago we got back from Courmayeur. The *popi*[22] are beautiful, tanned, and have good appetites." [23]

Six months after Mariolina was born, Gianna became pregnant for the third time. She announced the news excitedly to Father

---

20. Mariolina died on February 12, 1964, about two years after her mother's death.

21. John Paul II, *Gianna Beretta Molla. Una santa della quotidian ità,* ed. C.M. Martini (Milan: Centro Ambrosiano, 1994), 98.

22. *Popi* is a term for "babies" in the Lombard dialect. Gianna often used this expression to show her affection for her children. — Trans.

23. Letter to Father Alberto, September 24, 1958, her third wedding anniversary.

Alberto, who was coming back to Italy for the summer. Gianna wrote him: "I will have the great joy of having you baptize my third baby, who, if all goes well, should be born around the beginning of July. Are you happy, Uncle?" [24]

In late spring of 1959, Pietro had to take a business trip to the United States. He was gone from April 26 to June 16. Gianna suffered greatly from his absence, especially since during that time she had some serious pregnancy complications. On June 15 she was taken to the hospital in Monza for sharp pains and pre-term contractions that made her fear she was losing the baby. Only the prompt care of the doctors warded off the worst, and on June 17 Gianna was able to go to the airport to pick up Pietro who, knowing nothing about all this, had just returned.

While he was away, Gianna was greatly helped by her sister Zita, to whom she was forever grateful. On July 15, 1959, their third child was born: Laura Enrica Maria. Gianna gave the news to her friend Mariuccia Parmigiani: "Wednesday morning (July 15), Lauretta was born at 8:15. You can't imagine how happy we are: first of all because, thanks be to God, everything went well; secondly because she's beautiful, good, and healthy, and also because she's a girl—I really wanted Mariolina to have a little sister. I know from experience how precious sisters are, and the Lord has heard my prayers." [25]

This time was possibly the happiest time in the marriage of Gianna and Pietro. Gianna was happy: she loved her husband and children and enjoyed being with them. The year after Lauretta was born, she wrote to her husband from Courmayeur: ". . . [E]verything is quiet. Dear Pietro, how beautiful it is to be able to stay with them day and night, to watch and enjoy them. . . . It doesn't seem real to

24. Letter to Father Alberto, December 2, 1958.
25. Letter to her friend Mariuccia Parmigiani, July 18, 1959.

them to have their Mamma all to themselves all of the time. . . .
They're really three treasures. What a pity I don't have my fourth big
treasure, my most beloved and most affectionate Pedrin. . . ."[26]

Some months later, her wish to spend time with Pietro was ful-
filled. Leaving her children with her sister Zita, Gianna accompanied her husband on a business trip to England and Holland. They
left on December 10 and arrived in London on Sunday, December
11. Gianna wrote to Father Alberto: "From London, I went to a different place each day, either by train or by car, and thus I visited the
North, along the North Sea, Norwich, Great Yarmouth, and I was
able to get some idea of these people and their ways and life. From
London, it was only an hour and ten minutes by plane to Amsterdam,
the city crisscrossed with canals. . . . Tomorrow evening, or Monday
night at the latest, we'll be back with them (the babies) and will start
getting ready for Christmas."[27]

Months later, Gianna was in Courmayeur again with the children.
She wrote to Pietro one of her last known letters to him: "My dearest
Pietro, our three dearest treasures are asleep, after having walked,
played and skied all day—they were tired tonight. . . . My Pietro, how
often I think of you and how I wish you were here with us! Thank
you for everything, Pedrin *d'or:* for your great love, your care, for all
your goodness. Your treasures kiss you with much love, and together
with them your most affectionate Gianna."[28]

Spurred on by love and joy, Gianna wanted to have another
baby. After her third pregnancy, according to the testimony of her
brother Dr. Ferdinando, who was taking care of her, Gianna had
two miscarriages whose cause was never discovered.[29] After a trip to

---

26. Letter of June 27, 1960.
27. Letter to Father Alberto, December 17, 1960.
28. Letter of February 14, 1961.
29. *Posizione sulle virtù,* op. cit., 47.

Denmark and Sweden, in July 1961, the signs of her final pregnancy appeared. However, as early as the second month, a fibroma—a benign tumor—developed on the right side of the uterus. This necessitated surgery, which took place at the hospital in Monza in September 1961.

According to the medical knowledge of the time, it would have been necessary to abort the child in order to eliminate every risk, but Gianna refused. She knew every detail of what was coming and the dangers she was facing by only having the tumor removed, but her vocation as mother and doctor was to protect life, not to kill it. The head doctor at the hospital, Dr. Vitali, simply removed the tumor, and after eight days Gianna was able to return home. Her children were on vacation in Courmayeur with her friend Mariuccia Parmigiani, and she sent them a letter in which her maternal affection betrays her emotions at the time: "Dearest treasures, Papa will bring you many big kisses. I wish I could come too, but I have to stay in bed, because I have some *owies*. Be good, do what Mariuccia and Savina tell you. . . . I have you here in my heart and I'm thinking about you all the time. Say a Hail Mary for me, so our Lady will make me better soon, and so I can come up to Courmayeur to give you hugs and stay with you all the time."[30]

After her operation in September, life went back to normal. Gianna knew that a suture of the uterus during the first months of pregnancy could burst, with mortal danger to herself as well as to the child, but she tried to live calmly. Her husband and relatives all attest to this. She went back to work, although she was considering giving up her medical practice after the fourth child came. She lovingly saw to the growth and education of the children. At the same time, she prayed more and more intensely that she would be spared

---

30. Letter included with one to her friend Mariuccia Parmigiani on September 13, 1961.

having to sacrifice her life, in order to go on caring for her husband and children. On one point, however, she was extremely clear with Pietro and her relatives: in the event of their having to choose between her life and that of the baby, the preference must absolutely be given to the child's life. She refused to listen to those who reasoned otherwise with her, and repeated decisively, "This time my pregnancy will be difficult and they will have to save one or the other, and I want them to save my baby." [31]

Her trust in Divine Providence gave her the strength to keep hoping. Only once, according to her sister Zita, was she momentarily overcome with fear. "Finding herself alone, she called me in tears. I had Ferdinando go over there right away. He was not one for tears, and the Servant of God courageously turned the whole thing into a joke." [32]

The due date was approaching, and it seemed that once the baby was born, everything would be all right. Gianna checked into the hospital in Monza on April 20, 1962, Friday of Holy Week. It is not difficult to see the parallels between her sufferings and those of Jesus on the Cross. The next morning, Holy Saturday, Gianna had a C-section and her fourth child, Gianna Emanuela, was born. But just a few hours later, because of a septic infection, a rising fever and terrible abdominal pains set in. It was a slow agony, made infinitely more painful by [having to leave] the new baby,[33] and by the sufferings of her relatives and Pietro.[34]

---

31. In *Posizione sulle virtù*, op. cit., 79.

32. Ibid.

33. Her husband wrote later in the form of a last dialogue with his wife: "When you took our little one in your arms, you looked at her so lovingly, with a gaze that betrayed your unspeakable suffering at the thought of being unable to raise her, and never seeing her again," P. Molla-E. Guerriero, *Santa Gianna Beretta Molla,* op. cit., 68.

34. Again I will let Pietro explain in his own words: "I remember when you told me, that Wednesday morning, with such serenity that it seemed otherworldly to me:

On Wednesday morning Gianna asked to return to Ponte Nuovo to die with her loved ones at her side, in the house that had safeguarded the sacrament of her love. At dawn on April 28, she was taken home, where she breathed her last at 8:00 AM, probably after having heard the voices of her children who were just waking up.

After the funeral, it was necessary for Mr. Molla to quickly go back to daily life. There was the new baby to think of, and the three older siblings who missed their mother. The Berettas and the Mollas all gathered around him to help bring up the children, but the greatest responsibility fell to the father. The previous year, 1961, he had reached another level in his career when he was named vice general director of the large company, which at the time employed between 5,000 and 6,000 workers. He still needed to visit their many plants, installing and planning new machinery, some of which he had invented himself, and these machines were patented and exported to other countries.

In the midst of all these responsibilities, another death tried him sorely. At the beginning of 1964, Gianna and Pietro's second child, Mariolina, who was boarding at the Sorriso d'Italia School run by Pietro's sister, Sister Luigia, contracted a particularly virulent form of an illness which caused skin eruptions, complicated by an acute kidney infection. She was admitted to the hospital in Imperia, but continued to worsen. She was then taken by ambulance to Niguarda Hospital in Milan, but not even the Milanese doctors could save the little girl. Pietro told me, "I've had to convince myself that sorrow

---

'Pietro, I am healed now. Pietro, I was already on the other side, and if you only knew what I saw. Some day I'll tell you. But since we were too happy, too comfortable with our marvelous children, full of health and grace, with all of heaven's blessings, they sent me back here to suffer some more, because it is not right to appear before the Lord without having suffered much.' This was and remains for me your testament of joy and suffering," Ibid., 69.

remains a mystery even in the light of faith, and I have experienced that the only way to accept it is the way of the Crucified Jesus."[35]

Once again the engineer responded by devoting himself to his work, while at the same time he managed to stay close to his living children, as they have all attested. Pierluigi's testimony speaks for all three: "Within the space of two years, Papa had undergone two most painful losses, my mother's death in 1962 and my sister Mariolina's in 1964, and he remained the guide and support for me and my sisters, trying, if possible, to alleviate the suffering of our having to grow up without a mother figure. He succeeded very well, thanks to his great love, the care he took and his tact in bringing us up, and thanks to his counsel which was never imposed but always available."[36]

In spite of these deaths and the time he devoted to his family, Pietro continued to rise within SAFFA's ranks. In 1966, when he was fifty-four, he became general director; a few years later, in 1972, he became a member of SAFFA's administrative council. During these years, the first steps were taken toward Gianna's possible beatification. Among those who were with the saint during her final days was Father Olinto Marella,[37] an extraordinary priest, a witness to charity who, for love of the poor, had become a beggar and vagrant in Bologna. More than once he had gone to Ponte Nuovo with his truck to pick up all types of clothing and anything SAFFA was getting rid of. He made use of everything to build his town for boys.

---

35. Ibid., 71.

36. In the periodical published by the Saint Gianna Beretta Molla Foundation, in one special issue entirely dedicated to Pietro with testimonies from relatives and authorities, *Gianna sorriso di Dio*, January–December (2010), 10.

37. To learn more about Father Olinto Marella, whose beatification cause is nearly finished, see L. Bedeschi, *Padre Marella. Un prete accattone a Bologna* (Cinisello Balsamo: Edizioni San Paolo, 1998).

He knew Gianna well; he knew her love for children, her joy in living, and the great sacrifice of her death. As early as at Gianna's funeral he spoke of her holiness, and the following year, on the first anniversary of her death, he printed a small booklet[38] in which he gave public testimony to a mother who was able to give her life generously, without limit, and he spoke of veneration on the part of the faithful, hoping that the hierarchy would recognize her sanctity. The priest's invitation was quickly accepted by the ecclesiastical authorities. When Gianna died, Milan's archbishop was Cardinal Montini, who shortly thereafter was elected pope and took the name of Paul VI. With discreet attention he kept informed about Gianna's case, while Archbishop Carlo Colombo, who was very close to the pope, was among those promoting the beatification cause.

Pietro recounts: "In the spring of 1970, Bishop Carlo Colombo, when he came to my parish in Ponte Nuovo to confer Confirmation, had me called to the rectory and told me of the Church's desire to promote the cause of my wife's beatification, and asked what I thought about it. I was truly perplexed! . . . My reluctance arose from the fact that I understood immediately what this would mean: we would have to publicize our life, our affections, and our sufferings." [39] After having given Gianna up to the Lord once, he had to give her up again—this time to all the faithful. The process began in Milan in 1972. Testimonies were gathered and a critical biography was drawn up by Antonio Rimoldi.

---

38. In *Gianna Beretta Molla*, a booklet printed in 1963 at the Graphics School in Father Marella's Town for Boys in Bologna, the priest wrote: "In every home where her name will be spoken, her example will shine like that of a saint. If obedience to canonical prescriptions does not allow the use of that term in the sacred liturgy until the Church has decided and the highest authority has consented, we can still pray and invite others to pray to this victim of maternal love."

39. P. Molla-E. Guerriero, *Santa Gianna Beretta Molla*, op. cit., 77.

The year 1978 was the year of three popes. Paul VI died in the summer. John Paul I succeeded him for a month, and in October, John Paul II was elected. The Polish pope was the one destined, in 1980, to give the *nihil obstat* to the introduction of the cause. Authorized by Archbishop Martini, the diocesan process was concluded in 1986. In 1991 a decree was issued affirming Gianna's heroic virtue; in 1992 came the recognition of a miracle, and on April 24, 1994, the solemn proclamation of Gianna as Blessed by Pope John Paul II. On that occasion, Cardinal Martini declared: "Gianna's example, to which other examples of other mothers of yesterday and today can be added, is a sign of hope and an incentive to our families, and for all of us." [40]

In the meantime, Pietro, who had overcome his initial hesitation, put his organizational skills to good use and together with his brother-in-law, Father Giuseppe Beretta, in 1999 started the Blessed Gianna Beretta Molla Foundation whose purpose was to honor his wife and spread her story. More and more often, he accepted speaking invitations and, with his daughter Gianna Emanuela, published the magazine *Gianna Sorriso di Dio* (Gianna, God's Smile), which recorded the growing veneration of Gianna all over the world.

The canonization itself took place on May 16, 2004. For this occasion, the new saint's husband, children, and other relatives were present in Saint Peter's Square.

This whole process took some time, but in the end, the desire of many was realized: to see raised to the honors of the altar lay Catholic men and women, married spouses who had reached holiness through living the sacrament of Christian love in the Lord.

---

40. John Paul II, C. M. Martini, *Gianna Beretta Molla. Una santa della quotidianità,* op. cit., 82.

After his wife's canonization, Pietro Molla spent the last years of his life in fidelity, devotion, and giving witness to her holiness. In the foreword to the second edition of his wife's letters, he wrote: "Now, I kneel before her, a marvelous and strong woman, fiancée, wife, and mother, who, in her love for life and for the child in her womb, knew how to scale the heights of the greatest love which Jesus showed us."[41]

Nearly one hundred years old, Pietro died on April 3, 2010, surrounded by the love of children and grandchildren, his mind clear to the end. A year later, his youngest daughter, Gianna Emanuela, who cared for him during his last years, dedicated a special issue of *Gianna Sorriso di Dio* (which she edits) to him, including in its pages many testimonies and remembrances written by her siblings and relatives. She herself wrote: "I don't know how to thank the Lord for having given me, and allowing to remain with me so many years, a *papà d'oro*, a papa who was more than worthy of his dearly beloved and holy wife, a papa who was always close to me until the very last moment."[42] And since the daughter speaks of a papa worthy of the mother, after the time required by the Church has passed, it would be fitting to think of a beatification cause for Pietro as well. His Christian virtues require it, those virtues which I have only briefly sketched in this short biography: his foresight as a manager, who, while technological innovations reduced the necessary manpower for manufacturing, tried to diversify production in order to create new jobs; and his great love and perfect fidelity to his wife. In this manner, the couple will be reunited on the altars, giving the most beautiful witness to the family in this time of crisis.

---

41. Pietro's preface is included in this edition of the letters; see p. xiv.
42. See the already-cited issue, 12.

THE LETTERS

The Historical-Cultural Context

In Saint Gianna's *Positio*,[43] Antonio Rimoldi accurately reports on the letters, notes, and postcards written by Gianna Beretta Molla to her husband, family members, friends, and other acquaintances. The letters to her husband, which are presented in their entirety in this book, number seventy-three. As far as Pietro's letters are concerned, these were diligently saved by Mr. Molla himself, helped in his later years by his daughter Gianna Emanuela who also took on the arduous task of typing in the texts of the letters. This publication would not have been possible without her help. The original letters have been saved in the Pietro Molla Archive.

Pietro's letters to Gianna, and hers to him, which make up the body of this book, begin in 1955 and end in December 1961— seven years during which society as a whole, including the Church in Italy, underwent great changes, which are reflected in the letters.

The biggest change in Italy between 1950 and 1960 was economic in nature. Leaving behind the trauma of the war, the country saw rapid and surprising economic development. It was the period of industrialization and the spread of electronic devices, to which Pietro Molla contributed by his diligence, from the first San Remo Festivals to the first RAI transmissions.[44] It was also the time of the Cold War and the Communist Party that still looked to the Soviet Union as a model of political and social organization. From the political point of view, Italy was solidly governed by the Christian

---

43. A *Positio* is the official summary of documentation concerning the virtue of a person being considered for canonization. It is often referred to as the *Position on Virtue* in this book. —Ed.

44. RAI: Italy's public broadcaster: radio, television, Internet. —Ed.

Democrats, the Catholic party whose foremost members came from the ranks of Catholic Action and the FUCI,[45] organizations in which, as we have already mentioned, Gianna and Pietro were actively involved.

In the mid-1950s, however, there were already hints of disunity and changing viewpoints, signs of coming upheavals. In the previous years, De Gasperi,[46] urged on by Montini, had tried to "introduce in Italy the experience of [religious] diversity and tolerance, which was already consolidated in other European countries."[47] But those on the political right, supported by a fringe of the hierarchy, pushed for the foundation of a second Catholic political party, while others looked to new horizons "whose limits had not the necessary clarity."[48]

In the succeeding years, the growing success of the Communist Party and of the Left in general posed a problem for the Christian Democrats—the problem of "openness to the Left" and the government's collaboration with the socialist party. This was a political question that involved religious interests and caused great divisions among Catholics, including the hierarchy. It will be enough to recall the outcry that arose when, in early 1957, the future John XXIII sent a greeting to the National Congress of the Socialist Party that was meeting in Venice.[49]

The years between 1950 and 1960 were no less surprising in the religious sphere. In 1955, when Gianna and Pietro began

---

45. FUCI: Catholic Italian Federation of University Students. —Ed.

46. Alcide De Gasperi, Prime Minister of Italy 1945–1953. —Ed.

47. A. Giovagnoli, *I laici nella Chiesa del XX secolo,* in *La Chiesa in Italia dall'unità ai nostri giorni,* ed. E. Guerriero (Cinisello Balsamo: Edizioni San Paolo, 1996), 646.

48. G. Penco, *Storia della Chiesa in Italia, Vol. II, Dal concilio di Trento ai nostri giorni* (Milan: Jaca Book, 1978), 556.

49. G. Alberigo, *Angelo Giuseppe Roncalli patriarca di Venezia,* in *La Chiesa in Italia dall'unità ai nostri giorni,* op. cit., 434.

writing each other, the Church was still under the guidance of Pius XII, who had placed Catholicism on a path of marked presence in society and increasing opposition to the Leftist parties. During the postwar years, Catholic organizations like FUCI and the Catholic Graduates grew steadily. Toward the middle of the decade, however, the first internal difficulties surfaced, along with the first disagreements with the hierarchy. It was partly for this reason that, in 1954, the pro-secretary of ordinary affairs at the Secretariat of State, Giovanni Battista Montini, who had long been close to the FUCI and the Catholic Graduates, was banished from Rome. Named archbishop of Milan, he became the bishop of Gianna Beretta and Pietro Molla. The two young professionals came from the ranks of Catholic Action. They were closer to the views of Luigi Gedda[50] than to those of Mario Rossi, whose 1954 dismissal from the post of president of the young league of Catholic Action began a series of crises within the movement. Archbishop Montini, instead, was closer to Rossi, but this did not prevent Gianna and Pietro from loving and actively collaborating with their bishop.

On October 28, 1958, the elderly patriarch of Venice, Angelo Giuseppe Roncalli, succeeded Pius XII. Without contradicting the thought and practice of his predecessor, John XXIII introduced new accents into the Church's governance. He put the brakes on the activism promoted by the Jesuit Riccardo Lombardi,[51] placed his trust in the pastoral action of the bishops, and convoked Vatican Council II. At the heart of the Pope's actions was his Christocentric spirituality. His actions "pushed the Church to accept a poverty of

---

50. Luigi Gedda, 1902–2000, Italian geneticist, political activist, President of Catholic Action. —Ed.

51. Riccardo Lombardi, SJ, 1908–1979, known as "God's Microphone," was promoter of "Exercises for a Better World." —Ed.

means and to practice an habitual availability to men and their lives, coming to them as one poor in everything except in Christ."[52]

This was the program of *aggiornamento*[53] which would occupy the Church during the 1960s and long afterward.

Content of the Letters

After the publication of Saint Gianna's letters, which were received favorably by the Italian people and which were translated into five other languages, we now present the entire correspondence between the saint and her husband, Pietro Molla. The reader can thus better understand the circumstances that gave rise to the individual letters and can also appreciate the reciprocal loyalty and love between the two. As in the previous edition, the letters are divided into four chapters corresponding with the main periods of their married life. In addition to the letters, the new edition includes the postcards and notes as witnesses to the intensity of their relationship and the frequency with which they corresponded. The texts of the original handwritten letters are faithfully reproduced in this volume, including little differences in punctuation.

The Engagement Letters

Pietro wrote fourteen letters and Gianna wrote him eleven during this time. In these letters Gianna, who in numerous testimonies is described as a quiet and reflective young woman,[54] reveals her joy

---

52. G. Alberigo, *Il pontificato di Giovanni XXIII,* in *La Chiesa del Vaticano II,* ed. M. Guasco-E. Guerriero-Fr. Traniello, Vol. XXV/1 della *Storia della Chiesa* (Cinisello Balsamo: Edizioni San Paolo, 1994), 36.

53. *Aggiornamento*: process of updating. —Ed.

54. T. Lelièvre, *Madre. Gianna Beretta Molla* (Casale Monferrato: Piemme, 1994), 46.

and enthusiasm, her happiness at having found her vocation, at having discovered as her vocation what she had often spoken of to her young Catholic Action girls. She had said in one of her conferences on October 21, 1946: "To be called to family life does not mean getting engaged at fourteen. This would just be a bad sign. You have to start preparing yourself now to raise a family. One cannot enter this way without knowing how to love. To love means having a desire to become more perfect, to help the beloved become better, to overcome any selfishness, to give oneself." [55] This plan for her young disciples was not simply the fruit of her reflections. Gianna had done this herself since her adolescent years. Her preparation had begun in her family, where her parents had passed on to her their joy in living, their love of poverty and the simple life, and the acceptance of God's will.

When Gianna joined Catholic Action, she absorbed its spirit of collaboration with the hierarchy, but she also became convinced of the possibility of the laity offering something specific, a presence and a witness in a world that is sometimes closed to the priest's influence.[56] With the aid of her spiritual director, prayer, and a pilgrimage to Lourdes, Gianna found her vocation. In the mid 1950s, when she met Pietro, her search ended.

Though his path was different as far as external circumstances go, Pietro was inspired by the same cultural surroundings. His family values were the same as those of Gianna's family, and the basis on which he wished to found a family was again the same as hers. Pietro was forty-two when he had a life-changing encounter with Gianna. He describes it thus: "It was a marvelous time; Gianna and I

---

55. A. Rimoldi, *Gianna Beretta Molla*, op. cit., 238.

56. Reflection points on the beauty of the doctor's mission in P. Molla-E. Guerriero, *Santa Gianna Beretta Molla*, op. cit., 59ff.

were overflowing with joy. There are some photos from that period in which the fullness of Gianna's joy is captured, so to speak. For example, there is the photo taken in the summer of 1955 on the snows of Livrio at Bormio. Her joy was heartfelt, transparent, genuine."[57]

Gianna was a young woman fully aware of her times—in fact, ahead of the times in her thought and action. She loved the beauties of nature and sports, and tried to share this passion with Pietro. On March 23 she wrote: "After breakfast, we leave right away with our skis and down . . . to the slopes. I usually go skiing with the instructor for a little while around 11:00 AM, and . . . all modesty aside, I have learned to ski even some difficult slopes. But don't worry—wherever it's too steep, the instructor has us go down the easier way. It's marvelous on the mountain, though. When you're way at the top, with the clear sky and the very white snow, one cannot help but rejoice and praise God! Pietro, you know how happy I am when I'm surrounded by nature; I could spend hours contemplating the beauty of creation."[58]

This is a harmonious snapshot in which her fiancé is not a rival, but rather a companion on the way, the one in whom she places her trust. For his part, Pietro was caught up by this enthusiasm and conquered by Gianna's spontaneity and enthusiasm. She often wrote in her letters: "Tell me what I should do to make you happy." And Pietro reflected, "If she wanted to make me happy, what else could I want but to make her happy? That was how she helped me to come out of myself, to remove the mask I had when dealing with those around me."[59]

---

57. P. Molla-E. Guerriero, *Santa Gianna Beretta Molla,* op. cit., 44.
58. Letter of March 23, 1955.
59. P. Molla-E. Guerriero, *Santa Gianna Beretta Molla,* op. cit., 46.

Letters of the First Years of Marriage

These are letters mostly written during Pietro's business trips, from December 13, 1955 to February 18, 1959. During these three years, the first two children were born: Pierluigi and Maria Zita.

The most striking thing about these letters is the deepening of their mutual love, their joy at having children, and their love for the children. Additionally, the prejudiced notion that passion and love between spouses end with the marriage is roundly refuted. Two citations from Gianna's letters: On December 13, she wrote, "Pietro, you'll say I'm exaggerating, but the house is so empty and sad when you are not here! . . . My Pietro, I'm very happy because I love you, and you love me too, and I will always do everything I can to be a good, loving, understanding, and always smiling wife." [60]

And on July 20, 1958: "Dear Pietro, it would be so wonderful to be able to be together, united, all of the time. Luckily, your vacation begins in only ten days: what joy!" On his part, Pietro blends the best of these two sentiments in his letter of April 7, 1957: "I wouldn't be able to sleep if I didn't first lovingly communicate with you, always so loving and caring, whom I wish I could always have near me. . . . Right now I'm thinking of you with Pierluigi in your arms. . . . I kiss and embrace you with all my love, and together with you, I kiss our treasure very much." Love for their children, then, took nothing from the intensity of the love of husband and wife, but gave to the two the happiness of offspring, the cares of helping them grow and learn, and the intense joy of being parents, participants in God's creative work. Gianna also wrote: "The Lord has blessed our love once more by giving us another child—I am happy, and with the help of our Heavenly Mother, and with you close to

---

60. Letter of December 13, 1955.

me, you who are so good and understanding and affectionate, the sufferings of this new pregnancy no longer frighten me." [62] Therefore the children were not burdens on the parents or obstacles to their self-realization, but as Psalm 128 attests, a sign of God's blessing.

Letters from the United States

In 1959, from April 26 till June 16, Mr. Molla had to take a long business trip to the States. During these fifty-two days, Gianna and Pietro wrote to each other about every other day, which attests to an affection that, as the years passed, lost none of its intensity but instead matured and solidified. In spite of his constant traveling and the demands of his work in weather that was sometimes burdensome, Pietro answered Gianna's letters and tried to be present to her by sending postcards and some audiotapes. During these nearly two months, Gianna, with Pierluigi and Mariolina, went back to the house of her paternal grandparents in Magenta where her brother Francesco, her sister Zita, and her brother Ferdinando with his family all still lived. Zita especially was a great help to the saint who was expecting her third child.

There are three dominant themes in these letters: the maturity of their mutual affection; the pain caused by their being apart; and the first appearance of suffering, which gives love new authenticity. Here are three passages testifying to the fullness of the love between Gianna and Pietro, who, despite this, still faced and overcame difficulties that many other couples also experience—overcame them with full trust in God who clothes the lilies of the field and lovingly watches over each person:

61. All of her pregnancies were accompanied by illness and acute pains. —Ed.
62. Letter of April 11, 1957.

"Cecco took them to Lugano in the afternoon. So many sweet memories! I saw the long lake where you took your first picture of me at the Felix Hotel. I wish you could have been there with me again, so I could embrace you and kiss you and thank you for your great love for me and all the joys you've brought me these past three years." [63]

The sweetness then progresses to tenderness and wistfulness: "I preferred to stay at home where it's quiet, since the ninth month starts today and I get tired easily. All alone and with much emotion, I read and re-read the most affectionate letters you've sent me so faithfully every day from America. I am in your dear company, feeling better today . . . but yesterday, I will admit, I was a bit down. I wanted you here with me, and I missed you so much that I decided to write and tell you to come home right away. But the feeling passed. . . . Today I say, 'Come home as soon as possible, Pedrin *d'or*, as soon as you can.'" [64]

But it was not only her husband's absence that caused Gianna anxiety. She was having a difficult pregnancy, but of this one only catches a hint in her letters, so as not to worry her husband: "I always have the burning stomach pains, but at least I have some suffering to offer the Lord for you, my treasure, so you come back safe and sound—and soon." [65]

A month before the birth of her third child, she had a crisis. [66] Admitted to the hospital in Monza, she did so well that on June 17, she was discharged and was able to go to the airport to pick up her husband who was back from the States.

---

63. Letter of May 8, 1959.

64. Letter of May 24, 1959.

65. Letter of June 1, 1959.

66. Letter to her friend Mariuccia Parmigiani, July 18, 1959.

Letters of Maturity

These are the letters written between December 1959 and December 1961. During these two years Gianna watched over her children, practiced her medical profession, and was president of the women's Catholic Action. Ever in love with her husband, she attracted him by her sweetness. Her husband's trips became less frequent, and at times Gianna accompanied him, enjoying seeing new places as well as being together with him. In December 1960 they were in England and Holland; in July 1961 they traveled to Denmark and Sweden.

In these letters, the most prevalent theme is tenderness. Gianna wrote in July 1960: "I think of you every moment, in your travels and your work, and I am very close to you with all my affection and love." [67] On his part, Pietro replied, " . . .I keep thinking of the marvelous, unforgettable days in Naples and Capri when we fully relived our honeymoon; and it comforts me to think of the smiles and joyous happiness of our babies and how secure I feel since you are with them." [68]

In her second to last letter to him in February 1961, Gianna wrote to her husband: "My Pietro, how often I think of you and how I wish you were here with us! Thank you for everything, Pedrin d'or: for your great love, your care, for all your goodness. Your treasures kiss you with much love, and together with them your most affectionate Gianna." [69] This is a letter revealing the fullness of love filled with nostalgia and tenderness; it became what amounts to a testament to her children, and also to her many devotees.

---

67. Letter of July 4, 1960.
68. Letter of August 4, 1960.
69. Letter of February 14, 1961.

Looking over the correspondence as a whole, one cannot help admiring this couple who could reach the fullness of love in their mature years—the doctor who could give herself equally to her patients and to her family, and the manager who at the height of his career found time, energy, and much tenderness for his family.

Spirituality

I have already mentioned that Gianna and Pietro's letters, like the human and spiritual vision they reveal, were deeply influenced by their common formation in Catholic Action. After the fall of Fascism, Catholic Action represented an imposing force on the Italian political and social scene. The members were numerous among both men and women. Catholic Action provided formation for those at the head of the Christian Democrats, who, with the Church's aid, won the elections in 1948. Their time in power, under the guidance of De Gasperi, guaranteed civil and religious freedom in Italy, but only gave second place to social needs that some parts of the movement and some members of the clergy tried to meet (including Father Olinto Marella, who knew Pietro and Gianna). Generous and active, the members of Catholic Action did not distance themselves in any significant way from the traditional expression of Catholicism in Italy: devotion to the Blessed Sacrament, Marian devotion, and pilgrimages. In spite of this, we find ourselves face to face with a solid spirituality that was able to seriously motivate its members to action, witnessing to Christian presence in society. They had an acronym, PAS (prayer, action, sacrifice), which sums up their spirit and appears frequently in conferences Gianna gave the members, while at the same time we see in the letters published in this book that the husband and wife faithfully following this life plan.

Prayer

Gianna wrote to Pietro in her letter of September 4, 1955: "What would you say about our making a triduum to prepare spiritually to receive the Sacrament?" This is a rather curious suggestion coming from a young woman in love preparing to meet her beloved, a woman who had a thousand things to think about. But this young woman knew how to give prayer first place. Pietro did not show any surprise in response.[70] He made her suggestion his own, as we can see from the letters. In addition, the two made a habit of saying the Rosary and participating fully in the Church's liturgical life. Even when he was traveling, Pietro not only said his prayers but also attended Mass when he could.[71] Both husband and wife were devoted to the Blessed Virgin and consecrated each new baby to her as soon as it was born. All in all, their piety was not uncommon for their time, but it was earnest and enthusiastic, especially since they believed that the faith strengthened their love and communion.

Action

The second part of the trifold plan given to the members of Catholic Action was action. As we have already seen, during the tragedy of the war, the Catholic laity showed great ability to organize. They actively helped in the reconstruction of their homeland, and made obvious the Catholic contribution to public life in their country. Out of family habit and cultural influence, Gianna and Pietro were already inclined to action. To this inclination Gianna

---

70. Letter of September 4, 1955.
71. See especially his letter of May 16, 1959, from New York.

added her particular vocation of caring for her patients, whether these were children, adults, or the elderly, while Pietro was caught up in the whirlwind of SAFFA's expansion that rapidly unfolded during the 1940s and early 1950s. One unique characteristic of Pietro as an engineer and manager was his attention to technological advances. These advances made jobs fewer, so to avoid a loss of jobs he constantly pursued new avenues of production. In his case, charity led him to diversify production. It should also be noted that the sanctification of Sundays and living family life were effective antidotes to the excessive work schedule he had followed before meeting Gianna.

Sacrifice

The third and last distinctive part of Catholic Action's life plan was sacrifice. This was certainly not a exclusive or pietistic element, but a real pathway of formation that molded strong characters, able to tackle life with dedication and courage. This was certainly the case with Gianna. As her husband insistently stressed, the doctor was a beautiful, fascinating woman who skied, loved to be outdoors—especially in the mountains—and enjoyed a good classical music concert. Sacrifice was not pursued for its own sake, then, but out of love for her husband, children, and neighbors. The same decision that led her to sacrifice her life, taken with resolute, firm courage in the conviction that she must place her child's life above her own, seemed, in the days between her child's birth and her own death, to bring about such suffering that it seemed like the suffering of Jesus in the Garden of Gethsemane. Her husband remembered that Gianna's decision to give her life for her daughter was "dramatic. The more I think about it, the more I realize what a sacrifice it must have been for this woman." After Gianna Emanuela's birth, the mother "with difficulty took the baby in her arms, lifted her up, and kissed her, looking at her with such sadness that I knew she was aware that she would leave this child an orphan."[72]

Pietro, too, was called upon to give his assent to his wife's decision, to keep his word right up till her death, and after that, to bear the unbearable—the death of his second child. At the same time the need to continue providing for and raising his children left him no time to linger over his own sorrow or to fully give vent to his sufferings.

Conclusion

Up till now we have examined the characteristics the husband and wife gleaned from Catholic Action. These three distinctive characteristics, however, were supported and strengthened by their mutual love. In prayer, the couple's love was enlivened by communion with the eternal love of God who, like a spring of water, bubbled up and slaked the thirsting souls of the spouses, who continually drew new vigor for their love and reciprocal communion from liturgical and personal prayer. Benedict XVI wrote in his encyclical on charity: "The story of the love between God and man consists in the fact that this communion of wills grows in communion of thought and feeling and, thus, our will and God's will coincide more and more."[73] In marriage, then, the love between husband and wife is a sign and image of the love of Christ for his Church (Eph 5:23–33). It is a mystical love that also becomes an active love toward one's neighbor. There is "an unbreakable link between love for God and love for neighbor."[74] This was what motivated Gianna and Pietro in

---

72. P. Molla-E. Guerriero, *Santa Gianna Beretta Molla,* op. cit., 68.

73. *Deus Caritas Est,* no. 17.

74. Ibid., no. 16.

their professional lives and in what is now called volunteer work. We could also add that between the two forms of activity there was no disjoint but only continuity and complementarity. The very same communion with God was, in fact, the source of their love for their children. In the photos of Gianna with her children in her arms, she looks like a radiant woman, happy to have given them life and love. Pietro too, as can be seen in his letters, loved his children with generosity and dedication, thus weaving a net of love among the generations that is the foundation of transmitting life, but also of peace and future social harmony.

Benedict XVI writes in the aforementioned encyclical, "The lives of the saints are not limited to their earthly biographies but also include their being and working in God after death. In the saints one thing becomes clear: those who draw near to God do not withdraw from men, but rather become truly close to them."[75]

For this reason we can be sure that Saint Gianna and Pietro Molla are still close to us with their love, their prayers, their works, and their willingness to give.

---

75. Ibid., no. 42.

PART I

"I Really Want to Make You Happy"

The Engagement Letters

Kind Doctor,

An endless round of visits, meetings, and banquets with their endless and tiring ceremonies, typical of the Nordic countries, has left me little free time during the day and even forced me to wait till this evening before I could tell you again of my gratitude for the lovely evening we spent together.[1]

The memory of that evening has come back to me very often during these days.

My work[2] on this trip has turned out really well. I'll be finished by Friday and expect to be back Sunday or Monday.

The sky has been serene the whole time, even though its colors are pale from sunrise to sunset. The sun is nearly always shining, though it appears to be very far off; there is snow everywhere, but it's not as cold as I expected—only a few degrees below zero [Celsius].

When I return, I'll tell you all the interesting details of my trip.

With cordial greetings from,

Pietro Molla

---

1. Gianna and Pietro had become better acquainted toward the end of 1954, on the feast of the Immaculate Conception when they both attended the ordination of Father Lino Garavaglia, the future bishop of Cesena and Sarsina. For New Year's Eve they had attended a ballet at La Scala together, and at the beginning of 1955 they had begun to date.

2. In 1955, Pietro Molla, an engineer, was the central director of SAFFA (Societa per Azioni Fabbriche Fiammiferi ed Affini), a very large industrial enterprise whose head plant was in Ponte Nuovo di Magenta. Mr. Molla in particular was involved in planning expansion strategies.

FEBRUARY 21, 1955

MONDAY

Dearest Pietro,

I hope you don't mind if I begin this letter by calling you by your first name and using such familiar language. After sharing our thoughts so openly yesterday, I think we can assume this level of intimacy, which will help us to understand and to love each other more and more.

I really want to make you happy and be what you desire: good, understanding, and ready for the sacrifices that life will require of us. I haven't told you yet that I have always been very sensitive and eager for affection. While I had my parents,[3] their love was enough for me. Then, although remaining very united to the Lord and working for him, I felt the need for a mother, and I found her in the dear nun whom I told you about yesterday.[4]

Now there is you, whom I already love, and to whom I intend to give myself to form a truly Christian family.

Ciao, dear Pietro. Pardon my familiarity, but that's how I am. *Arrivederci.*

With affection,

Gianna

---

3. Her mother died April 29, 1942, and her father died September 10 of the same year.

4. The saint refers to Sister Marianna Meregalli, whom she knew at Magenta in the years 1945–1949. The letters give evidence that Sister Marianna was particularly close to her in those years of research and apostolic work among the young women of Catholic Action.

MAGENTA, FEBRUARY 22, 1955
TUESDAY

My dearest Gianna,

I've read your letter over and over, and kissed it.

A new life is beginning for me: the life of your great (and greatly desired) affection and of your radiant goodness. We are starting the journey of our love.

I love you, my dearest Gianna.

I could not have received a greater or more ardently desired grace from our Heavenly Mother, Our Lady of Good Counsel, as she is invoked in my little church in Ponte Nuovo.[5]

I so wanted and needed love and a family of my own. Now I have you, your love and affection, and I am happy.

My love is yours, and I want to raise a family with you. I too want to make you happy and understand you well.

Forgive me for not beginning a closer confidence sooner than I did.[6] Thank you for your help and trust.

With all my love,

Pietro

MARCH 11, 1955

Dearest Pietro,

I don't have words to thank you for all your thoughtfulness and kindness toward me. Thank you for the beautiful roses and for the

---

5. Starting in the 1940s, Pietro had lived in Ponte Nuovo di Magenta, and had a particular devotion to Our Lady of Good Counsel, to whom the church was dedicated.

6. Pietro, who was more reserved by nature, had been pleasantly surprised by Gianna's spontaneity; she had moved ahead more quickly in the direction of greater trust and familiarity.

hours we spent together last night. You know, I feel bad because I'm stealing your precious hours of sleep, when you need to rest after a day of work and worry. On the other hand, I am so happy in your company that I wish time would stand still when I'm with you.

Pietro, if only I could tell you all I feel for you! But I can't—you will have to read between the lines. The Lord has truly blessed me. You are the man I had wished for, but I often ask myself, "Will I be worthy of him?" Yes, worthy of you, Pietro, because I want so much to make you happy, but I fear not being able to do so, and I often feel I am unable to do anything. When this happens, I ask God, "Lord, you see my desire and my good will. Supply what is lacking and help me to become the wife and mother you desire and which I think Pietro wants, too."[7] Is that all right, Pietro?

I greet you with so, so much love, your

Gianna

SESTRIÈRE, MARCH 21, 1955[8]

Very best regards

Gianna

MAGENTA, MARCH 21, 1955

Dearest Gianna,

Why thank me for my efforts and kindness, which come easily to me because of our great love, and which I really owe you because of how good you are to me?

---

7. Mention should be made of her attentiveness and availability to the holy will of God. It is a characteristic trait of her person and her spirituality.

8. On holiday at Sestrière [an alpine resort], Gianna sent Pietro a postcard. On the same day, he responded to the letter dated March 11.

Gianna and Pietro on the day of their engagement, April 11, 1955.

On an outing in the snow at Livrio, August 1955.

I would like to always cover you with affectionate attention, because I would like to see you always filled with joy, the same joy I have.

I was in the plant and office a long time today, from 6:30 AM to 4:00 PM.

If you only knew, Gianna, how peaceful I am, tonight too, and how dear to me and vivid is the sweet memory of the hours I've spent with you, in the evenings and on our outings—the sweet memory of sharing our dreams and promises, of confiding our joys and hopes to each other! How I love remembering your dear, sweet face, and that smile only you have!

Your gentle humility makes your gifts more beautiful and your love sweeter.

That's the answer to the question you asked me: You are everything to me, dearest Gianna.

You have already filled my life with yourself, in both affection and desires.

I already feel that you are the worthy spouse I hoped for and the incomparable mother of the children with whom God will bless us.

I pray that the Lord will make me always worthy of you.

I am with you in spirit, and I can just picture you beautiful and serene, happy and full of life on those snowy slopes you love so much.

I'm thinking of you, and I hope you're having a really good time with your cousin.[9]

---

9. Pier Angela Beretta, Gianna's cousin. The two had been friends mainly since October 1942 when Gianna, who was about to start her medical studies, returned to Magenta with her siblings after the death of their parents and lived in the same big house where Pier Angela already lived.

With the greatest affection I remember you, and I'm so looking forward to seeing you again Saturday.

Your

Pietro

Cordial greetings to Miss Piera.

SESTRIÈRE
MARCH 21, 1955
MONDAY EVENING

Dearest Pietro,

Now I feel happier because I heard your voice on the phone. As I told you, it snowed all day today, but I skied for about four hours[10] anyway. To make up for the cloudy day, all the stars are out this evening, so I hope tomorrow will be nice. I am really enjoying the wonderful atmosphere and service of the hotel—the only thing missing is you, Pietro. I'm already looking forward to the joy of having you with me this weekend. I will pick you up so that I can spend the last hours of my vacation with you. Thank you for the beautiful outing in Switzerland on Saturday. You're too good to me—I don't deserve it at all, but I promise to do all I can for you in return.

Do you still have a lot of work to do? It doesn't seem fair that you're there working, while I am here doing nothing. If only I could send you a little bit of this fresh air, I would do it with all my heart!

Ciao, dear Pietro, greet your dear parents for me, and *arrivederci*. With much love, your

Gianna

---

10. The saint, who had from childhood frequented the mountains, was a good skier. Her genuine appreciation of the alpine scenery, and of nature in general, should be emphasized because in contemplating it she found God.

SESTRIÈRE
MARCH 23, 1955
WEDNESDAY EVENING

Dearest Pietro,

I found your letter today at lunchtime when I came back from skiing. You can imagine how happy you made me with all of your sweet and affectionate expressions of love. Thank you, dear Pietro, I love you too, very much, and I know we will always love each other. You're so good and intelligent that you'll always understand me and we won't be able to disagree. I'm sorry you were so busy with work on Monday. My thoughts are always with you, Pietro, and if I could help you I would do it with all my heart.

Yesterday and today we had beautiful, sunny weather. I get up at 8:00 in the morning (what a lazybones! you are already in the office!) and go to Holy Mass[11] at 8:30. I have never enjoyed Holy Mass and Holy Communion as much as I do here. The beautiful little church is always quiet and empty. The celebrant doesn't even have an altar boy, so I have the Lord all to myself, and all for you, Pietro, because already, where I am, you are too.[12]

After breakfast, we leave right away with our skis and down . . . to the slopes. I usually go skiing with the instructor for a little while around 11:00 AM, and . . . all modesty aside, I have learned to ski even some difficult slopes. But don't worry—wherever it's too steep, the instructor has us go down the easier way. It's marvelous on the mountain, though. When you're way at the top, with the clear sky and the very white snow, one cannot help but rejoice and praise God!

---

11. The saint was eager to attend Mass every day. As we see, she did not even miss daily Mass during vacation.

12. The two young people were preparing now for their engagement and lived a spiritual union that anticipated their sacramental union.

Pietro, you know how happy I am when I'm surrounded by nature; I could spend hours contemplating the beauty of creation.

Around 3:00 PM, after lunch, a brief nap, and a little walk, I go back to the slopes until about 6:00 PM. After that, the time drags; I'm lucky to have Piera here—she's so much fun and we laugh so much!

So that is how my days go—a little bit different from yours, poor Pietro, always working.

Two more days and then we will see each other, what joy!

Ciao, dear Pietro, greet your dear parents and your sister Adelaide for me, and a big hug from your most beloved

Gianna

Piera thanks you and returns your greetings.

SESTRIÈRE
MARCH 25, 1955
FRIDAY

Dearest Pietro,

I'm sending you some pictures[13] of me, and I hope you will like them. The weather is always beautiful here—we are very sunburned! . . .

You won't recognize me when you see me, my face is so burned— here red, there black, a little of every color. Creams are useless. Our attraction to the ski slopes is so strong that we ignore our burned faces and go back anyway.

My dear Pietro, my happiness would be complete if you were here with me to enjoy this fresh air, but we will spend our next vacation together, right?

---

13. Gianna Beretta Molla is one of the first saints of whom we have ordinary everyday photographs. It is possible to see in these frequent pictures, and in her profound gaze, the radiant joy of a face illuminated by Christian love.

I want to be a joy and comfort to you because you deserve it and need it with all your work and preoccupations.[14] This means you have to pull my ears whenever I fail in this respect! *Ciao*, dearest Pietro. Waiting to embrace you again tomorrow, I send you the most affectionate and cordial greetings.

Your

Gianna

MAGENTA, MARCH 28, 1955
MONDAY

Most beloved Gianna,

After your phone call at noon today, I received the letter you sent Friday, and the lovely photos. You couldn't have sent me a more beautiful gift from Sestrière, or one I would have liked more!

I have them here in front of me, and I'm keeping them with me. How many times I've already looked at them today, and how often I'll be looking at them during the coming days—especially during these months when I can't have you here with me every day, as I would like to—and whenever I have the greatest need of your joy and support!

Looking at you, dearest Gianna, seeing your sweet loveliness and reading the great love in your eyes is like a balm of serenity and life.

Thank you from my heart, and with all my love, for making the long trip to meet me on the road to Sestrière.[15]

---

14. In regard to this her husband has said, "From the beginning and in almost every letter she repeated this request: 'Tell me what I must do to make you happy.' It was not difficult for me to match this love of hers. If she wanted to make me happy, what could I possibly do but make her happy?"

15. Over the weekend Pietro had visited his fiancée, who had come to meet him as he arrived by car.

I love to remember your affectionate embrace when we met and the restful tranquility of the unforgettable hours we spent together. I want to thank you again for taking me up to the snowy peaks, surrounded by sky and sun.

I am very happy to receive the invitation to take our next vacation together. It will be the most beautiful, joyful, and restful vacation.

For the first time together, we heard Holy Mass and received Jesus in Holy Communion.[16]

"Thank you for giving me Gianna as the sweet companion of my life. Make our love grow ever greater, sweeter, and purer.

"Make me worthy of her, and may our family receive Heaven's blessings; may we and our children be holy": this was my prayer to Jesus as soon as he had come into my heart, while at the same time I was moved by your devout recollection while you were talking to Jesus.

With the greatest love, I embrace you,

Your

Pietro

APRIL 9, 1955

My dearest Pietro,

How can I thank you for the magnificent ring?[17] Pietro dear, in exchange, I give you my heart and I will always love you as I love you now. You are the dearest person to me, and my thoughts,

---

16. Pietro had gone to Mass with Gianna. He too reveals a firm and devout faith, as his prayer after Communion shows.

17. Pietro gave Gianna the engagement ring a few days before the date they had set of April 11.

affections, and desires are continually turning toward you on this eve of our engagement. I can't wait for the moment when I can be yours forever. Pietro dearest, you know that I want to see and to know that you are happy; tell me what I should be and what I should do to make you so. I have great trust in the Lord, and I am certain that he will help me to become your worthy spouse.

I often meditate on the words of the Epistle of the Mass of Saint Anne: "A strong woman, who will find her? . . . The heart of her husband can trust in her . . . she will do only good things for him and never bring evil upon him throughout all of his life" (Prov 31:10).

Pietro, I want to be that strong woman of the Gospel! Instead, I think and feel myself weak. This means that I must lean on your strong arm. I feel so safe, so close to you! I ask you a favor: from now on, Pietro, if you see me doing something wrong, tell me, okay? I will always be grateful to you if you do this.

With much, much love, I embrace you, and I wish you a Holy Easter.

Your

Gianna

MAGENTA, APRIL 11, 1955[18]

OUR ENGAGEMENT DAY

With sweetest joy, and all my love,

Your Pietro

---

18. This note probably came with some flowers from Pietro.

MAGENTA, APRIL 15, 1955

My dearest Gianna,

I'm still beside myself with the joy you have given me by our engagement, that sweet joy renewed at every moment knowing that your thoughts, affections, and desires are directed toward me, that sweetest joy which I hope will be just as great in you, the beloved object of my thoughts, of all my love and desires.

In return for the gift of your heart and your love, my heart is all yours, and my love will be only and always for you, O my dearest Gianna.

You are my jewel, delicate and so beautiful in virtue and goodness, in the beauty of your smile.

My love for you will always be brighter than the light reflecting from our engagement ring!

The lovely watch you gave me will be with me during the most beautiful time of my life: the time of our love, of our family.[19]

You are the strong woman I begged Heaven for, and whom our Heavenly Mother has given me.

I entrust my whole heart to you forever, and I will receive everything good from you.

Always love me as you do now; always be affectionate and good, thoughtful, sweet and understanding as you are now—that is how you have made me happy and how I ask you to always make me happy.

To me you are the strong woman of the Gospel.

When I am with you, my joy is full.

---

19. "The time of our love and of our family": an expression of rare incisiveness which half a century later seems prophetic since now the love of family life seems almost forgotten.

I am sure you will never give me any reason to have to correct you. To your question, I answer with the same request on my part.

I still see you, so devout during our engagement Holy Mass, and I am certain of the divine blessing called down on us by dear Father Giuse.[20]

I see you, and I again rejoice in thinking how beautiful and sweet you were to everyone on our engagement afternoon.

I am thinking of you and embrace you with all my love,

Your Pietro

APRIL 18, 1955

MONDAY EVENING

My dearest Pietro,

Today of all days, when I wasn't expecting to enjoy your dear company, I have you even closer to me: I received your letter. Pietro, thank you for being so good and affectionate. Your words touched me, and I'm happy that in answer to my question, "How should I be to make you happy?" you answer I should continue to be good, affectionate, and understanding as I am now. I will, dearest Pietro, and it will be easy, because you are so good to me.

I already knew that you loved me, but being reminded of your love through your letter today filled my heart with joy. Just think, Pietro, what a great gift the Lord has given to us—how thankful we must always be for it![21]

---

20. Father Giuseppe Beretta, Gianna's priest-brother.

21. After expressing her love fully, the saint turns her thoughts to God, not that human love needs to be corrected and disowned before God. Just the opposite: when it is authentic, love between Christians leads to God in spontaneity and gratitude. We recall Benedict XVI's words to engaged couples: "The experience of love has within it the movement toward God" (Ancona, September 11, 2011).

Pietro, I promised you that I would always tell you my worries. I must tell you about something that causes me to suffer.

I'm afraid your parents[22] aren't satisfied with me, that I am not what they wanted for you. I know you always have been and still are the center of their affections, and now I feel like I'm taking you away from them. And while I love them because they're your dear parents, I don't feel for them the affection I think I should because they have always shown me such delicacy and kindness.

If I made you sad by telling you this, forgive me.

Ciao, dear Pietro, be happy, and many big kisses from your

Gianna

MAGENTA, APRIL 20, 1955

My dearest Gianna,

There's no reason for your doubts or fears.

Mamma, Papa, and my sisters believe I could not have found anyone better than you, anyone more suited to their hopes and mine, anyone better suited to my character and life.

Mamma, Papa, and my sisters[23] hoped and prayed so much that we would meet and become engaged much sooner than last December, and they couldn't be happier about our love, our engagement and upcoming marriage.

---

22. Pietro's parents, Luigi Molla (1884–1956) and Maria Salmoiraghi (1885–1978), were very close to their son. This attachment was the cause of a slight misunderstanding that was quickly clarified, as evident from the letter that follows.

23. As we have already seen, Pietro had four sisters: Maria Rosa (b. November 2, 1914), Adelaide (b. April 27, 1920), Sister Luigia (b. March 16, 1922), and Teresina. Teresina, who was born April 1, 1927, died of nephritis at only twenty-three, on April 21, 1950. At the time of this sister's illness, Pietro and Gianna met for the second time at the hospital in Magenta.

You are the woman my loved ones hoped I would find.

That I am the center of their affection—that's true. But it's just as true that for years they strongly urged me to start a family, so they are well prepared to accept and bear the sacrifice of my no longer being all theirs. They will be greatly rewarded by knowing how happy I am with my sweet companion in the family I shall form with you.

Mamma and Papa are very good people, made in the best of the old mold.

They're only comfortable speaking in their dialect, and they only feel completely at ease in their own environment.

Sometimes they can look or act as though they're uncomfortable, but having to speak in Italian, with people whom they don't yet know well, makes them seem embarrassed or almost fearful of making mistakes, or of not being equal to the persons, places, or circumstances in which they find themselves.

These worries and embarrassment, which I think are groundless, will disappear once they get to know [your family] and when loving familiarity develops.

If you only knew how many inner treasures of the heart and what a sacrificial spirit Papa and Mamma have!

Is it too much, O my dearest Gianna, if I dare to ask—in fact if I certainly wish—that you would be Papa's and Mamma's most loving daughter and best-loved sister of my sisters?

You are the welcome one, the one all my loved ones wanted me to have.

You are my most beloved Gianna, whom I wish I had here beside me to press close to my heart and tell you again, with my kisses, of all my love.

Your Pietro

JUNE 10, 1955

My dearest Pietro,

Knowing that it gives you so much pleasure to receive my scribbles, I am sending you these few lines to tell you again how happy I am and I am sure that it is the same with you. You've got a heart so big, good, and understanding, we will always agree and we will want always what's best.

Dear Pietro, last Sunday when your mother said that if she should ever see you unhappy, she wouldn't know what to do, I began to wonder if perhaps I'm not the right person for you, that I'm not good or understanding enough. Now, though, after your repeated reassuring words, I am at peace and rejoice to know that you are happy.[24]

Dearest Pietro, I don't know how to thank you for the beautiful doctor's office [25] you're preparing for me with so much love. When it's finished and I move in, I will have you even closer to me in my work; in this way, you, too, will alleviate suffering and give joy to my dear patients.

I love you so, so much, Pietro, and you are always with me, starting in the morning during Holy Mass. At the Offertory, I offer your work, your joys, and your sufferings along with mine; then I repeat the offering all day long until evening.[26]

---

24. Her delicacy and firm desire to make her husband happy should be noted.

25. This is the doctor's office (commonly called "ambulanza" in their dialect) that, after their engagement, Pietro began to prepare near her home. It was more spacious and better equipped than the one rented in Mesero.

26. It is the Catholic understanding that spouses should be examples for the whole Church. The sacrament of Matrimony allows them to actually live out the exchange of joys and sufferings, sacrifices and serenity which is proper to the life of grace. It also invites the comparison between engagement and the trial period in

I wish I could see you every day, but . . . that would be too greedy of me. When you're tired, you must tell me and not beat around the bush, so I'll send you home earlier—do you understand? You're already tired from work, and I wouldn't want to be a cause of your falling apart.

Ciao, take care of yourself, and big, big kisses, your

Gianna

MAGENTA, JUNE 24, 1955

THE NAME DAY[27] OF MY MOST BELOVED GIANNA

May you always be very happy, just as you are today, and I embrace and kiss you, with all my love and with the strongest emotion, since it's your feast day, in fact the dearest and sweetest of your feasts, the first joyous anniversary in the life of our most sweet love.

Your Pietro

SAINT PETER, 1955[28]

With all my affection I wish, dearest Pietro, that you may always be happy next to your

Gianna

---

the life of religious. Similar to the fervor of the novice is the exaltation of the couple's engagement, to be followed by a marriage that does not forget the tenderness of youth, but can face daily life, which requires the virtues of strength and perseverance, of discretion and justice.

27. June 24 is the feast of Saint John the Baptist, Gianna's patron saint.

28. This note of greeting was for June 29, the feast of the saints Peter and Paul.

JULY 5, 1955
TUESDAY EVENING

My dearest Pietro,

It's 9:00 PM, the time when my dear Pietro generally arrives. But not tonight—it's Tuesday! You'll tell me I'm too greedy and that I exaggerate, but the more I'm with you, the longer I want to stay; the more I know you, the more I love you. Dear Pietro, that's life. And I write to you tonight so that I can visit with you a little.[29]

Pietro, thank you for your love for me; I wanted a good, kind man, and the Lord has placed one by my side. I so want to be a joy and a comfort to you, but I sometimes wonder whether I am a burden to you. You're tired and weary, and I always keep you with me for hours!

While we were choosing furniture on Sunday, I could already feel the warmth of our little house, all beautiful, new, and shining. Thank you for your perfect understanding and efforts to satisfy my desires.

Think, Pietro, about our nest,[30] warmed by our love, and joyful with all the beautiful *popi* [31] the Lord will send us! There will be sorrows, too, of course, but if we always love each other as we do now, then, with God's help, we'll know how to bear them together. Don't you think so?

For now, though, let's enjoy the happiness of loving each other. I was always told that the secret of happiness lay in living one

---

29. On Tuesday Pietro, detained by work commitments, could not make their evening appointment.

30. There is a sense of discretion that must be cultivated around the house. Although open to everyone, it is above all the place of the family, where life encounters the love of the family members.

31. "Popi" is a term of the Lombard dialect for babies. The saint used it often as an expression of affection. In this case it emphasizes the joyful serenity of one accustomed to doing God's will.

moment at a time and in thanking the Lord for everything he sends us.[32] So, let's lift up our hearts and be happy!

Ciao, dearest Pietro. I'm not expecting an answer; I wrote only to pass the evening with you and to tell you another time I love you so, so much.

Big kisses, your

Gianna

SEPTEMBER 3, 1955

SATURDAY EVENING

Dearest Pietro,

I was waiting for you and was beginning to think something had happened to you, but your phone call relieved my fears. My Pietro, you know how happy I am when I can see you and be with you, and when anything prevents us from being together—even though the reasons are just—my heart . . . protests, though my mind says, "It's right, this is the right thing to do." Tonight, then, I'm writing to you in order to chase the blues away.

Pietro dearest, I want you to feel me very close to you these days, because you can't imagine how much I miss you when you are so far away. You'll say I'm exaggerating, but it's true. You are my Pietro, and I am already one with you in heart and soul.

You are so good, dearest; you love me so much, and I love you so, so much. Your joys are mine, and all that worries you or makes you sad worries me and makes me sad, too.[33]

When I think of our great, reciprocal love, I can do nothing but thank the Lord. It's true that love is the most beautiful sentiment that

---

32. Gianna is remembering what she learned from Sister Marianna Meregalli and Catholic Action. However, even before that she had the example of her parents.

33. She returns to the sense of human communion that faith not only recognizes, but also deepens and strengthens.

God has given to us.[34] And we'll always love each other as we do now, Pietro.

In only twenty days, I'll be . . . Gianna Molla! What would you say about our making a triduum[35] to prepare spiritually to receive this Sacrament? Holy Mass and Holy Communion on the twenty-first, twenty-second, and twenty-third, you at Ponte Nuovo, I at the Shrine of the Assumption.[36] The Blessed Mother will unite our prayers and, because strength is found in unity, Jesus can't help but listen to us and answer our prayers.[37]

I'm sure you will say yes, and I thank you.

Just think, the next time you travel, I will be there, right beside you, telling you over and over—until you're tired of it—that you are my whole life.

A thousand thanks, Pietro, for the magnificent little house you have prepared for me. I couldn't have wished for anything more beautiful. Soon it will be my turn to give to you by making it always warm and cozy.

---

34. Love and sentiment are the foundations of Christian aesthetics studied by the theologian Hans Urs von Balthasar.

35. Gianna invited her husband to a shared spiritual journey. She gradually revealed to him her deep Christian piety and invited him to follow her. Her husband spoke about it as a complete pedagogy because "at the very moment she invited me to these celebrations of liturgy and piety, she proposed to me a new model of human life" (P. Molla-E. Guerriero, *Santa Gianna Beretta Molla*, op. cit., 46).

36. The wedding was set for September 24. On the three days prior, the couple prepared with a triduum focused on Mass and Holy Communion. With this they were able to break away from the anxiety of everything involved in the wedding preparations in order to benefit from spiritual preparation.

37. Pietro went to the shrine of Our Lady of Good Counsel at Ponte Nuovo, Gianna to the Assumption at Magenta. The couple entrusted themselves to the Virgin Mary asking her to hear their prayers, and, as at Cana, to present them to Jesus with holy insistence.

Buon viaggio, dearest Pietro, and . . . don't miss the train next Sunday!

Big, big kisses, your

Gianna

SEPTEMBER 4, 1955

SUNDAY NIGHT

ON THE JOURNEY TO BASEL

Most beloved Gianna,

I can't sleep before telling you once more of my love for you.

Thank you, most affectionately, thank you for having given me such wonderful companions on my trip—your sweet, precious photos,[38] a tangible expression of your great love.

You wanted to lighten the sadness of my leaving with your dear greeting, and I am imagining you again next to me, in my compartment, so full of love.

In reading, reading, and re-reading your letter with growing joy, I wanted to have you close to me to embrace and kiss you and tell you again of all my love, of my thanks for the infinite joy you give me, to repeat again, with you, our deepest gratitude toward the Lord for having loved us so much.

Thank you for the holy suggestion of making a triduum.[39] I welcome it with all my enthusiasm.

I, at the little Church of Our Lady of Good Counsel, and you at the Shrine of the Assumption, will whisper our desires, hopes, promises, and prayers. Our Lady of Good Counsel will be a witness

---

38. Some photos of Gianna that Pietro carried in his briefcase.

39. In the preceding day's letter, Gianna had suggested to Pietro that they prepare for their wedding with three days of recollection and prayer, participating in the Eucharist each day. Pietro enthusiastically took Gianna up on this suggestion.

that my desires, my hopes, and my promises will only be for you, and my prayers will all be for you and your happiness.

Everything reminds me of you.

Pausing in Como, Brunate, lit up by the rose-colored sunset, was for me the first meeting of our sentiments, our hearts and our souls.[40] And I have blessed and thanked God that now we are only one heart and one soul, joined together by the greatest and most joyful love.

I saw you there with me on the lake once more, and at Lugano I thought of you again, so recollected in prayer, before Our Lady of Locarno, and I thanked God for having given me, in you, such a model of devout piety and saintly virtue.

Now it is night, but I have your beloved picture here before me, in all its lovely beauty, with your smile, full of light and affection for me who loves you with the same immense love.

I'm thinking of my next trip when I'll have you with me; and the more you'll tell me over and over that I'm your whole life, the happier I'll be, because you, Gianna, are my life, my joy, and my love.

And I thank you; most lovingly I thank you. I think of you always and I kiss you with a long, most sweet kiss.

Your Pietro

SEPTEMBER 5, 1955
MONDAY EVENING, AROUND 10:00 PM
ABOARD THE *KING FREDERICK IX*
ON THE WAY TO DENMARK

Dearest Gianna,

I had nine good hours of sleep the first night on the train, and today was a long day going through Germany. It was longer than

---

40. When they were newly engaged, Pietro and Gianna had taken a trip to Lugano, passing through Como.

usual since we had a five-hour delay caused by storms in the Saint Gotthard Pass, right at Basel.

Dr. Busnelli buried himself in his books today, devouring, with great irony, Salter's *Processo all Psicanalisi* [The Case Against Psychoanalysis], published by Vita e Pensiero.[41]

I only read Papini's *"Schegge"*[42] on the third page of yesterday's *Corriere [della Sera].*

We left Germany for Denmark this evening, six hours late.

Today was a calm succession of all shades of green in the fields and woods, studded with red, pink, and white houses, up high, all beautifully lined up.

And in every one of those houses I saw our little house, the one I've prepared with so much love for you, and the one that will always be happy and precious to me because of you, O my sweetest Gianna.

Dr. Busnelli told me the Holy Father receives newlyweds at Castel Gandolfo[43] on Wednesdays and possibly Sunday afternoons, too. We'll want to go Sunday afternoon.[44] Or do we want to ask (through Monsignor Bertoglio[45]) for a private audience?

My friend Busnelli recommended Villa Borghese and Villa Sciarra with their gardens, and a drive through the Roman hills and lakes.

Gianna, today you were the most wonderful of all my thoughts.

---

41. Andrew Salter, *Processo alla Psicanalisi* (Milan: Vita e Pensiero, 1954).

42. "Schegge" (Splinters) a newspaper column by Giovanni Papini. —Ed.

43. Pope Pius XII (1876–1958), who was nearing eighty, was in poor health; thus at the time he prolonged his stays in the pontifical villa of Castel Gandolfo.

44. Pietro is alluding to a pontifical audience during their honeymoon.

45. Bishop Francesco Bertoglio (1900–1977), a native of Magenta, was rector of the Pontifical Lombard Seminary, Rome, 1933–1960, when ordained auxiliary bishop of Milan. His cousin, Serafino Bertoglio, married Carla Beretta, Piera's sister and Gianna's cousin. In 2010, Bishop Bertoglio was awarded the title "Righteous Among the Nations" by the State of Israel for having saved sixty-five Jews during World War II.

On the prow of this ship, which is sailing quietly on a peaceful sea, I'm saying the Holy Rosary and begging every grace for you and our family from Our Lady of the Sea, the Mother of Good Counsel in the little church at Ponte Nuovo, and Our Lady of the Assumption of your fervent daily prayers.

Here, with the sea as my witness and under the gaze of the stars, I kiss and re-kiss your sweet picture to keep you close to me, even though the prow is headed north.

And I feel you as close to me as you were in the sweet hours we passed together, when our gazes met; you became almost transfigured, and your beautiful, luminous eyes, and your look of infinite love, radiated the light of happiness: your happiness, Gianna, because of my equally great joy.

A kiss as deep and sweet as the sea from

Your Pietro

Remember me to Zita, Cecco, Nando, and his family for me.

SEPTEMBER 6, 1955

TUESDAY EVENING

ON THE TRAIN FROM STOCKHOLM TO SÖDERHAMN

My dearest Gianna,

Another day traveling north, but now there's one day less separating us from the divine blessing on our love. And the farther north I have to go, the more I feel you and keep you with me, most beloved Gianna, always with me in heart and soul.

Last night, before midnight but after I had written you, I climbed up to the highest part of the ship. The clouds had dispersed, and the moon, with a silver sheen, was mirrored in the waves that were shimmering under the Baltic breeze. The moon's reflection seemed to me like a bright river, an infinite number of tiny flames: a river that, starting from my ship, traveled far, far away—all the way to you. And I felt you very close to me as you were on those moonlit evenings we spent together in your garden. I sent you another kiss, a long kiss, with a wish for a peaceful night like the night on these quivering waters kissed by the moon.[46]

I slept from the time our ship reached Denmark, along the Danish coast up to Copenhagen, through the border crossing between Denmark and Sweden, and for about 100 km past there. It was beautiful and sunny till 10:00 AM, but after that the sun only peeked out now and then; toward evening it was completely cloudy.

We passed countless pine and birch forests, interspersed here and there with small grassy fields, small orchards where they're only now collecting the fruit, and small lakes colored green by the reflections of the pines.

In between the cities we passed, there were little wooden houses of the woodsmen and peasants, beautiful but not neatly lined up as they are in Germany.

Having left at 8:00 AM, I arrived in Stockholm at 4:00 PM. On the train, as dusk was falling, I tried to take a few color pictures of the Royal Palace in the sunset, an enchanting vision of nature entwined together with the work of man.

See, Gianna, your love makes everything more beautiful to me, because in creation's beauty I see your wonderful beauty and your goodness and virtue, and because I am anticipating the joy of seeing all this again with you.

In the time between our arrival in Stockholm and leaving for Söderhamn at 5:00 PM, I sent you a postcard from the Grand Hotel.

---

46. The beauties of nature acquired even greater significance through the love of the engaged couple.

From here I wrote you my first letter.[47] Do you remember, Gianna? At that time I was dreaming of your being mine; today you *are* mine, and we are so happy.

Söderhamn, 10:00 PM

I was traveling again until 9:00 PM and after . . . fifty-two hours of travel and . . . wishing I could fly, I'm finally here. At last, tonight I won't have a bed on wheels.

I have a nice room.

With all my love, I kiss your photo from which you smile with joy at me, framed by the whiteness of the snows and the deep blue of the sky.

Good night, Gianna, and many, many kisses from

Your Pietro

SÖDERHAMN, SEPTEMBER 7, 1955

Most beloved Gianna,

My first thought this morning was of you, and the next was a "thank you" to the Lord for the past good night—yours and mine—and a great desire to see you again as soon as possible.

This morning, we drove 250 km along curves and endless hills and valleys. We had a wonderful, well-built Mercedes that sped more than 120 km an hour on the very few straight parts of the road, and almost 100 km on the curves and mountain ascents and descents. After a long train ride, there was another auto ride.

In the afternoon we drove another 80 km or so. This morning we had a very interesting visit to a plywood factory,[48] and in the

---

47. Letter of January 12, 1955, written on the letterhead of the Grand Hotel in Stockholm.

48. This was during the post-World War II reconstruction years when the foundation was being laid for the Italian economic boom of the 1960s. Pietro had

afternoon we had fine results on the test of our tree trunks[49] in the bark-stripping machine.

The sky was beautiful and clear all day long; the sunshine was splendid, and so were the lakes, forests, pastures, and houses; the flowers were really magnificent. If my color photos come out looking as beautiful as the things I was photographing, they will be splendid.

The Swedes lunch at . . . 1:00 PM; tea and . . . shrimp at 5:00; dinner at 9:00 and . . . a movie which I was invited to, so I couldn't refuse, from 7:00 to 9:00, *On the Waterfront* with Marlon Brando, in English with Swedish subtitles.

At supper tonight, Mr. and Mrs. Wistawuosi toasted us: "We wish you all happiness and many children" for our wedding on September 24. They will put us up when we come here on our first trip to Sweden.

Today I was able to say every single word in English. I took this on myself, since I had the foresight to bring a dictionary.

Tomorrow morning will be the second and final test of the bark-stripper on our tree trunks. I think I'll be able to leave for Stockholm Friday and be in Milan Sunday or Monday. I'll send you a telegram with the exact time I'll arrive.

I have here before me your splendid photo which smiles with goodness and love. You are with me in this beautiful city north of the 61° parallel. Today, after the test results, I was satisfied enough to go ahead with the mechanization of bark removal, which will eliminate some of our workers' heavy labor. I was and am glad because this way I can make a small contribution to your work that alleviates so much suffering.

---

gone to Sweden to research new materials (plywood, Formica) and new technologies for accelerating production.

49. Tree trunks like those used at SAFFA for making wooden matches.

I have your letter here in front of me, and as I do every night, I will re-read it before going to bed. If you only knew, my dearest Gianna, how close I feel you, just one heart and one soul with me, and how much I want to see you again and never leave your side! I embrace you, pressed to my heart, and kiss you with all my love. Good night, Gianna!

Your Pietro

SÖDERHAMN, SEPTEMBER 8, 1955

My most beloved Gianna,

Another 400 km with the Mercedes racing 100–120 km per hour down the road, which is all curves and mountains. The sky is still gorgeous; the temperature could be the same as August in Italy; enchanting little towns, lakes, forests, and villages.

From 9:00 AM to 5:30 PM we were on the road and had tests on the cutter that were conclusive and satisfactory.

Midday, lunch in Sandviken and, in the evening, supper in Söderhamn. Up here you really have to have a stomach of iron! Imagine all this on one plate: raw chopped onions, raw chopped green onions, whipped cream, fish in a sweet-and-sour sauce, etc.

Tonight I'll be staying in this very cozy hotel again. Tomorrow morning I'll be up at 5:15 AM and from 6:26 till 11:00, I'll travel 250 km to Stockholm by train. In the afternoon, a quick visit to the international fair in Stockholm, and at 9:10 PM I have to be sure not to miss the train bringing me back to my Gianna. I'll be in Milan on Sunday at 1:00 PM. I can't wait to see you right away at the station.

How you would have enjoyed traveling with me today, you who are so open to the beauties of creation and folklore![50]

---

50. As we know, Gianna had a great love for the beauty of nature (see her letter of March 23, 1955).

I have you here before me in the lovely photo Sister Virginia took at the shrine above Bormio. I am beside you. How wonderful your smile is, so joyful and affectionate! It has reached me again up here, new and so loving, and it does me so much good.

Gianna, I will see you again on Sunday after being gone for what seems like forever to me. I want to press you to my heart and kiss you, a long, long kiss to tell you again of my love.

I hope we'll see each other every day, and then we'll be together for good and we'll always love each other. You tell me this very often; I too am certain of it.

Dearest Gianna, I'm your Pietro who desires nothing more than to see you again soon, to be with you always, to love you very, very much and always make you as happy as you are now.

Your Pietro who is giving you a bigger kiss than ever because he is too far away.

Buona notte, Gianna!

STOCKHOLM, SEPTEMBER 9, 1955[51]

A most loving *arrivederci.*

Pietro

SEPTEMBER 10, 1955
THE MORNING OF THE SECOND TO LAST
SATURDAY BEFORE OUR WEDDING
ON THE NORTH SEA, EN ROUTE TO COPENHAGEN

Most beloved Gianna,

Last night as we left Stockholm, before going to bed in my little berth, and this morning as I woke up early on the ship between

---

51. Postcard.

Sweden and Denmark, my first and last prayers were to Jesus and our Heavenly Mother that they might bless you, and that they might always bless us, especially this month.

I spent a long time looking at your photos again, trying to alleviate, at least for a moment, the loneliness caused by the distance between us. I sought comfort in your gaze[52] that always speaks to me of a great, pure, and serene joy, of a gentle goodness which moves me, of an immense affection that gives me so much joy because I too, Gianna, love you immensely.

And I kissed your most sweet picture that brought sunshine into my day, even though this morning the sky was completely clouded over and the waves of the Danish sea were an autumn grey.

I'm so very happy, Gianna, because the train is heading south, bringing me to you.

I embrace and give you a great big kiss with all my love.

Your Pietro

SEPTEMBER 10, 1955
SATURDAY, AROUND 3:00 PM
ON THE BALTIC SEA, EN ROUTE
FROM DENMARK TO GERMANY

Dearest Gianna,

I'm writing you at sea, under your affectionate gaze, which for me is the harmony and life of the green shades[53] and snowy slopes of Valtellina. (Forgive me if I'm using some paper that isn't meant for letter writing.)

---

52. The photographs prove what witnesses say about the deep gaze of Saint Gianna, which reflected serenity, joy, and affection.

53. The varying shades of green in the fields and woods in Valtellina.

Tomorrow we'll see each other and be together again after a long separation. Even though I didn't promise in Milan to write you every day,[54] I did so anyway, because I couldn't contain my great desire to keep this conversation with you going, at least once a day—this silent conversation, which for that reason is all the warmer in affection.

During these Nordic days, how many times have I looked at your dearest pictures!

I already wrote you, O Gianna, that the houses in Sweden, with flowers at all their windows—almost as if to radiate outward the intimate warmth of their hearths—always spoke to me of our little house and of the sweet affection with which you will enrich it.

In the Swedish children who call out "Mamma!" just as they do in our language, I saw the gifts of Heaven: your jewels, O Gianna, the children God will bless us with.[55]

In the people at all the different stations who were bidding fond good-byes to their loved ones, I saw you again, O Gianna, and your most affectionate greeting.

And I saw with new eyes, with new feeling, every created thing and every fact, for you and with you, O Gianna.

Just one more Saturday, and you'll be my wife.[56]

Gianna, I want to be the husband you always dreamed of in your most beautiful dreams, the one you desired in your most joyous and holy dreams, a husband worthy of your virtues, your goodness, and your great love.

---

54. In this sentence Pietro shows that, even though he had not promised Gianna he would write her every day, he had done so because of his great desire to remain in communion with her.

55. See Gianna's letter of July 5, 1955. The engaged couple looked upon children as gifts and not as obstacles to their own well-being.

56. Pietro repeats a sentence Gianna had written in her letter of September 3, 1955, in order to emphasize the reciprocity of their love.

More than ever during these days, and above all during our triduum, I will pray to Jesus, to our Heavenly Mother, and to my sister[57] whom I feel is in Heaven, that they might bless my intentions and be most generous in granting graces to our new family.

Gianna, you and I have undertaken our new life with the certainty that God wanted us together.

These months have all been a crescendo of understanding and affection.

Now we understand each other perfectly, because Heaven is our light and the Divine Law our guide; because Heaven and the Divine Law find in you the most beautiful virtues and the greatest good, while I have the greatest desire and the immense joy of making you happy always.

Now our love is full because we are one heart and soul, one feeling and love, because our love, strong and pure, knows how to wait for the blessing of Heaven.

Dearest Gianna, how many more things I and, maybe, you too, wanted to tell each other these past few months!

But we did not do so, because we were immediately sure of all that God wanted of us, and we had the certainty of our love for each other, and we let ourselves be guided by our hearts and our love.

I will draw near the altar, asking Jesus to supply for my deficiencies and make me able to make you always, always happy.

Gianna, you who are my love, my life, my sweetest Gianna, always wipe out my failings with your understanding, your goodness, and your love.

I press you sweetly to my heart, I lovingly kiss you in your virtues and beauty that remind me of the beauty and goodness of

---

57. Teresina, Pietro's younger sister, had died of nephritis at age twenty-three.

Heaven, and, looking into your eyes full of light and love, I tell you
again: Gianna, see, here's your Pietro. He wants to make you very
happy, always. Always make him as happy as he is now!

With ardent longing and all my love to you,

Your Pietro

SEPTEMBER 13, 1955

My dearest Pietro,

I can't find the words to thank you for the wonderful and loving
letters that you have sent so faithfully these past few days. Every letter, every expression gave me so much joy. You are a treasure, Pietro,
and the more I read your letters, the more I know that you are so
good and you have within you many virtues hidden by your humility, but seen and appreciated by your Gianna.

Thank you for everything, Pietro. I want to tell you all that I
feel, all that is in my heart, but I can't. But you already know what
my feelings are, so you must know how to understand me.

Dearest Pietro, I'm sure that you will always make me as happy as
I am now and that the Lord will listen to your prayers, coming from a
heart that has always loved him and served him in a saintly way.

Pietro, how much I have to learn from you! You are such a fine
example for me, and I thank you for it. With God's help and blessing, we will do all we can to make our new family a little cenacle[58]
where Jesus will reign over all our affections, desires, and actions.

My Pietro, our wedding is just a few days away now, and I feel
very moved to be so near receiving the Sacrament of Love. We will

---

58. This particularly impressive expression was a favorite of Pietro's. It was a
visual image to which the spouses often referred.

be working with God in his creation; in this way we can give him children who will love and serve him.[59]

Pietro, will I be able to be the wife and mother [of your children] you have always wanted? I hope so, because you deserve it and I love you so much.

I kiss you and embrace you with all my love, your

Gianna

MAGENTA, SEPTEMBER 23, 1955
THE DAY BEFORE OUR WEDDING [60]

Gianna,

May these [pearls] crown the wonder
and purity of your beauty and virtue on our wedding day,
in order that the one gift [a watch] may always mark
the most beautiful and serene time of our lives,
and that the other, the pearl necklace, signify the enchanting
    light of our love,
your Mamma and mine, with a mother's love, give you these
    gifts,
as do I, with the greatest love.

Your Pietro

---

59. Here is expressed a pre-conciliar theology of marriage, however, with feminine grace and delicacy typical of the saint: she often repeated almost verbatim statements in use at the time, but softened and transformed with her finesse.

60. This note accompanied two gifts sent to Gianna from Pietro, his mother, and, symbolically, from Gianna's own mother on their wedding eve.

PART II

"Your Great Love Will Help Me to Be Strong"

Letters of the First Years of Marriage

Your Pietro wishes you every happiness, today and always, and he embraces and kisses you with all his love, deeply moved on this, the dearest and most beloved of all your anniversaries,[1] the first joyful, dearest occasion in the life of our sweetest love.

NOVEMBER 24, 1955[2]

To my dearest Pietro with all my love

DECEMBER 13, 1955
TUESDAY AFTERNOON

My dearest Pietro,

You have been gone now for a whole night and half a day, but I'm thinking of you every moment and you are always present to me. When I got home from Milan last night, I stopped by your parents' house to reassure them and say hello to them again for you. Then after I had supper with my family, Zita came back to our house with me.

Pietro, you'll say I'm exaggerating, but the house is so empty and sad when you are not here! I started to write holy Christmas cards while I waited for the nightly news, but my Pietro did not

---

1. Gianna's birthday.
2. A note.

appear on the show. I said the Rosary, prayed for our family, and with my dear treasure in my heart and mind, I went to sleep.[3]

I was planning to get up for the 6:00 AM Holy Mass, but guess what woke me up instead? . . . The nice sound of your [factory] sirens! So I went to Mass in Magenta with Zita at 8:30 AM. Then I picked up Iucci and returned to Ponte Nuovo with Zita.

Iucci,[4] all excited, brought her pajamas with her. She will stay for a day and then it will be Maria Vittoria's turn. As you can tell, I have plenty of company. You, on the other hand, have to travel all alone in that cold Switzerland. Dress warmly, Pietro, and don't get too tired. I wish I could help you in your work, but I can't do anything except pray that God will always protect and help you.

My Pietro, I'm very happy because I love you, and you love me too, and I will always do everything I can to be a good, loving, understanding, and always smiling wife.

A big, big kiss and a most affectionate hug from your

Gianna

ZURICH, DECEMBER 13, 1955[5]

Dearest wife,

I had a great trip and slept well last night. Work went well this morning and this afternoon. Our Swedish friends in Zurich welcomed me and treated me to an exquisite breakfast on the lakeshore. There was no sunshine, but it wasn't too cold.

---

3. This brief aside reveals the personal piety of the saint and her deep familial spirituality.

4. Iucci (Amalia), as well as Maria Vittoria mentioned below, is the daughter of Ferdinando. Saint Gianna, in her husband's absence, brings her nieces to the house.

5. Another trip to Sweden. On the way, Pietro stopped over in Zurich.

At 9:43 PM I'll be on the train again with Mr. Fkmark as far as Basel; from there we'll take a sleeper car with Dr. Bombig,[6] and tomorrow evening at 8:30, we'll be in Copenhagen.

This is the first letter from your husband since our wedding.

Not even a day has gone by since your affectionate goodbye, and already our separation seems so long to me—too long.

You've been my wife less than three months, and how greatly the understanding, love, and joy of our union increase day by day!

I have you here before me, smiling at me, happy in your radiant smile of goodness and beauty, just like at the seaside in Taormina and in the greens and blues of Ischia![7]

Last night, at every Joyful Mystery of the Holy Rosary I had a special prayer for you and for our new family.

May the Lord and our Heavenly Mother bless our love and render it fruitful!

Hasten the day when Gianna, happier than she has ever been before, can share with me and our loved ones the holy news that a new life stirs within her!

After this Christmas, may the Christmases to come see our children praying before Baby Jesus!

O Lord, O Heavenly Mother, give us the grace and joy of bringing our children to your altar and consecrating them to you!

O Lord, keep us always vigilant, like the Holy Family of Nazareth, to give our children a holy education!

Please also pray the beautiful prayer to the Holy Family every evening for me.

Good Gianna, please try to make up to my parents for the sadness of my frequent trips, and say hello to your family and mine from me.

---

6. Giorgio Bombig directed the export department at SAFFA.

7. Places where they had stopped on their honeymoon. The prayer that follows reveals Pietro's profound spirituality.

I embrace you and kiss you with all my love,

Your Pietro

Today I also wrote to our far-away loved ones: Father Alberto,[8] Sister Luigia,[9] and Sister Virginia.[10]

DECEMBER 14, 1955

WEDNESDAY, 4:40 PM

ON THE BALTIC SEA EN ROUTE TO DENMARK

Most beloved Gianna,

I'm writing you right when I miss you and our little house the most. Almost complete darkness has fallen over the sea, and the ship is moving forward silently, rocked by the wind.

I see you diligently working among your patients in Mesero, just as this morning I thought of you devoutly in prayer before the dear Mother of Good Counsel.

When we passed near Hanover, about 10:30 this morning, I remembered how you were with me, always so loving, good, and dear, on that unforgettable trip.[11]

Last night's journey was restful.

Around 10:00 this morning, Dr. Bombig knocked on my compartment door and asked, "Why haven't you invented a machine to wake up loafers?" "Because it's already been invented," I answered;

---

8. Father Alberto Maria, brother of Gianna, a Capuchin medical missionary to Grajaú, Brazil. On June 18, 2008, the Curia in Bergamo officially opened the diocesan process for his beatification.

9. Sister Luigia, Pietro's sister, worked in a boys' school named "Sorriso d'Italia" in Imperia-Porto Marizio.

10. Sister Virginia, Gianna's sister, was a doctor and a Canossian missionary in India.

11. Gianna had accompanied Pietro on one of his previous work trips to Germany, which they made into an extension of their honeymoon.

"I left it behind in Ponte Nuovo. A few days without sirens[12] won't hurt me."

We had a good trip to Germany: very little snow, but it was almost everywhere.

In the *Corriere della Sera* we read about the accident that happened to the Italian-Leandinovisen Express Monday/Tuesday night. Perhaps you were worried about me! I was safe and sound in Zurich.

In the German and Swiss cities, there are Christmas trees and lights.

This will be our first Christmas, Gianna. How much sweetness and intimate serenity it will bring me!

I embrace you, give you a great big kiss, and live for you.

Your Pietro

DECEMBER 14, 1955
WEDNESDAY EVENING

My dearest Pietro,

You're traveling as I write—I wish I could be with you to help pass the hours on the train!

Today was a dreary day, rainy and foggy; it was dark outside, and a little dark in my heart, too, knowing you're so far away. But time will pass, and soon it will be Tuesday . . . and we'll take up our life again, the beautiful hours of intimacy and affection that I wish would never end. How are you? Is it very cold there? I think of you so often, Pietro, and now that you are so far away, I realize more than ever how much I love you and how I can't live without you. I went to Holy Mass and Holy Communion this morning in our little

---

12. The 8:00 AM siren signals the beginning of the workday at SAFFA in Ponte Nuovo di Magenta. Gianna mentions this siren in her letter of the previous day.

church and I prayed to our beautiful Heavenly Mother for you, Pietro, that she would help and protect you.

Mariuccia[13] came at noon and wanted me to go to lunch with her and Zita in Bernate, and I had to go to please her.

After lunch I went to the Crespi farm on a call, and then I went to Mesero. I visited Papa and Mamma,[14] explained your itinerary again, and eased their worry by telling them that you would be staying in a hotel tonight.

Pietro, I would like to write to you every day, but I'm afraid you might not get my letters. I think of you all the time, and I can't wait to hold you again.

Take care of yourself, and don't get too tired. With much love, I kiss and embrace you.

Your

Gianna

Many greetings from Zita.

COPENHAGEN, DECEMBER 15, 1955

12:10 AM

Dearest Gianna,

Copenhagen came into sight yesterday evening, the most light-filled city I've ever seen: lights of every imaginable color, enormous Christmas trees, and people who don't seem to feel the intense cold and icy wind. From my window I can see the splendid panorama of the City Palace and its magnificent tower.

---

13. Mariuccia (Maria Bambina Parmigiani, widow of Mainini) was born in Magenta October 19, 1925 and died in November 2001, and was a close friend from 1942 until Gianna's death.

14. These are her in-laws, Luigi Molla and Maria Salmoiraghi.

If there had been any sun, how I would have regretted not bringing my Rolleiflex [camera]! But I'll be back up here with you when the weather is nice. Dr. Bombig told us this is an unforgettable city. He visited here in the summer with Mr. Lazzari.[15] The hotel is magnificent: carpets, tapestries, paintings, wonderful chandeliers, very fine taste. There are vases of evergreen and cyclamen at every window. Last night we were at supper from 9:30 to 11:00. Viking chicken and vegetables; I'll bring you the recipe. Tomorrow morning around 9:30 we will start on the final stretch to Jönköping.[16] According to today's paper, we're in for some cold weather. But I'm well dressed for it.

I accompany you throughout your day and I'm always thinking of you with great love.

I embrace and kiss you at length,

Your Pietro

7:00 AM —The square in front of City Hall is all covered with snow. It's still snowing, and the wind is blowing fiercely. These people are more morning people than we are. So many cars, trolleys, and pedestrians. It's better to be here in the summer.

Another kiss,

Pietro

---

15. Mr. Temistocle Lazzari was SAFFA's general director and Mr. Molla's immediate superior. He was the best man at the wedding of Gianna and Pietro.
16. A city in southern Sweden, the capital of a county of the same name. The city is located on Lake Vättern.

COPENHAGEN, DECEMBER 15, 1955[17]

Great trip so far.

Remembering you with love,

Pietro

JÖNKÖPING, DECEMBER 15, 1955

My good and most beloved Gianna,

This morning from 9:30 to 10:00, challenging . . . cold and snow. In Copenhagen I picked up three knickknacks and a big silver spoon.[18]

A rainy hour and a half at sea brought me to Sweden around 12:30. Then a six-hour train ride, through towns and woods covered with snow, and here I am finally at my destination at 6:00 PM.

We were welcomed by snow that sometimes flies horizontally because of the strong wind. It was terribly cold yesterday—sixteen degrees below zero [Celsius]; tonight only two below zero, thanks to the snow which started falling again after a few days' lull.

One of STAB's[19] directors met us at the station with cordial greetings and a very luxurious car—with white and blue leather inside—he brought us to the Stora Hotel as usual.

Here we were welcomed by those who had already arrived for the conference regarding the future plant in Peru:[20] the directors from Algeria, Portugal, Tunisia, from the Augustins factory, and two directors from Jönköping.

At the bar, instead of a dry martini, I had some tomato juice. From 8:00 PM to 10:00 PM we had our first banquet. I tried a little

---

17. Postcard.
18. He was buying Christmas presents.
19. A Swedish wooden match factory.
20. A match factory planned for Peru.

of everything: hors d'oeuvres of caviar, raw salmon, shrimp; roast deer with many things around it; cheeses with celery, croquettes, cookies, etc.; ice cream, coffee, liqueurs.

And there is silver everywhere: silver trays for the deer, for the cheeses, and the ice cream. The flower vase in the middle of the table is made of silver, and so are the candelabra holding lighted candles.

But everything I saw made me think of our little house, our table, and how very well you take care of me.

Tomorrow morning we'll begin our work.

Here I am, alone in my little room, with you before me, smiling, good, affectionate, and happy.

I am alone just as on so many other trips, but this is a solitude different than any other time: harder because now I have you whom I would like to have with me all the time to enjoy your love and make you happy, but at the same time, easier because now I have you to think about every moment, you who are following me with your affection, who love me so much, you to whom I long to return.[21] Now there is our little house that you make so lovely and a source of so many joys.

Anxiously looking forward to seeing you again, I kiss at length your sweetest picture and send you many, many kisses, with all my love.

Good night, Gianna.

Your

Pietro

Remember me to our loved ones.

---

21. Feeling that the pain of being apart is both harder and easier at the same time is typical of one who desires only to be with his beloved.

JÖNKÖPING, DECEMBER 17, 1955

SATURDAY

Gianna, most beloved Gianna,

Here I am, finally, after the Peru plant conference with Dr. Bombig and sixteen STAB directors, after tonight's banquet, returning to my daily, loving, silent colloquy with you before I go to sleep: you who are my life, my sweetest wife.

I'm looking southward out of my window, and beyond the snow and the lake, beyond the darkness, I love to think of you peacefully sleeping after praying a long time for me and wishing me well. Sleep well, my Treasure!

All last night and most of the day it snowed. The afternoon conference ended at 5:00 PM.

Our work turned out well. Tomorrow morning we have more conferences till 11:00 AM.

How I wished you were here last night! In the hotel's great parlor, with the lights turned low, we saw the Saint Lucy procession. While the orchestra played, the hymn *Santa Lucia* was sung: "*Sul mare luccica . . .*" followed by a group humming quietly. Then five children dressed in white, with lighted candles in their right hands, followed "Saint Lucy" who, with her hands folded, with five lit candles on her head, slowly led the little procession. I hope to be able to bring you some pictures. The songs and saints of our homeland speak much more powerfully to our hearts and our feelings when we see them in the frigid North, which is cold by nature, and also in regard to religion.[22]

---

22. Mr. Molla was referring to the diversity of religious sentiment and practice between the Nordic and the Latin countries. It should be noted that the great majority of Swedes are Lutheran and that the veneration of the saints is not very common among them. One should also keep in mind that, at the time, Vatican Council II, with its emphasis on ecumenism, had not yet taken place.

At supper last night, and at breakfast and supper today, I was surrounded by friends from . . . ONU.[23] Seated near Dr. Bombig and me, in addition to our Swedish friends, were a Jewish industrialist from Israel, a Peruvian PhD, a Portuguese engineer, a French engineer from Algeria, an American official, and a French director. Everyone was friendly. They wanted to drink to your and my happiness.

Mr. Thiluse, the general director from France, said we can stay with him in Paris whenever we like.

He can let us use a lovely apartment for as long as we care to stay.

Dr. Aramhuns wants us to visit him in Lima.

So . . . I am most anxious to return to you in the sweet intimacy of our little house, so I can have you always near me, so I can tell you again and again of my love, so I can make you happy, so I can hug and kiss you at length. . . .

Your

Pietro

Say hello to all our loved ones for me.

NÄSSJÖ, DECEMBER 20, 1955

Dearest Gianna,

Today, at 6:00 PM, I finished my work in Jönköping with the final plenary conference. Everything turned out well. Yesterday we worked both morning and afternoon, something uncommon in Switzerland—maybe it's the fault of us Latins who wanted to end the discussions and get back to our families.

---

23. Organizzazione delle Nazioni Unite (United Nations Organization).

Yesterday I received Jesus in the plain but very pious little Catholic chapel in Jönköping, from the hands of the good Father Ducher, a French Dominican. I thanked Jesus again for having given me you as a dearest spouse, and I prayed above all for you.

Tonight I will finally start traveling south, coming back to you.

I'm writing you from the station in Nässjö, where STAB had me driven in a very comfortable car from midnight till 1:00 AM, through a countryside covered with snow and ice while the temperature is sixteen degrees below zero. The sky is clear and the North Star seems very close.

It's already 4:30 AM and I'm still waiting for the 1:45 sleeper car from Stockholm, which they tell me will only get here at 5:00. Oh well. A little inconvenience doesn't hurt anyone.

I'm saying my Rosary.

I'm thinking of you, looking again and again at your sweet picture, and reading and re-reading the loving letter you wrote on my return from Sweden in September.[24]

And I pray again, as you prayed, that God's help and blessing may make our new family a little cenacle where Jesus will always reign over all our affections, desires, and actions, as he has from our wedding day until now.

And I tell you again, as you tell me over and over, that I love you very, very much.

And with all my love I send you many kisses, as intense and sweet as ever . . . but quietly so as not to wake you up.

Your

Pietro

---

24. See Gianna's letter of September 13, 1955.

MAGENTA, DECEMBER 31, 1955[25]

A remembrance of our first meeting,[26]
with the most affectionate wishes
and all my love

Pietro

IMPERIA, MARCH 18, 1956[27]

A most loving remembrance

Pietro

PARIS, APRIL 10, 1956
11:30 PM

Dearest Gianna,

Finally it's my last evening far from you.

We had a big gala banquet that ended around 11:00 PM, in a luxurious locale on the Champs Élysées.

Spaniards, Portuguese, French, Swedes, and . . . Italians, too.

Furs to die for and endless jewels, champagne, and dancing.[28]

It was all indifferent to me.

---

25. A note.

26. On New Year's Eve 1954, Pietro had attended a ballet at La Scala in Milan with Gianna and her family, and had brought in the New Year at their house in Magenta. Writing in his diary that day, he recorded: "This evening may represent an important day in my life and in my hopes. I entrust myself to Our Lady of Good Counsel and to Teresina."

27. A postcard. Pietro had gone to visit his sister, Sister Luigia, who headed a boarding school for boys in Imperia.

28. This was ten years after the end of the war, and a time of great prosperity was approaching (see Pietro's letter of December 15, 1955 written from Jönköping).

I thought of you, of our baby,[29] and of our boundless love. And in this wrenching homesickness, I think of you as peaceful, and here in my little room I kiss your photograph.

Today we finished our work at 7:30 PM, and if I had not already seen Paris other times, tomorrow morning when I catch the 8:10 train, the only part of this splendid city that I would know would be Opera Square and the view from my window. I didn't take any pictures.

I'll tell you more when I return to you.

I kiss and embrace you tightly, tightly, with all my love.

Your

Pietro

APRIL 11, 1955 . . . APRIL 11, 1956[30]

My dearest Pietro,

One year has passed since the day we were engaged:[31] a year of intimate joys, understanding, and great love.

The most beautiful thing I can wish for you with all my heart is this: many, many more years like this one, and may the Lord always bless and preserve our great love.

I kiss you with all my affection,

Your Gianna

---

29. Gianna was then expecting their first child, Pierluigi.

30. A note.

31. Gianna recalls the first anniversary of their engagement. Beyond the freshness of tone, one can imagine the power of love with its origin and foundation in Christ.

Marriage of Gianna and Pietro, basilica of Magenta, September 24, 1955.

Pietro and Gianna on their honeymoon, Capri, October 1955.

MAGENTA, JUNE 24, 1956[32]
SAINT JOHN [THE BAPTIST]

With all my love, I wish you
the most wonderful joys
on the day of your most sweet name,
the same day that reminds us of our yes,[33]
and we bless Heaven in the joyous anxiety
of the Divine Gift[34] we are awaiting.

Pietro

MAGENTA, SEPTEMBER 24, 1956[35]

With all my heart, with all my love
and with my gratitude, in the trembling expectation
of the sweetest Fruit of our Love.

Pietro

MAGENTA, OCTOBER 4, 1956[36]

With all my love and the most beautiful wishes,

Pietro

---

32. A note for Gianna's feast day, Saint John the Baptist.

33. Pietro and Gianna were married on the twenty-fourth of another month, September 1955.

34. Gianna was expecting Pierluigi.

35. A note for their first wedding anniversary.

36. This was a note for Gianna's birthday; she turned thirty-four that year.

PARIS, JANUARY 29, 1957

Dearest Gianna,

I slept well enough last night, in spite of the "click-click" of the wheels right under my bed.[37]

The weather is lovely in Paris, almost like the weather yesterday in Ponte Nuovo.

This morning we did almost all the work we came here to do, and this afternoon we finished it. We'll be sleeping in a beautiful hotel very close to the Gare du Nord,[38] so we can leave for London around 8:00 tomorrow morning.

In the few hours since I left, how many times have I kissed the photo of you and Pierluigi![39] I feel your love, your affectionate care, your radiant serenity very close, comforting and guiding—all the things that make me so happy when I am with you.

Thank you with all my heart and all my love for the joy you give me through Pierluigi!

Thank you too for your affectionate care for Mamma.[40]

Give Pierluigi a great big kiss for me, and remember me to Mamma.

I kiss you with all my love.

Your

Pietro

---

37. Pietro was on the train.

38. One of the main train stations in Paris.

39. Pierluigi was born on November 19, 1956, at home in Ponte Nuovo. At the time of this letter he was two months old.

40. Pietro's mother.

LONDON, JANUARY 31, 1957

My most beloved Gianna,

I fell asleep last night thinking of you and with our "family prayer"[41] on my lips, and this morning, as soon as I awoke, I gave your picture with Pierluigi many big kisses.

I always see his precious smile, the way he sleeps like a little angel and his Mommy near him, full of love and affectionate care.

Yesterday when we arrived at the Victoria Station in London,[42] we had a reception hosted by important people. Mr. Backwitt and Colonel Maretini were waiting for us in a luxurious and aristocratic Rolls-Royce. On our trip from the station to our hotel, we received our first gift, a beautiful book of photos of London; then we received a welcome letter from the president of Spicers. Then a schedule for today, tomorrow, and Saturday.

The Connaught Hotel has a royal atmosphere from the Victorian era. Do you want a description of my . . . apartment? A bedroom with every comfort, even goose down comforters. The bathroom is all mirrors and even has . . . a scale. A sitting room with a couch, armchairs, lamps, a desk, exquisite antique side tables. A very English cabinet with a mobile bar holding an assortment that would last me at least a hundred years, but maybe only a few days for these English: seven bottles of liquor, twenty bottles of soda water, and crystals.

Yesterday afternoon, we drove around seeing the most important sites: Trafalgar Square, Buckingham Palace, Parliament, the Tower of London, and Westminster Abbey.

---

41. Every evening before going to bed, Gianna and Pietro recited a prayer of thanksgiving to God and of petition for their family (cf. P. Molla-E. Guerriero, *Santa Gianna Beretta Molla,* op. cit., 48).

42. The London station for trains arriving from all over Europe.

And in the evening we had the first banquet, in typical English surroundings.

These are all beautiful things, but far from both of you, the only joy would be to see this whole splendid city again with you.

Smile a lot, and give Pierluigi big kisses for me.

Kisses to Mamma, and to you lots and lots of kisses and a most affectionate hug from

Pietro

Affectionate greetings to Zita, Cecco, Nando, and Laura, and the little nephew and nieces.

Affectionate greetings to Adelaide, Rosetta, and their families.

Great weather, not cold . . . just as I predicted with certainty.

LUGANO, MARCH 8, 1957[43]

A most affectionate remembrance and big kisses to you and Pierluigi.

Pietro

ON THE FERRY FROM
GERMANY TO SWEDEN, APRIL 7, 1957[44]

Great trip, good health. From the sunshine of the Baltic Sea, I send you and Pierluigi many big kisses and many, many wishes.

Pietro

Greetings to Savina.[45]

---

43. Postcard. Lugano, situated on the lake of the same name, is about 70 km from Milan. Gianna and Pietro had taken a trip there in early 1955, shortly after they had become better acquainted.

44. Postcard.

45. Savina Passeri was their domestic helper from 1956 to 1962.

COPENHAGEN, APRIL 7, 1957

Dearest Gianna,

My long trip is over. I had the kindest welcome from Mr. and Mrs. Hastmann who waited two hours at the airport in vain . . . not thinking we would have the patience to travel twenty-seven hours by train.[46] It ended with a dinner in Tivoli, to the sound of classical Italian piano music. Now I'm here—it's already 11:30 PM—in my cozy room in this very modern and hospitable Hotel Europa.

I wouldn't be able to sleep if I didn't first lovingly communicate with you, always so loving and caring, whom I wish I could always have near me.

Right now I'm thinking of you with Pierluigi in your arms, as he's eating in between your mamma kisses.

I kiss and re-kiss with all my love the photo I have of both of you, and with all my love I wish you a good and peaceful night.

The trip here was good. I slept well at night, partly thanks to the wonderful sleeping car, the latest version, which is much better than the older ones.

When I saw Brunate, still lit by the sun, it spoke to me more vividly than ever about our first loving meeting: the beginning of our joy.

Hanover, with its sunshine, reminded me of the splendid days I spent there with you.[47]

And here in Copenhagen I dream of you and I hope soon in the coming years to see you resting happily from your daily labors.

---

46. Another tiring trip to Denmark by train. Pietro often took the train in order not to worry his wife who was fearful of his flying (see Pietro's letter of April 12, 1957, and Gianna's of April 28, 1959).

47. Gianna and Pietro had spent some days in Germany as an extension of their honeymoon while Pietro was on a business trip.

Today I wrote in my diary, which I write as a sort of affectionate conversation with Pierluigi:

"May Heaven grant us again the immense divine gift of a treasure like you: a little sister or brother!"

Immense good wishes and good night, Gianna! My Treasure, my Love!

I kiss and embrace you with all my love, and together with you, I kiss our treasure very much.

Your

Pietro

APRIL 11, 1957

THURSDAY EVENING

My dearest Pietro,

How could I fail to respond to your beautiful letter? Dear Pietro, what a great comfort your love is to me!

The Lord has blessed our love once more by giving us another child[48]—I am happy, and with the help of our Heavenly Mother,[49] and with you close to me, you who are so good and understanding and affectionate, the sufferings of this new pregnancy no longer frighten me.

Thank you, dearest Pietro, for your prayers. The Blessed Mother will surely listen to us, and we will have another beautiful child like our little Pierluigi. What a dear little angel he is! Every day he becomes more beautiful, livelier, and he seems to understand when we talk to him. Isn't it a consolation, Pietro? Every time I kiss him

---

48. Gianna announces the new pregnancy to her husband. Mariolina, of whom she speaks, would be born on December 11, 1957.

49. This emphasizes how quickly her love moves from her husband and family to Marian devotion and vice versa.

when you're away, I kiss him for you, too. Who knows how often you must think of him when you're away and wish he were near you! I'm so glad there are only four days left until you come back; I'm already looking forward to the joy of seeing you again, of embracing you, of finally seeing you with some free time to spend with your little angel. How sweet you always look when you have your little boy in your arms and you make him smile! And when he reaches out his little arms to caress you, what a beautiful picture you make! When he lisps his first words, he will be even more precious. Now he speaks with his little blue eyes, always smiling and waving his arms and legs.

And now, Pietro, I have a great favor to ask of you. Please forgive me when I am in a bad mood or sad; I try to be cheerful, but I don't always succeed. I hope it's just a result of these first months [of pregnancy]. Your great love will help me to be strong and conquer myself.

I am waiting for you, Pietro, with all my love.

I kiss you and embrace you, along with our dear little angel,

Your most affectionate

Gianna

LONDON, APRIL 12, 1957

Most beloved Gianna,

Finally (it's already 11:30 PM) I'm free, in my room at the Savoy, after the dinner given by the Lords of Spicers. Since Monday it's been nothing but a long chain of meetings, visits, travels of every possible kind by sea, on land, and . . . [50] and it's not easy to get used to such banquets.

---

50. Pietro leaves out the word "air," having taken a plane. Gianna was afraid of airplanes and always worried if her husband was flying.

Tomorrow we'll finish our work in London, and Sunday I'll happily start my journey back home.

I've seen with interest many important things for my company, but I believe this trip will bear good fruit in another area as well.

These people in Denmark, Germany, and especially in England, who know how to stop working at 5:30 or 6:00 every evening and even more on Saturdays, and who know how to pass long hours at home, taking care of their own gardens and enjoying their own flowers, have taught me to do everything possible to change my ways.[51]

I'll try to follow this teaching, especially because you and Pierluigi really deserve it.

I've written to all our relatives.

Anxiously waiting to see you again, to embrace you and spend time with you. An ardent, ardent kiss to you and Pierluigi.

Your

Pietro

I wanted to write more, but tiredness and especially this cold are keeping me in bed.

BRUSSELS, JUNE 21, 1957

Most beloved Gianna,

The thought of your great love and your loving kindness stays with me and is my joy in these days far from you.

Yesterday, as I admired the beautiful furniture and flowers at the villa where we had breakfast, I started planning how to make our own house more comfortable and beautiful, so as to contribute more

---

51. Once again the theme of Pietro's workaholism comes up. Gianna had already spoken to him about it during their engagement (cf. P. Molla-E. Guerriero, *Santa Gianna Beretta Molla,* op. cit., 46). Now Pietro himself realizes the need to spend more time with his wife and son.

and more to your joy and that of our children. There was a child there, like Pierluigi, seven months old.

This morning I prayed and prayed for Pierluigi, for you, and for the child in your womb. I served Holy Mass at the altar of the Sacred Heart of Mary, which seemed like a good omen to me.[52] Up above was the Blessed Mother with the Child Jesus next to her; he was taking his first steps. On the altar piece, again in a beautiful bas-relief, was the Nativity.

Your name day[53] is coming up soon: I send you the most affectionate wishes for joy and everything good.

Dearest Gianna, you always make me completely happy. I wish you happiness always and I want to be your joy, and with our children I want to always respond lovingly to your care for us, to your daily motherly sacrifices, true Treasure.

I embrace you and kiss you with all my love,

Your,

Pietro

Kiss Pierluigi for me.

MAGENTA, JULY 9, 1957

Dearest Gianna,

With all my heart I hope that today and tonight you and Pierluigi[54] will have quiet and restful hours without the usual problems. I'm always thinking of you; I wish I could always be with you and do much more for you both than the little or nothing that I do manage to do.

---

52. Devotion to our Lady was the foundation of the family's love and piety.

53. Saint John the Baptist, June 24.

54. Gianna and Pierluigi were on vacation at Courmayeur in Val d'Aosta. Pietro, whose vacation had not yet started, visited them on weekends.

I talked to Dr. Maciocchi today.[55] He was very firm and told me again *not* to take off the brace during the night, and he advised me to try a mild painkiller. Nando[56] immediately got one ready for me and I'm sending it to you. I'm so sorry for him [Pierluigi] and you.

Today Dr. Bottoni[57] asked me to find out whether the Miramonti Hotel has a honeymoon room with a bathroom from Sunday, August 11 till Sunday, August 25.*

Could you ask them today so you could give me an answer tomorrow night?

Since Nando's maid[58] stopped by, I'm taking advantage of the opportunity to send you the cord for the radio/record player and the pick-up mechanism.

I had a good ride in this morning. I was at work by 9:30.

At 4:00 PM I gave the Laminated Plastics[59] report to the general director.

Many affectionate greetings to you and Pierluigi from Mamma, Zita, Cecco, Nando, and Rosetta.[60]

Best wishes and most affectionate kisses to you and Pierluigi.

Your

Pietro

---

55. Dr. Maciocchi, an orthopedic doctor, had prescribed a brace for Pierluigi, who had a dislocated hip. The child was unable to sleep at night with the brace on. The doctor, however, insisted that it had to stay on at night, and ordered a mild painkiller rather than allow the parents to remove the brace.

56. "Nando" is short for Ferdinando, Gianna's brother who was also a doctor. He was nine years older than Gianna.

57. Dr. Franco Bottoni, central director of SAFFA.

58. Ferdinando and his wife's (Laura Viola) domestic helper.

59. A company producing laminate plastics, or Formica, used in the production of furniture and electronics, begun in 1950 at Mr. Molla's initiative. Associates in the company were SAFFA, Gerli, and the English Formica company Thomas de la Rue of London. The headquarters were in Magenta.

60. Zita and Cecco (nickname for Francesco) were Gianna's sister and brother. Rosetta (nickname for Maria Rosa) was Pietro's sister.

My warm greetings to Adelaide, to . . . the little rascal and . . . the big rascal.[61]

* Please also ask them what their daily rate is.

JULY 15, 1957
MONDAY

Dearest Pietro,

I just got home from the Visitor's Residence Enterprise with the coupons for eighty liters of gas,[62] which I am sending to you right away in the hopes that they'll arrive on Saturday. They'll give me the rest after July 25.

It is 5:30 PM now and little Pierluigi has been sleeping peacefully for almost two hours. If only he would always sleep that way!

It's a bit chilly outside today. The sun comes out for a little while and then disappears. I took Pierluigi for a walk in the woods with Adelaide and the children for about an hour. He had such a good time, the little angel! I hope you're feeling better.[63] Take care of yourself and don't overdo it, understand, my dear Pedrin?

When you come, please bring me my rosary. Thank you. Greet Mamma[64] a lot for me and thank her for all she does for us and for you while we're away.

I'll be expecting you early Saturday morning, you can imagine how eagerly! It's too bad we will only have two days . . . but the 28th will come soon!

---

61. The "little rascal" was Flavio, and the "big" one was Gianfranco. These were the sons of Pietro's sister Adelaide. All three were on vacation in Courmayeur with Gianna and Pierluigi.

62. To promote tourism in those years, the Tourist Office of the Autonomous Region of Val d'Aosta gave free gas coupons.

63. The previous day Pietro had not been feeling well.

64. Gianna refers to Pietro's mother who, in the absence of his wife, takes care of her son and his house.

Many, many big kisses from your Pierluigi and from your most affectionate

Gianna

MAGENTA, JULY 15, 1957

MONDAY EVENING

My dearest Gianna,

My first care this morning when I arrived in Ponte Nuovo[65] was to look for your letter. It only got here with Armi[66] when he arrived at 10:30 AM. I was very moved by it. Reading of your most loving feelings toward our Pierluigi and me salved this morning's suffering at leaving our little angel quiet, in his bed, with his legs bound,[67] and you. You could not be more affectionate with me and more anxious about our little treasure.

We are all receiving blessings from our Heavenly Mother whom you pray to every day, so devoutly, in her fifteen mysteries.

Mamma burst into tears on reading your letter.

I'm always thinking of you, of Pierluigi, and of the immense treasure[68] you are carrying and nurturing in your womb, and I pray for you.

I'm looking forward to seeing and being with all of you again on Saturday. I offer with you, for Pierluigi and for the treasure we are expecting, the sacrifice of being so far apart.

The trip went well. I got to Ponte Nuovo at 8:40 AM, and Zita arrived at Laminated at 8:45.[69]

---

65. On his return from a weekend in Courmayeur with Gianna and Pierluigi.

66. Armando Armi was SAFFA's deliveryman.

67. Pierluigi had to wear the orthopedic brace. See Pietro's letter of July 9, 1957.

68. Mariolina, who would be born December 11.

69. Zita, Gianna's older sister, who was a pharmacist, worked in the Laminated Plastic's lab in Magenta. She too had been in Courmayeur over the weekend.

Please forgive me, Gianna, and Pierluigi too, if I was not able to be as good company to you yesterday as I wished to be. I wasn't feeling well.

The medicine did me good last night; I was able to drive the three hours and then go to work.

After some time in Benevento, Mr. De Petri, the accountant, came back today. This will save me from hours and hours of work at the office.

Tomorrow morning at 7:30 I leave Milan for Este[70] with Mr. Lazzari.[71]

Good night, Gianna, and sleep well, you and our little angel. Kiss him every night for me too.

A most affectionate embrace and many, many big kisses to you and Pierluigi.

Your

Pietro

Many, many affectionate greetings from Mamma. She wants you to kiss Pierluigi for her.

Say hello to Adelaide and the kids.

JULY 16, 1957
TUESDAY EVENING

My dearest Pietro,

It's only 8:30 PM, but we have already finished supper. Our treasure has just fallen asleep, after a little bit of fussing while trying to get comfortable. You are, however, unfortunately still in Milan. Dear Pietro, it would be too beautiful if we could be together all of the

---

70. One of SAFFA's match factories was in Este.

71. Mr. Temistocle Lazzari, SAFFA's general director.

time; everything seems more beautiful when you are with me, and all my worries over Pierluigi decrease with you by my side. Patience! Let's offer it to the Lord so he will help our dear little one bear his first suffering and get perfectly well. I promised a daily Rosary to the Madonna of Guérison[72] for him. What I wouldn't do to keep him from suffering! He did manage to sleep a few hours today with his brace on, though.

Let's hope for the best.

Ciao, my dearest Pietro, and good night,

Your

Gianna

MAGENTA, JULY 16, 1957
TUESDAY EVENING

Dearest Gianna,

I almost thought I could see you this evening around 8:20 as I looked past the quiet horizon and the few distant clouds that hid the mountains of Val d'Aosta. As I was driving back from Este, I got off the ramp from the highway passing by the road you take to Mesero[73] every day.

It was right at the time our treasure goes to sleep, and I loved thinking of him smiling in your arms. How many times today, in my eight hours in the car, I thought of you in that cozy little house or in the green meadows! Most of all I was imagining how our little one was playing in freedom.

---

72. This is a small shrine in Val Veny at the foot of Mont Blanc, about 2 km from the center of Courmayeur. Gianna often went there to pray.

73. Pietro's birthplace, where Gianna traveled daily to her medical office. Pietro had had the house of his parents remodeled into a clinic for her.

In the comfortable car "1400" . . . I placed you and the children in my programs and desires, driving through the same roads today again and enjoying the peaceful landscapes and parks . . . at San Vigilio,[74] in the hills of Brescia or among the Mantuan castles.

Very spontaneously, I stopped in front of the door of our house and went to the little church[75] where Father Augustine[76] was reciting the litany. I received, on your behalf and that of our children, the blessing of Our Lady of Mount Carmel. I had you all with me.

Good night, and I wish you and Pierluigi a good day tomorrow.

I embrace and kiss you both with all my love,

Your

Pietro

Most affectionate greetings from Mamma to you and Adelaide.

Kisses to Pierluigi, Flavio, and Gianfranco.[77]

Last night and this morning, it was nearly cold: fourteen degrees [Celsius]. In the afternoon it was warm again but breezy.

JULY 17, 1957
WEDNESDAY MORNING

Dearest Pietro,

Before sending this out,[78] I wanted to let you know how Pierluigi is doing. He slept with his brace on last night, and he woke

---

74. In Upper Bergamo, where the home of Gianna's maternal grandparents was located.

75. The little Church of Our Lady of Good Counsel at Ponte Nuovo di Magenta.

76. Father Augustine Cerri, who at the time was the archbishop's delegate and later the pastor of the church.

77. Flavio and Gianfranco are sons of Adelaide, Pietro's sister.

78. It is, therefore, a note sent together with the previous letter.

up every hour, but without crying or fussing. He always went right back to sleep in my arms with his little smile. I gave him his bottle at 6:00 AM, and he drank it all; then I took his brace off, and he wriggled happily until 8:00 AM. He's asleep now.

I can't wait to hear your voice on the phone today.

But for now, many, many big kisses from your dear Pierluigi and your

Gianna

Many, many dear greetings to Mamma.

JULY 18, 1957
THURSDAY EVENING

My dearest Pietro,

Yesterday, I got your express letter from Monday, and today I received the one from Tuesday. My Pietro, you really are a treasure. You know how much I love your letters and how much comfort they bring me, so you never fail to write to me. Thank you so much.

Our dear little angel is getting used to his brace; he puts up with it very well during the day (we try to distract him as much as possible), and he doesn't cry very much at night, even though he wakes up every few hours to turn over. He has a good appetite now, and a rosy little face, just like a little shepherd. And all this is because of his dear Papa, who chose an enchanting little place with lots of sunshine from morning till night for us to have our vacation. I love to think that in fifteen days, you will be here with us to rest and enjoy this wonderful fresh air.

We all went to the pine woods yesterday from 1:30 to 3:00 in a beautiful spot, only about fifteen minutes from the house; Pierluigi loved it! He came home in a very good mood, and even though he can't talk yet, he shows how happy he is by wriggling and squirming in his brace. Then he slept well for a couple of hours. We went to church at 6:30 to say the Holy Rosary, and when we got home, he ate his cereal and fruit with a great appetite. His day ended at 8:30. I gave him a big kiss from his Papa and then, off to sleep!

Today, we spent the day at Checrouit.[79] When we got up this morning, there was marvelous sunshine and a clear, bright sky, and it was not at all cold. We packed up the bags and took the cableway up—Flavio and Gianfranco were very excited. Pierluigi was very lively, and everyone in the car smiled at his shrieks of joy.

At the top of the mountain, I put his brace on and he slept for about an hour. Then, since it was getting a little bit windy, we went down to the meadows, where Pierluigi drank his bottle with great appetite. You'll see what a tanned little face he has on Saturday!

I found your second express letter when we got home. What a dear little husband and saintly Papa our children have! Even though your work keeps you busy, you always find time to think of us and pray for your dear family! I can never thank the Lord enough for giving me a companion as dear, good, and affectionate as my Pietro.[80]

I hope your pain is gone and that your toothache doesn't keep you from eating and resting.

I'm sorry I forgot to give you the little bottles of medicine. But I think resting in the peace of Courmayeur will do you the most good.

Thank Mamma for her affectionate greetings and please give her mine and Pierluigi's. Tell her I'm very tranquil because I'm sure no one can ease the separation from your family like she can.

---

79. This is the hill above Courmayeur, in front of the tunnel at Mont Blanc. Gianna, who loved the mountain, brought her children there often.

80. Her joy in her husband leads to praise of the Lord, a sign that true love leads to God.

Ciao, dearest Pietro, many, many, most affectionate and big kisses from your Pierluigi and from your most loving

Gianna

SEPTEMBER 17, 1957
TUESDAY MORNING

My dearest Pietro,

Before I go to Ponte Nuovo[81] to air out our beautiful house, I'm sending many, many kisses to you and to our dear little angel who will be ten months old on Thursday! I'm glad Gigetto's cold is almost gone. I kissed him before I left yesterday morning and even though he was asleep, he smiled; seeing that smile, I felt a little less sad at having to leave.

I wish we could always be together, but unfortunately . . .

I have a lot of patients right now—I'm in the office a good two hours every day. Tonsillitis, bronchitis: the Asian fever has probably reached Mesero. But it's nothing serious; it's gone in two days.

The weather here is beautiful, though it's a bit chilly in the morning and evening. I hope it's nice at Courmayeur, too, because good weather makes people happy and is good for their health. In any case, if it gets too cold, let me know and I'll come pick you both up right away.

I'll call Sister Luigia tonight before 6:00, so I can tell you what she says. Rosetta is starting her vacation, which will last until the end of the month. Adelaide[82] is tired of begging for work and

---

81. The situation was reversed: Gianna had resumed her work as a doctor, while Pietro was at Courmayeur with their son. Because of this, Gianna slept at the house of her paternal grandparents in Magenta. Her brother Francesco, her sister Zita, and her brother Ferdinando and his family were also there.

82. Luigia, Rosetta, and Adelaide were Pietro's sisters.

stayed home yesterday. I told her to relax, that even she wouldn't be hurt by a little rest. Flavio is always riding his bike on the new paths and zooms around like a madman, as usual.

I'm glad those gentlemen came to visit you yesterday. Visits from good people are always a pleasure. If Mr. Marzola,[83] the engineer, should come, let me know ahead of time so I can bring everything we need for lunch.

Ciao, dear Pedrin, many beautiful kisses to my Gigetto and to you, and affectionate greetings to Mamma and Savina, [84]

Your

Gianna

COURMAYEUR, SEPTEMBER 17, 1957
TUESDAY

Most beloved Gianna,

Thank you with all my heart for your most affectionate letter.

I was so happy yesterday evening that you could hear Pierluigi's moving "Mamma, Mamma," and his shrieks of joy.

He's practically over his cold now, thanks to the wise care of his Mommy. Yesterday morning his forehead was a bit warmer than usual and I was somewhat worried; but in the afternoon his temperature went back down to normal.

Last night he slept well and was watched over, as always, by the dear image of your saintly parents.

Today is just beautiful: blue skies, just a few wisps of clouds; a clear and splendid view of Mont Blanc; a slight breeze up till noon, and sunshine as warm as August.

---

83. The engineer Ivo Giovanni Marzola was manager of the glue factory that was part of the SAFFA group at Ponte Tresa.

84. Savina Passeri worked for the Mollas from 1956 to 1962.

It's too bad the sun sets before 5:00 PM here, too.

During the day we were glad to open the kitchen windows; in the evenings it feels good to have a fire lit.

If only you could be here, too! How much lovelier our days would be! Distance is to love and affection as sickness is to health. We appreciate the great comfort, serenity, and perfect joy which that beloved person gives us when we're far apart and the beloved is always present in spirit, in an atmosphere of deep longing.

Fortunately, we'll be seeing each other often, and I have here with me our splendid treasure, for whom we can never thank our Lord and our Heavenly Mother enough.

What a joy it is to see him and hear him always adding to every expression of joy and admiration an affectionate appeal to his Mamma! And how moving it is when I hear him calling you whenever he's upset!

As for his stiff neck[85] that worries you so much, let's keep trusting the Madonna of Guérison!

We can offer to her also the sacrifice of our being apart.

Dearest Gianna, I promise you I'll take better care of my health, or rather, I'll have every necessary care.

This should be a good lesson. I understand that this is my great duty toward you, who love me so much and make me so happy, toward our treasure who is such a joy to us, and to the little one we are awaiting with so much joy and eagerness.

If only I could dissolve all your anxieties with my prayers! Our Heavenly Mother will surely bless you in the most perfect way.

Thank you again and again for your special efforts on my behalf as I'm convalescing.

---

85. Pierluigi had a stiff neck that refused to heal.

I'm glad of Zita's caring company. I'm very grateful to her for this and for all the most affectionate care she gives our family. Many, many greetings to Sister Virginia for me.

Innumerable "Mamma, Mamma, Mammas" and big kisses from our treasure.

Affectionate greetings from Mamma, and many, many greetings to Savina too.

A strong, most affectionate embrace and a big kiss from

Your

Pietro

Most cordial greetings and best wishes from Cav. Bordone.[86]

SEPTEMBER 20, 1957
FRIDAY EVENING

Dearest Pietro,

When I got back from Mesero, Rosetta told me you had called. I was so disappointed not to hear your voice and Gigetto's! You had just missed me; it's better if you call me between 6:00 and 6:30 PM, that way I'll be sure to receive the phone call myself.

Anyway, thank you for letting me know everything is fine. How hard it is to be away from you! My thoughts are always with both of you: I imagine you, all loving with our treasure, and our dearest Pierluigi filling the house with his shrieks of joy.

How beautiful he is! Everyone who sees him admires him. Thanks be to God that he's so healthy and is such a lively and sweet baby.

Your faith, dearest Pietro, gives me hope for a complete healing of his stiff neck. I must admit that I worry a lot about that problem.

---

86. Cavaliere Francesco Bordone, SAFFA's general director before Pietro.

May the dear little Madonna of "Notre Dame de la Guérison" hear our prayers!

They are broadcasting the *Manon Lescaut* of Puccini from Spoleto as I write to you—that music is always so beautiful and touching![87]

Zita and Cecco[88] left for Bergamo at 7:00 AM. Cecco had to pick up a tool that he had left in Brazil from a man who has just returned from there. I decided to stay home because I was afraid I would get too tired. I sent the film to Bergamo, though, and asked them to develop it as soon as possible.

And so I'm all alone with you, dearest Pietro. Try to stay well, darling, and promise me that you'll take better care of your health.[89] Medicine helps, yes, but what counts the most—you know it very well—is rest. Think of Gigetto and the little one that we're expecting so eagerly, of your Gianna who loves you so much, and who wants to see you healthy and always happy.

Don't worry about me; I try not to tire myself, partly because my feet are starting to swell. I go over to the house every day to clean up a little and give the plants some light and air. Zita takes good care of me and is happy to have me here with her.

Mother Virginia comes almost every day, too, because Nando[90] is teaching her how to do x-rays. She is hoping the Reverend Mother Provincial will buy an x-ray machine.

---

87. Gianna and Pietro both loved classical music and they had subscribed to the concert season at the Conservatory of Milan.

88. Cecco, an engineer and the brother of Gianna, had been for a time in Brazil where he was working with their brother, Father Alberto, on the construction of a hospital in Grajaú.

89. Concerned for her husband's health, Gianna asked him to take time for rest and for his growing family.

90. Mother Virginia and Nando are Gianna's siblings. The first, a doctor and a Canossian religious, was particularly close to Gianna although three years younger

It's 11:00 AM, so I'll stop my rambling. Please excuse my bad handwriting.

Big, big kisses to my Gigetto, special greetings to Mamma and Savina, and a big hug to you from your

Gianna

COURMAYEUR, SEPTEMBER 24, 1957[91]

My most beloved Gianna,

Together with our beautiful treasure, I'm entrusting to these flowers the hugs, kisses, and thoughts I want to send you on this, our second wedding anniversary.

May we always bring as much joy to each other as we have in these first two years, and may your next delivery be the happiest ever! This is the wish I send you and the prayer I offered to our Lord and our Heavenly Mother this morning.

Our dearest Pierluigi sends you many big kisses and harder and harder squeezes, and calls his Mommy.

I kiss you and embrace you with all my love,

Your Pietro

Many best wishes from Mamma.

---

than her. She testified: "I know that Gianna was very concerned about the education of the children and considered it a continuation of their procreation. She devoted the entire morning to it," from the *Position on Virtue*, op. cit., 111 for the canonization process.

91. Letter which accompanied flowers sent by Pietro to Gianna on their second wedding anniversary.

SEPTEMBER 25, 1957

My dearest Pietro,

Your magnificent flowers and your sweet words were very touching. Infinite thanks to you, to my Gigetto, and above all to the Lord who loves us so much.

I'm enclosing the note from Father Agostino so you can reply as you see fit.

Zita will be happy to come on Saturday,[92] and we should be there around 5:30 PM, if we leave here around 2:30 PM.

I'm so happy you're both coming back because . . . having you close is [so much better than only writing letters].

Many greetings to Mamma and Savina.

Big kisses to my Gigetto and to his dearest Papa,

your most affectionate

Gianna

DÜSSELDORF, JANUARY 28, 1958[93]

Thinking of the unforgettable days spent up here[94] with you, I kiss you and our little angels with all my love.

Pietro

IMPERIA, FEBRUARY 18, 1958[95]

A most loving remembrance and big kisses to you, Pierluigi, and Mariolina.

Pietro

---

92. Gianna and her sister Zita were joining Pietro and the children for the weekend and then all would return home.

93. Postcard.

94. Gianna and Pietro had visited the city soon after their marriage.

95. Postcard. While in Sanremo for a rest, Pietro had visited his sister, Sister Luigia.

FEBRUARY 18, 1958
TUESDAY

Dearest Pietro,

I was happy to hear last night on the phone that everything is fine. I hope the weather stays nice so that you can stay outside in the sunshine as much as possible. Here, it's cold and snowy, so Pierluigi can't go outside. He's venting his energy by playing records and dancing. He seems to be feeling better, as I told you—he didn't throw up at all yesterday.[96] Unfortunately, he did earlier today, but his color is back and he looks more rested; let's hope he's just feeling sick because he's teething. But he has been sick now for ten days, and he should be better by now. Dear Pietro, I could never have imagined how much I would suffer being a mother! I always want to see our children beautiful and healthy, without having to suffer, but instead, there is a little thorn in our happiness every day. . . . It's a good thing you're more optimistic than I am, so you can encourage me—otherwise, my morale would be almost below zero.

As I write, I have Mariolina[97] here beside me, looking at me with her beautiful big eyes and smiling every time I say her name. She cried a little bit last night; I don't know why. Fortunately, Zita was here to take care of her. I wish I could comfort her myself during the night, but it is still impossible for now—the two of them are still too little and they would disturb each other too much.

Does it bother you that Zita is coming to help me a little while longer? I ask you this, Pietro dear, because I sometimes feel like you're not happy about it.[98]

---

96. The child suffered from hyperesthesia of the pharynx, which caused frequent vomiting.

97. Mariolina (Maria Zita) was born on December 11, 1957. At the moment mentioned here she is about two and a half months.

98. Pietro wrote "far from it" on the letter after receiving it.

I keep thinking how happy Sister Luigia[99] must have been to have you with her for almost a whole day. When you see her again, give her many, many greetings from me.

Many big, big kisses from your dear little angels.

Stay well and happy, rest and eat. Understand, Pedrin dear? With all my love I embrace and kiss you,

Your most affectionate

Gianna

Many big kisses, Papa, from your Pierluigi.[100]

FEBRUARY 19, 1958
WEDNESDAY AFTERNOON

Dearest Pietro,

A little note today too, and a big, big kiss from your *popi*[101] and from your Gianna. Both Pierluigi and Mariolina had a good night last night. Gigetto ate a big lunch today with a good appetite and didn't throw up. Let's hope he continues that way. Mariolina spits up a little and is a bit cranky, but she is asleep for now. Whenever he sees your hat, Pierluigi says "Ma . . . ma . . ." which for him means "Papa." Zita says that in the evening he goes to the hall and pounds on the storm door with his little hand, calling "Mamma" and "Ma"! What a treasure! He tries to express all his thoughts with these two little words.

It snowed yesterday afternoon, but today is clear and beautiful, though there's a strong wind.

---

99. Sister Luigia, Pietro's sister and a religious of the Congregation of the Precious Blood, was directress of the boarding school "Smile of Italy" in Imperia.

100. This sentence was written by Pierluigi.

101. In the Lombard dialect, children are affectionately called "popi."

Pierluigi has been invited to visit his cousins in Magenta on Friday.[102] I haven't been able to get to Milan yet, so I'll have to buy him a hat and mask [for Mardi Gras] in Magenta.

I saw your Mamma, and she told me to say hello for her and tell you to rest because you need it.

I would like to bring Pierluigi with me when I come to pick you up. What do you think? Will it be too tiring for him? Many, many big kisses from the *popi* and from your

Gianna

Are you all right? And your teeth?

Greetings from Zita, Cecco, and Savina

SAN REMO, FEBRUARY 19, 1958
WEDNESDAY

Dearest Gianna,

I have here, in the silence of my little room, your affectionate letter of Tuesday—you and Pierluigi are smiling at me from your wonderful pictures, and in Mariolina's photos I can enjoy all her different moods: serious, self-confident, almost smiling—all of you are so lovable.

Tonight too, I have the joy of hearing from you that all is well.

I wish every day could be spent without health problems and not even the slightest hurt to our two little angels—and that you can always be strong, healthy, and serenely happy in your constant, daily work as Mamma!

Above all, please don't fear the worst for Pierluigi. When his teeth are all in, he'll stop throwing up. Don't worry. You know I'm

102. They are Amalia and Maria Vittoria, daughters of Ferdinando, Gianna's brother.

not naturally an optimist, but that I tend toward pessimism. We can't do much about all these things, but everything—or nearly everything—depends on the Lord's Providence: things like health and children. I'm trying to trust completely and pray to Providence with the greatest possible confidence. I have a trust that almost gives me an intuition and a certainty that the clouds will lift and these problems will go away. So in these things I'm an optimist.[103]

Far from my family, I feel a greater need of divine help, and I can't manage a day without Holy Communion. I dearly love saying the Rosary and the Angelus along the seashore, when the sun is setting over the sea, before the wide and silent horizon.

There's a lot of sun in the mornings until 10:00, but often little or none in the afternoon. I try to walk out in the fresh air, far from the streets where cars are driving.

Here you smell gasoline, not fresh air.

I really, really appreciate how Zita is helping you. She's really a fairy godmother.

I fully understand that you can't manage alone at night yet with our two little angels. Please tell Zita I am so thankful to her.

Sister Luigia is pretty well, except for some digestion problems. She doesn't have a constant headache anymore. The Superior and Sister Luigia thank you sincerely for the wonderful medicine.

I wasn't expecting to have Sister Luigia spend the last day of Carnival with me and to enjoy the children's school. You can imagine how happy Luigia was to be able to share a good bottle of sparkling wine and a cake with me (a present of her superior and another sister, a colleague who teaches with her)!

---

103. As Pietro explains so well, trust in Providence comes from prayer, not simply from a natural disposition.

That same Tuesday afternoon I enjoyed myself on the pier in Porto Maurizio, admiring the fishermen's patience with their hooks and bait. I enjoyed some splendid sunshine, together with sprays of water and air that smelled like iodine.

For supper Tuesday evening, Mr. and Mrs. Bornè[104] offered exquisite hospitality: a hotel, the Savoy, with marquises and countesses and jewels that—so said Mrs. Bornè—were so plentiful they almost lost all their value.

Today I explored Bordighera: the shoreline and the old, quaint part of the upper town. The sun was out, but there was still a cold wind.

I'm resting all I can, and I have to make an effort to stay in a good mood. So far my appetite is good and my teeth aren't bothering me.

And you, Mamma and little wife *d'oro*, take very good care of yourself. Smile, and kiss Pierluigi and Mariolina for me, and many kisses and a loving embrace from

Your

Pietro

Affectionate greetings to Zita and Cecco.
Cordial greetings to Savina.

FEBRUARY 20, 1958
THURSDAY EVENING

My dearest Pietro,

I hope you're still doing well. Today I received—or rather, we received—your cards. Thank you, and many big kisses from your little ones.

---

104. Luigi Bornè was the director of SAFFA's plant in Ponte Nuovo during the difficult period after the war. He was a member of SAFFA's administrative council.

Mariolina cried non-stop yesterday afternoon, and didn't quiet down until 2:00 AM. She was vomiting a lot, so I had Mr. Crotti[105] take us to Milan to see Dr. Cislaghi[106] today. Nando came with us, and since Mariolina had to go, I brought Gigetto along as well.

Unfortunately, nothing can be done for Mariolina; we just have to wait until she can eat cereal, when she's about five months old. The doctor gave me some drops to relieve her stomach pains, but said there's nothing to worry about: she looks healthy and rosy, not a bit pale, and he said that whenever she cries a lot, we can use some small suppositories to calm her.

In Gigetto's case, though, the doctor found him well and strong; the vomiting is due to hyperesthesia, so any little irritation (from a cough, a bread crumb, etc.) will cause vomiting. This will pass, too, as he gets older.

Now I feel better, and with the help of God and all my good will, I'll try to be patient[107] and wait for them to get older! I brought Pierluigi over to your Mamma's this morning, since I had to go to Cuggiono to see one of my patients in the hospital. She was delighted to take care of him for me; she said he didn't cry, but he pouted and refused to talk. As soon as I got back, though, he started jumping and playing as usual. Today he wanted to eat and he didn't throw up. He went to nursery school, but he didn't like the [Mardi Gras] masks—he was a little afraid of them.

---

105. Adolfo Crotti was Pietro's trusted driver.

106. Dr. Cislaghi was a well-known pediatrician at that time.

107. In February of 1958 Gianna lived a difficult time: her husband had to go to San Remo for care, and both children were afflicted by small but annoying problems. Encouraged by the pediatrician, Gianna immediately thanked the Lord and promised to be more patient.

We always remember you and are waiting for the day we can embrace you again. Try to stay well, dear Pedrin, and "catch" the many, many big kisses from your little angels and your

Gianna

Best greetings from Zita and Cecco.

SAN REMO, FEBRUARY 21, 1958
FRIDAY

My dearest Gianna,

Thank you again for your most loving letter on Wednesday. I'm very relieved to know you're all in good health. And now I'm even more relieved since Dr. Cislaghi was able to put all your doubts and anxieties to rest: the ones I too shared and . . . the ones I had about you.

I'm doing well. Between nighttime and a nap after breakfast, I sleep as much as twelve hours a day. Isn't that a bit too much? I must need to catch up because I do sleep twelve hours altogether and I fall asleep in two or three minutes at night.

The "enough" that I inadvertently dropped this evening after the word "well" when I was on the phone with you wasn't referring to my health, but rather to some sad moments I have now and then (they'll pass, I assure you)—that I can't just get over because I'm so far away from you and our little angels. I wish I could have you all with me. I make up for it by thinking of you and constantly looking at your dearest photographs and kissing them.

This morning the sun was out and the sea was a magnificent blue. You should have seen me sitting on the rocks by the shore, enjoying the sun and fresh air, which smelled like seaweed. Unfortunately, when you walk along the main street that goes all the way through San Remo (and I assure you, I do that as seldom as possible), there are such fumes from the cars that the air is anything but healthful.

With Mr. Bornè (while his wife, just as on every other afternoon, was at the casino losing the 65,000 lire she won in 1957), I enjoyed a good symphony concert at the Opera Theater of Casinò: an overture by Mozart, a triptych by Respighi, *Three Symphonic Preludes* by Pizzetti, Beethoven's Fourth Symphony, and an overture by Rossini. The orchestra, the maestro, and the acoustics were outstanding, in my opinion.

Tomorrow afternoon I'll be enjoying the seashore at Porto Maurizio and visiting with Sister Luigia.

I often see Mr. Stradella:[108] he's such a polite, nice person.

Along with a "Good Night," I send you many most affectionate greetings and big kisses for you, Pierluigi, and Mariolina.

Your affectionate

Pietro

Remember me to Mamma and reassure her that I'm really resting.

Cordial greetings to Zita, Cecco, Adelaide, and Savina.

Please ask Adelaide to inquire of Dr. Ruginè and then tell me the address for Mr. Lancetti,[109] who is taking some time off in Nervi.

---

108. Giovanni Stradella, a cousin of Gianna. He had married Amalia Beretta, whose father was Gianna's paternal uncle.

109. The accountant Luigi Lancetti was SAFFA's vice director general.

FEBRUARY 22, 1958

SATURDAY AFTERNOON

My dearest Pietro,

The 1:00 PM siren [signaling the end of lunchtime at the factory] just sounded, so while the little ones take their nap, I will take advantage of this time to send you our love.

I hope you're all right, and that your "I'm okay" last night on the phone wasn't hiding anything. I've been thinking of you visiting with Sister Luigia—how sad she'll be not to see you so often after your vacation! But everything comes to an end—both the good things and the bad.

Pierluigi was very rambunctious during lunch and didn't want to eat; halfway through, he threw up. What a shame, Pietro dear! I loved watching him eat two or three little bowls of cereal. Now I never know what to give him . . . patience! It will pass, as the doctor says. Mariolina is doing well today—she slept through the night and hasn't cried.

There's a ball at the Nuovo Hotel in Magenta today for "Fat Saturday." Mr. Molla and his wife were invited, too. It begins with refreshments at five, and the ball will take place in the evening. I'm glad to hear you went to the concert—time will pass more quickly for you if you go out. Only one more week, dear Pietro, and then we'll be together again.

Nothing new is happening [at the factory], Adelaide says, so don't worry and just stay healthy.

Warm greetings from all of us and big kisses from your *popi*.

With all my love I embrace you, your

Gianna

I just now received your long, affectionate letter of Wednesday and the one addressed to your beloved Gigetto. Infinite thanks. You can't imagine my joy and consolation at your sweet words. As I have told you other times, your faith and your piety are a great example to me:[110] I want to learn to pray as you do, dear Pietro. I recommend to you: stay happy, understand? I think about you every moment of the day and the distance between us seems less difficult.

With all my affection I kiss you together with your dearest little angels, your

Gianna

Greetings from Zita, Cecco, and Savina.

SAN REMO, FEBRUARY 22, 1958
SATURDAY EVENING

My dearest Gianna,

I just got back from Porto Maurizio where I spent the afternoon on the beach and at the pier with Sister Luigia, and when I reached the hotel, I wished so much for a letter from you in my little post box—and there it was. Thank you from my heart for your most welcome letter of Thursday evening. To see confirmed the good news of last night, the very reassuring answer of Dr. Cislaghi, renews my joy and peace about our little angels.

I'm sure their little health problems, in the meantime, will be minimized by your loving care, by your wisdom and competence, and by Zita's welcome help.

I'm glad to hear that Pierluigi didn't cry when he was with Mamma; that way, when the weather's nice, you can take him to Mesero with you.

---

110. The reciprocal help that the spouses can give one another both in everyday life and in the spiritual realm is an important support and one of the most significant fruits of the sacrament of Marriage.

I can just picture Pierluigi at the nursery school—just as I saw him that day— sitting in the front row, intent on his tasks like the other children, looking important like a pupil well aware of his duties. He's truly a treasure in all his expressions.

This morning, too, I slept in till 9:30, and from 10:30 to noon I walked along the beach.

Luigia was very happy to be able to spend some down time with me. As usual, she confided a little in me. In my opinion, the biggest cause, if not the only one, of her headaches, her poor digestion, and her aches and pains, is her having too much work, which never leaves her a moment to rest any day of the year. Last week, the sisters, who had been seven, went down to five because two were more needed at Borgio Verezzi.[111] Luigia is resigned because, she says, this is life in the convent. I got her some more Saridon because she still has frequent bad headaches.

She would love to see Pierluigi. I told her that we'll bring him to Milan later on when she comes with the children over Easter break.

Kiss and caress Pierluigi and Mariolina for me, and for you, a big, big hug and a very loving kiss.

Your affectionate

Pietro

Greetings to Zita and Cecco, and to Adelaide and the family.

Most affectionate greetings and kisses from Sister Luigia, to you and our little angels.

---

111. An old Ligurian town in the province of Savona. Two of the sisters had been transferred there, making the workload even heavier for the remaining five.

FEBRUARY 23, 1958
SUNDAY AFTERNOON

Dearest Pietro,

Finally, I have a moment of peace. Mariolina is having a bad day today—after two days of quiet, she cried a lot today, but now she's asleep. Gigetto wants to go outside in the garden all day to play with the little stones. Just think how much fun he'll have at the beach! Your Mamma[112] is here visiting Adelaide and helping me, since Rosetta is on vacation this week.

It's 10:00 PM now, so I'll start over. I was happy to hear your voice on the phone, to know you're doing well and that your spirits are high. I'm sorry Pierluigi didn't say "Mamma" or "Ma." The poor little thing had just finished throwing up. It's a good thing he likes milk and doesn't throw it up, otherwise I don't know how he'd survive.

Mariolina has settled down a bit. I gave her some chamomile tea and that seemed to calm her.

Pietro, please forgive me if I cause you pain by telling you these things,[113] but you are my Pietro, the Papa, and telling you about things helps to lessen my worries.

You were right to switch hotels. Besides, you're closer to Sister Luigia now.

---

112. Signora Maria lived in Mesero. She came for a few days, as a guest of her daughter Adelaide, in order to assist her daughter-in-law with the two small children while Rosetta, who helped her with domestic tasks, was away.

113. She continues to be uncertain about sharing with her husband or remaining silent about small, but lighter news. It is a situation well known to spouses. The beauty of Gianna's holiness derives from the experiences of everyday life familiar to every Christian couple.

I'm sorry I won't be able to come to pick you up; I'll do it the next time.[114]

Ciao, Pedrin, one more week and then you'll be back with us again.

Big kisses from Gigetto, little smiles from Mariolina, and a most affectionate embrace from your

Gianna

SAN REMO, FEBRUARY 25, 1958
TUESDAY EVENING

My dearest Gianna,

I've come to my room earlier than usual tonight, because we can't watch television. The wind is blowing wildly and the antennas are covered with sea salt, so the picture disappears almost completely.

I have here before me Pierluigi and Mariolina who are smiling at me, and the blustery wind and thundering waves seem very far away, almost non-existent. I'm happy and peaceful here with all of you.

I'm still worried about Gigetto. I'm confident it will pass sooner than we think. It's good that you tell me everything. It's really true that, when people truly love each other, the joys are greater and worries lighter. With a Mamma like you, who takes things seriously and gets right to work, illnesses are quickly relieved and in the best possible way. I will never be able to thank you enough for this.

---

114. In her letter of February 19 Gianna had manifested the intention of driving to San Remo with her son and returning with her husband. Due to her work commitments she was later forced to give up this intention.

I really like this hotel. There's a wonderful view of the sea from my room and the dining room. From the hotel's garden I can step right onto the beach and the pier.

My digestion is good and I'm eating well. Even my teeth and gums are fine, as if I had never had any problem.

I was so happy to hear your dear voice this evening and to hear that all is well with our little angels.

How comforting it is to read and re-read your dear letters. I have here before me your letter of Sunday afternoon, and I too can't wait to see you all again and embrace you.

Wednesday evening

Thank you for phoning me today, and let's hope things continue to go well for our little angels.

I was out in the sunshine this morning from 10:00 to noon, even though the wind was strong.

The waves are very high; we can't go out on the pier.

In the afternoon there were the usual clouds and very strong winds. I hope tomorrow we'll have some sun with no wind.

I visited with Luigia from 3:00 to 4:30 PM; she mended my coat and . . . sewed on two buttons for me, button-popper that I am.

She absolutely had to take at least two of my shirts to iron them, even though I had already made arrangements for the hotel to take care of that.

She's not looking forward to my having to leave soon.

Thursday morning

I went back to the Casinò Theater in San Remo until 1:00. Maybe I'm too harsh and demanding in judging theatrical plays. The only good part—and I do understand that it is not a little thing—was the last five minutes in which all of the comedy's protagonists (two couples and a seventeen-year-old daughter) finally agreed, after fifteen years of marriage, that they must put aside all their differences and live as good couples, and the daughter decided to get married.

Gino Cervi[115] played "Patata." I did not even recognize Padovani,[116] maybe because of the part she had: no life, no soul, she just recited her lines vacantly.

This morning it was cloudy and windy, with flurries, and only around 11:00 did a few rays of the sun peek out.

Just two more days and I'll be back with you again. Many kisses to Gigetto and Mariolina for me, and many big kisses and a most affectionate *arrivederci* to you.

Your

Pietro

Affectionate greetings to Mamma, Adelaide, Zita, Cecco, and Savina.

FEBRUARY 26, 1958
WEDNESDAY EVENING

My dearest Pietro,

Pierluigi and Mariolina are asleep. I'm listening to *Everyone's Songs* on TV[117] as I write. Tagliavini[118] is singing "You will come back to me," etc., you know, from "Patata." You will have to tell me

---

115. Stage name of Luigi Cervi (1901–1974), a well-known actor.

116. Lea Padovani (1920–1991), a well-known actress.

117. RAI began to broadcast in Italy in 1954. We are, therefore, at the very beginning of the history of Italian television programming.

118. Renzo Tagliavini was a well-known crooner of that time.

later why it is titled the "potato." My dearest Pedrin, I'm sorry your days of rest are already over, but I'm glad I'll be able to embrace you again in a few days. Every night, whenever the doorbell rings, Pierluigi rushes to the door, hoping to see his *paparino*. Every time, he shakes his head and comes back into the hall protesting. When he saw me leaving the house this morning to go to the nursery school,[119] he started to cry so loudly that I couldn't bear to leave him home.

So he came along with me. At first, he played with the other children and the toys, but then he began to call for me, so they brought him to my office. When he saw me in my doctor's coat, he was frightened and began to cry. He did get used to seeing me dressed that way, though, and when the children who came to see me cried, tears welled up in his eyes, too. My poor little doctor!

Today he seems to be feeling better; he only threw up a little bit this evening, but he looks pale and isn't hungry.

Mamma was here for supper, and she was hoping to talk to you, but she didn't realize I was planning to call you tomorrow evening instead. She is well and says hello. She constantly speaks to Pierluigi about you, and Gigetto answers by shaking his little head "no," as if to say you're not here.

I ran in to Father Luigi[120] in Magenta today and he asked if you were home. He wanted to stop by and tell you that Monsignor's eightieth birthday (I believe) is on Tuesday, March 9,[121] and he

---

119. Gianna specialized in pediatrics, as well as being owner of a medical clinic in Mesero. She was chief physician for the nursery and counselor for the mothers of Ponte Nuovo, where she always took care of the medical needs of the children of the kindergarten and the elementary school free of charge.

120. Father Luigi Gallazzi was the assistant at Magenta from 1931 to 1967.

121. Msgr. Luigi Crespi, pastor of Magenta.

would like you and Nando to serve Mass at 6:00 PM. Nando called and asked me whether you would accept. I thought you would—will you? Anyway, you can talk with him when you come back.

Ciao, my dearest little husband, stay merry. The most beautiful big kisses from your three treasures, your

Gianna

MAGENTA, JUNE 24, 1958[122]

SAINT JOHN

With all my love, I wish you the most beautiful joys and I kiss you.

Your Pietro, with Pierluigi and Mariolina

MAGENTA

SUMMER 1958[123]

Dearest Pietro,

Maciocchi (the orthopedist) said everything is okay.[124] However, given her weight, he recommends that Mariolina wear the brace at night for two more months. Thanks be to God!

Ciao, dearest Pedrin, don't get too tired. I'll call you Monday night at 7:30.

Big kisses,

Gianna

---

122. Feast day note.

123. This letter was written before leaving for summer vacation without Pietro.

124. Because the girl, who was seven months old, ran the same risk as her brother of growing up with a dislocated hip, she had to wear a brace.

[JULY 6, 1958][125]

SUNDAY EVENING

My dearest Pietro,

I'm glad to hear everything went well, and I'm eagerly waiting for you to arrive here. Gigetto has been waiting for you[126] since yesterday, when Zita arrived. He called to you from the window for a good fifteen minutes. To console him, I took him down the road as far as the Blessed Mother statue, where we said a Hail Mary for his Papa and then returned home,[127] hoping that Zita would come in time for supper. She and Nando didn't arrive until midnight, though.

I'm sending you the thermos with Zita because it fell and broke. I bought it in a shop on the corner of Orefici Street and the Piazza Cordusio; they told me they would replace the glass inside if it ever broke.[128] It would be good if you could buy another thermos, even a small one, with a wide mouth, for Gigetto's risotto—it's so hard to get it out of narrow ones.

Then don't forget your clothes: overcoat, umbrella, shoes.

I'm also sending you the coupons for gas, and *buon viaggio!*

Many big kisses from your beautiful and precious little ones. Everyone admires them and compliments us for them.

A most affectionate embrace and an *arrivederci* soon, from,

Your

Gianna

---

125. Gianna indicated only the day of the week, but not the precise date. The date was established based on data of Monsignor Rimoldi. There is however some uncertainty about it being Sunday the sixth or the thirteenth.

126. It was Saturday, July 5, and Pietro was expected to arrive for the weekend.

127. This refers to that same Saturday afternoon when Gianna and her son waited in vain for the arrival of family members. Zita and Nando arrived at midnight, while her husband was not able to come.

128. Although well-to-do, Gianna was careful in the use of earthly goods.

JULY 9, 1958
WEDNESDAY

Dearest Pietro,

We're all fine here. The babies are already tanned and are eating well. Mariolina is making me a little desperate, though, because she doesn't want to wear the brace anymore.[129] I had to take it off last night so she would go to sleep; let's hope she won't have to wear it much longer.

I took them to the pine woods above Villair yesterday. Mariolina wriggled her legs in the sun, happy to be free of the brace for a while. Pierluigi spent his time energetically throwing little stones in a ditch. Poor Gigetto, he calls you fifty times a day, and every time he hears a car, he says "Mamma . . . Papa," then shakes his head and says "Grandma," since he thinks you have gone to Grandma's in Magenta.

The record player[130] isn't working today. Tell Menescardi he's a fine trickster and have him give you another one. Pierluigi loves his music, and if it starts to rain, we won't be able to settle him down without it.[131]

We forgot the white centerpiece for the 45 rpm records.[132]

I'm waiting for the booklet [of gas coupons] for the Fiat 1100; I'm sending you fifteen of the twenty-five liters that I've gotten, since I already used the other ten. Remind Cecco to let me have his car's log book.

---

129. The orthopedic device was ordered by Dr. Maciocchi. See the letter of Pietro to Gianna dated summer of 1958.

130. By the end of the fifties the turntable began to appear and by the sixties it had invaded Italian homes.

131. The life of faith does not eliminate the difficulties of daily life. However, it offers help to live them, as Saint Paul says, in the Lord.

132. As some readers may recall, at a certain point the insert was needed to go from 33 rpm to 45 rpm.

I haven't seen Mrs. Valle[133] yet.

How come Nando hasn't arrived yet? Are the children sick?[134]

Don't worry about the white polish for Pierluigi's shoes; I found some here at Courmayeur. The weather is mixed today: some sun, some rain, some wind. Fortunately, the children haven't caught anything—not even a sneeze.

Try to take care of yourself, dear Pietro, and don't work after supper—rest. Remember what happened last year?[135]

Looking forward to hearing your voice tonight, I greet you and kiss you with all my affection along with our beautiful *popi,*

Gianna

Greetings to Mamma.

JULY 14, 1958

MONDAY EVENING

Dearest Pietro,

I'm sending you the gas coupons now so that they'll arrive in time for you to use them. I hope you had a good trip and that you won't feel too much of a difference in temperature when you get to Ponte Nuovo. We finally had some sunshine this afternoon. Father Giuse[136] and Father Piero[137] went up to the Turin lookout[138] to

---

133. Mrs. Valle was the owner of the house the Molla family rented.

134. Indeed, as the following letters show, Nando's children had come down with some form of rash.

135. This is a reference to the extraordinary period of rest Pietro had to take because of recurring fevers brought on by excessive work.

136. Father Giuseppe Beretta, an engineer and priest of the diocese of Bergamo, was one of two brothers of Gianna who were priests.

137. Father Piero, of the diocese of Bergamo, was a friend of Father Giuseppe.

138. The Turin tower, at over three thousand meters, is one of the favorite places for those who love mountain hikes.

enjoy the sun and the gorgeous view while I took the little ones for a short walk. As usual, Pierluigi greeted each car that passed with a hopeful "Papa." I put him in your bed this morning to make him feel better, so he wouldn't miss his "paparino" quite so much.

Mrs. Valle stopped in to ask what we're planning to do next year. I told her I had to talk to you about it before giving her an answer. Someone asked to rent the house year-round, but she prefers to give it to us because we only rent it for a couple of months in the summer. I really don't know what to tell you: if we intend to come to Courmayeur again next year, it would be best to stay here, since it's so nice and all the rents are about the same around here. Come to think of it, fifteen days at the beach are enough—any longer and the children would just get cranky and overtired. What do you think?

Ciao, my dearest Pietro, *arrivederci* on Friday evening.

Big kisses from your *popi* and from your

Gianna

JULY 16, 1958
WEDNESDAY AFTERNOON

My dearest Pietro,

There have been thunderstorms since this morning. Pierluigi is asleep now, and Mariolina is here chattering to me, mamma . . . papa—she gets more mischievous every day! When she's not wearing her brace, she likes to sit and play on the swing or the high chair.

I went to Morgex[139] with Gigetto and Gianfranco[140] to get some meat—I also bought some for Laura and Mr. Furlan;[141] then I

---

139. A tourist resort about 10 km south of Courmayeur.

140. Son of Adelaide, Pietro and Gianna's nephew.

141. Laura Viola, wife of Ferdinando, is Gianna's sister-in-law. Luigi Furlan was a textile industrialist of Mesero.

bought a laminated blue-and-white checked tablecloth at the market so the white tablecloths won't have to be washed so often. Pierluigi was very pleased to be able to walk in the rain with his umbrella. Laura's children are feeling better; the fever is gone, but they're full of little scabs.[142] They have to be quarantined for fifteen more days before they can go out.

Gronchi[143] is arriving on Saturday; everyone was going crazy on the phone Monday. They hired four extra phone operators, two for daytime, two for nighttime at the Royal, where they had to put in a direct line to Rome. There were officials at the Stipel who had to talk to Rome and Turin, so we poor unimportant beings had to wait over an hour to place a call.

Amalia de Zoverallo[144] wrote to me and said the Sisters tried the SAFFA "Lily" soap and liked it so much that they want to buy it in bulk. Does it still cost sixty lire if they buy a lot[145] of it at once? I'll write to Amalia and then give the order to Adelaide.

I'm sorry it's so hot in Rome and that you have to stay in the city. When you come back from Rome you should come up here for a few days to rest before leaving for Spain. Can you?

Ciao, say hello to Mamma for me; many big kisses from your *popi*, from Gigetto, who, when he calls you, shakes his head, and then blows you a kiss.

A hug from your

Gianna

---

142. The children of Laura and Ferdinando were also suffering from the same malady (cf. letter of July 9, 1958).

143. Giovanni Gronchi, an Italian politician, was president of the Republic 1955–1962.

144. Amalia Beretta, who lived in Zoverallo, was the unmarried cousin of Gianna's father. She was Gianna's godmother at Baptism and her Confirmation sponsor.

145. This probably alludes to a community of religious who, having received a gift of the soap produced by SAFFA, desired to acquire a certain quantity.

ROME, JULY 19, 1958[146]
ST. MARY MAJOR

Remembering our honeymoon, I kiss you, Pierluigi, and Mariolina with all my love.

Pietro

I'm anxiously awaiting the express.

SANTA MARGHERITA LIGURE, JULY 20, 1958[147]

Dearest Gianna,

I was so happy to hear this morning from Vittoria[148] at Sestri Levante that Mariolina only has to wear the brace at night for another month.

Thanks be to our Lady.

Big kisses to you, Pierluigi, and Mariolina.

Pietro

JULY 20, 1958
SUNDAY EVENING

My dearest Pietro,

It's about 10:30 PM and our beautiful little ones are sleeping tranquilly after enjoying the sunshine almost all day long. I say "almost" because it rained for a little while this afternoon. It's calm and clear now, though, and I can see the beautiful starry Heavens. Adelaide, Cecco, and Zita left half an hour ago, happy after spending a lovely day with their beloved nephew and niece. I'm thinking

---

146. Postcard.

147. Postcard.

148. Maria Vittoria, daughter of Gianna's brother Ferdinando.

of you traveling right now, your heart here with us.[149] Dear Pietro, it would be so wonderful to be able to be together, united, all of the time. Luckily, your vacation begins in only ten days: what joy! Pierluigi misses you very much. How often he calls for you! How affectionate he is! When you're not here, he won't leave me for a moment: "Mamma . . . Mamma . . ." Maybe he's afraid I'll leave him like I did on Friday. How beautiful they are! Mrs. Valle was here for a while the other day and compared her three-year-old girl, who is much smaller and thinner than Pierluigi, to them. We must always be so grateful to the Lord for giving us two great treasures who are beautiful, healthy, and robust. Mariolina is even doing better now— thanks be to God! I go to church every morning to thank God for all the graces he is continually giving us, and to ask him to help me be a good mother and to make you happy every moment.[150]

I'm including a list of things for you to bring when you come, and also Gigetto and Mariolina's sizes [for clothing].

Take care of yourself, my Pietro. I wish you *buon viaggio* in Spain: enjoy your trip and don't feel sad about being far away from us.

Many big kisses from your three big treasures, your

Gianna

---

149. As mentioned in Gianna's letter of July 16, 1958, Pietro was due to go to Rome, and because of this he could not join his family in the mountains.

150. Every now and then we get a glimpse of how what is apparently neutral in everyday life is sustained and vivified. Gianna had written in a conference to the youth of Catholic Action: "We perfect Charity in ourselves, in our soul, by increasing grace, and the source is the Eucharist, the Sacrament of Love."

JULY 21, 1958
MONDAY EVENING

My dearest Pietro,

Today was a gorgeous, sunny day. As I already told you [on the phone], I took everyone to Checrouit.[151] Pierluigi held his breath until the cable car started moving, then he began chattering—you can imagine how the other passengers watched and complimented him. When we went in the chair lift, he observed everything from up high: the fields, the flowers, the cows, and he liked it so much that he didn't want to get off at the end!

Mariolina didn't cry at all. I made her some cereal on the little camp stove, while Gianfranco "took care" of the fire.[152] All in all, we had a wonderful day, completed by your telephone call. Did you hear how loudly Gigetto called you, and what big kisses he sent you!

I thought you had already gone to Barcelona by plane. If it tires you less and you get there faster, it would certainly be better [than the train].

I'll be waiting for your telegram and, above all, we'll be waiting for you with open arms on Tuesday the twenty-ninth. Tell Mr. Lazzari[153] that the doctor has ordered you to take another month of complete rest. If you don't take it now, when will you rest? Remember to bring the calcium injections (in the kitchen cabinet).

Ciao, dear Pietro, have a nice journey.

---

151. As can be seen from what follows, it is a cable car ride. Gianna transmitted her own love of mountains and nature to her children.

152. The boy is standing by the stove. Gianna is being affectionately ironic toward her nephew.

153. Temistocle Lazzari, general director of SAFFA, was Pietro's immediate supervisor. Gianna exhorts her husband not to neglect his time off.

Big kisses and hugs from your dear *popi* and from your
Gianna

Greetings to Mamma.
Gianfranco wants to remind you to bring him the stamps.

NICE, JULY 24, 1958[154]
11:48 AM

Dearest Gianna,

A great fifty-minute flight at an altitude of 3,000 meters.
My heart and thoughts are with you and our two wonderful
treasures.
Today, the twenty-fourth, I'm looking forward to the joy of
September 24, the third anniversary of our "yes."
Thank you and infinite gratitude for the joy you have always
given me and for being the incomparable little mother to our
treasures.
With all my love I kiss you, Pierluigi, and Mariolina.
Pietro

Affectionate greetings to Gianfranco.
Cordial greetings to Savina.

BARCELONA, JULY 24, 1958
11:20 PM

My dearest Gianna,

Here I am in my very comfortable room at the Arycasa [Hotel];
there's a radio, a door that opens and closes electronically, a safe for
jewelry, etc.

---

154. Postcard.

I'm thinking of all of you sweetly sleeping: Mariolina and Pierluigi in their characteristic poses, which are so like those of little angels, and you with the calm joy of having our treasures with you. We had a very cordial welcome from the Spanish gentlemen. The president and secretary of the Ibérica del Carbión[155] were waiting to pick me up at the airport.

I had breakfast at the secretary's house, a pleasant old-style place, formerly the home of a Spanish count, and . . . with six children, the oldest of whom is nine.

In the afternoon I browsed in Barcelona's shops, looking for baby clothes and records of authentic Spanish music. It was an immense joy to be able to do something, even from afar, for you and our babies.

At eight o'clock Jesus in the Eucharist blessed me, and along with me, all of you, in a beautiful Jesuit church.

At nine o'clock we had supper at the hotel. There were even a religious sister and a priest among the guests, and the orchestra was playing.

Today on the plane there was a little baby about two or three months old, and two children who were about two or three years old.[156]

Our children are so marvelous!

Sweet dreams, my dearest Gianna.

I kiss you with all my love and, with you, I kiss Pierluigi and Mariolina. Just a few more days and we'll be together again.

A big, big hug from

Your Pietro

---

155. Manufacturer of packaging materials.

156. This particular detail might have been included to reassure Gianna, who worried about Pietro's frequent flights.

BARCELONA, JULY 25, 1958

My dearest Gianna,

Today is Spain's national holiday: the feast of its patron, Saint James of Compostela.

Along with many, many of the faithful, I will be receiving Jesus at the Jesuit church. I can see you kneeling devoutly, with the same Jesus in your heart: the same prayers, the same invocations, even— and above all—when we are so far apart.[157]

Everything here starts late: our appointment at 11:00, the grand opening of the plant[158] at 1:00 PM, refreshments from 2:00–3:00 PM and a meal on the beach at Tarragon at 3:30.

All the Spaniards I met, men and women, gave us wonderful compliments on our precious children. They want us all to come and visit as soon as we can.

For the grand opening, I too had to give a little speech—in Italian, naturally.

If you could just hear how fast the Spanish talk when they give speeches! If only they were as quick in action.

Rome, with its arches and ruins, is present even in this city. These people are true Latins—and how they love and admire Italy.

How I wished you were with me this evening to admire a marvelous fountain in Barcelona's biggest square. How our babies would have turned heads, and how enchanted Pierluigi would have been.

Imagine a huge fountain whose waters are always changing to different colors of the rainbow, always changing the shape, number, height, and angles of its countless spouts of water. Even I was

---

157. Pietro stresses their sacramental communion. Even over great distances, the Eucharist and the sacrament of Matrimony unite spouses more and more deeply in Christ.

158. The packaging materials plant in Tarragona.

amazed by it just like a child, and I enjoyed this marvelous kaleidoscope of light and color from 10:30 till midnight.

I am always picturing you in the best of health, and what a joy it will be to embrace you again in a few days!

The day after tomorrow, Sunday, I'll be flying again.

Tomorrow I'm going to the Shrine of Our Lady of Montserrat.

Kiss at length Pierluigi and Mariolina for me.

I kiss and embrace you with all my love,

Your Pietro

Affectionate greetings to Gianfranco.

Cordial greetings to Savina.

MAGENTA, AUGUST 18, 1958[159]

Dearest Gianna,

I'm making up for forgetting something else—here are the receipts for the books and some money to buy good gasoline.

Knowing that you are all well, and knowing that Pierluigi is happy and doubly attached to his "little mamma d'oro" because his papa is far away, I don't even feel the heat and humidity of Ponte Nuovo.

Today I managed to leave work at six. The essential thing—you will say—is to persevere.

I can still hear Pierluigi saying, "Papa, papa!" and I love to think of Mariolina's smiles and of how the villagers look so admiringly at our beautiful children.

With all my affection, I kiss you, Pierluigi, and Mariolina.

Pietro

---

159. After their summer vacation in Courmayeur, Pietro had returned to work, while Gianna stayed on a few extra days with her children and relatives.

Affectionate greetings to Teresina, Zita, and to Father Giuse, whom I will be so happy to see again.

Affectionate greetings from Mamma.

MAGENTA, OCTOBER 4, 1958[160]

Infinite, most loving wishes and big kisses

From your Pietro and the popi

ASSISI, OCTOBER 11, 1958[161]

I remembered all of you with boundless love,

Pietro

JESI, 1958[162]

Most affectionate and big kisses to you, Pierluigi, and Mariolina

Pietro

STUTTGART, FEBRUARY 15, 1959

11:30 PM

My dearest Gianna,

I had a good trip on a train of the latest type, a triumph of Formica[163] and our railway system. I have a very nice room in this hotel.

I have here before me, on my worktable, the wondrous smiling expressions of you, of Pierluigi, when he was a year old, who's hugging you, and of Mariolina with her usual joyous outlook.

---

160. Note for Gianna's thirty-sixth birthday.

161. Postcard.

162. Postcard. One of SAFFA's match factories was in Jesi.

163. Namely of laminated plastic, which Mr. Molla had helped introduce to Italy.

This morning, too, in our little church,[164] next to you, I renewed my most fervent thanks to Jesus for the immeasurable gift of you as my wife, of Pierluigi, Mariolina, and the new little one[165] in your womb. I have always rejoiced to find in you the ideal wife I dreamed of, and an incomparable mother to our children. I am still finding in you new virtues of sacrifice, patience, understanding, and goodness, and always of so much loving affection.

And up here, so far away, your virtues and your affection seem even more real and dear, and I feel them very near me.

I can still hear you sweetly calling me "Pietro," and the affectionate "Papa, papa!" from our children. Right now I can just see you all sleeping, and I hope it is a sound sleep.

The weather is nice here and not too cold.

With all my love, I kiss you and our treasures.

Your affectionate,

Pietro

Affectionate greetings and most heartfelt thanks to Zita, who is such a very good "assistant mother," and to Cecco.

BERLIN, FEBRUARY 18, 1959
WEDNESDAY, 11:50 PM

Dearest Gianna,

Being so far away from you and the children is always hard for me. In this city, so grandiose and triumphant in its monuments from the past, but divided up into two zones, isolated in the Communist

---

164. The little Church of Our Lady of Good Counsel in Ponte Nuovo di Magenta. Before leaving for Stuttgart, Pietro had prayed with Gianna in this church.

165. Gianna was expecting their third child, Laura, who would be born five months later, on July 15.

world, with ruins that speak of apocalyptic tragedy, the distance is even more painful, and I long all the more to see you all again and be with you.

Today I read in the Berlin newspaper that Khrushchev would not even tolerate an airlift.[166] Let's hope it happens after we leave.

I received a cordial welcome both from the East Germans and from the West Germans.

My work has turned out well so far, and it's almost finished.

In my room, even here in Berlin, you and our treasures are smiling at me from those radiant photographs. Before I go to bed, I will say the same prayers that we say together every night, and the fullness of joy and warmth that you know how to bring to the intimacy of our family will seem even more luminous.

I give the photo of you and our *popi's* a great big kiss, and I wish you every good and every joy.

A big hug from your most loving

Pietro

HANOVER, FEBRUARY 20, 1959[167]

Remembering our unforgettable honeymoon, I kiss you and our wonderful children with all my love.

Pietro

---

166. During the Cold War, Soviet Premier Nikita Khrushchev launched a blockade of Berlin in opposition to the efforts of Western Allies to unite west and east Berlin. Western Allies responded with a massive airlift of supplies to the people of Berlin. A few years later, Pope John XXIII would usher in a time of greater openness between Russia and the United States after the Cuban missile crisis which brought the world to the threshold of a new world war.

167. Postcard.

PART III

"I'm Already Looking Forward to the Joy of Seeing You Again"

Letters from Pietro's Trip to the United States

Dearest Gianna,

We've been in the air only a few minutes, and my heart and my thoughts are with you and our marvelous Gigetto, whom I saw again out of my little window as our plane turned to taxi to the runway, still waving frantically, and you too in your warm and moving good-bye, and with Mariolina, sleeping right now with the serene sweetness of an angel.

I prayed to Jesus, our Blessed Mother, and to my guardian angel when the plane, with its fiery jets, was already in the air and passed over the gate where you were.

And now I'm going far, far away. . . . But I'm strong and peaceful because of your deep love, your sweet kisses, the dear kisses and "*Ciao, ciao*" of our treasures, your prayers and those of our dear ones, and the many good people who are praying to the Lord for me.

Thank you, my beloved Gianna, for having come with me and waiting until the plane left, despite your condition, which really calls for rest.[2]

---

1. From April 26 to June 16, 1959, Mr. Molla took a long business trip to the United States to visit various producers of matches, packaging materials, and other items. He and Gianna kept in touch by very frequent letters. Their early enthusiastic letters give way here to correspondence revealing a more mature concept of family life—one that is, however, still permeated by constant affection.

2. Gianna was expecting their third child, Laura.

Kiss Gigetto for me in return for his loving goodbye to his papa, and kiss Mariolina.

Thank Mamma, Zita, Cecco, Adelaide, and all our other relatives, especially Father Giuse, for having come with me to the airport.

In a few minutes I'll say my Rosary, then our usual family prayers, and finally, just as on every other evening, even those when I'm traveling, before going to sleep I will say to Jesus, to our Blessed Mother, and to our guardian angels: Bless Gianna, and help me know how to always make her happy.[3] Bless the new little one we are expecting with so much love and eagerness. Bless and watch over Pierluigi and Mariolina. Protect them from every accident and illness. Please help them grow up healthy and good!

We are already on the descent to Geneva.

Good night, my Love! Don't worry at all about me. Stay always very, very well and my thoughts will be with you at every moment.

With all my love, I kiss you and our treasures.

Your

Pietro

Affectionate greetings to Mamma, Zita, Cecco, and all our loved ones.

APRIL 27, 1959
MONDAY, 10:30 ITALIAN TIME
ON THE FLIGHT TO BOSTON

Dearest Gianna,

I'm flying about 4,500 km from home, above a sea of bright clouds, in the blue sky with bright sunshine as far as the eye can see. The wind was only in the airport's forecast. We took off again

---

3. Intense prayer makes family life peaceful, giving the members strength.

from Paris around 1:40. We had a quiet flight and I slept well all night.

Now the moon is also accompanying us in the blue sky.

I woke up at 8:30 this morning. I thought of you covered with the hugs and kisses of our babies. Did Gigi dream of Papa far away last night?

I still feel the boundless affection and emotion of your good-bye, and I thank Jesus for the great gift of you and our treasures and of the little one we are expecting.

Kiss them every morning and night for me.

It is 12:40 and I'm sure you will have called TWA at Malpensa [airport in Milan] by now. Unfortunately it's still about two hours till we land, but we are still flying in blue skies and sunshine, and everything's going just fine.

I'll telegraph you as soon as we arrive.

I kiss you, Pierluigi, and Mariolina with all my love, and send you all my best wishes.

Your

Pietro

An affectionate greeting to Zita, Cecco, Nando and family, and Liberata.[4]

Remember me to Mamma, Adelaide, and Rosetta.

1:00 PM—The clouds have disappeared. The sky and ocean are blue. We are getting close to Newfoundland. We can see white icebergs—those majestic solitary islands of ice—glistening in the sun.

2:25—After almost thirteen hours of flying over the ocean, we are landing at Gander for our last stop before Boston.

2:47—We landed safely in Gander.

Big kisses.

---

4. Liberata Villa was the domestic helper of the Berettas for over fifty years.

APRIL 28, 1959
TUESDAY, 8:30 AM

My dearest Pietro,

I was finally able to find out this morning that your plane reached Boston after a nine-hour delay. I had called TWA in Milan at 9:00 last night, but the latest news they had was from 3:00. You can imagine how slowly time passed while we waited.[5] Adelaide just called to tell me your telegram from Boston had arrived. Thanks be to God! I'll wait for more detailed news; I can't write anymore now, the little ones won't leave me alone. I'll write more later when they've gone to sleep.

2:00 PM

My Pietro,

I just received your first letter that you wrote on the plane Sunday night. Thank you for your sweet words. Gigetto was pleased with his postcard and fell asleep saying, "Papa got there, Papa didn't crash." You should have heard him on Sunday when he saw the plane take off: "*Ciao*, Papa . . . Papa's in the sky . . . *buon viaggio*, Papa . . . Papa, come back soon." Everyone around us was listening, and he explained, "Papa's up in the airplane; Papa's going far, far away. . . ." Then, every time I called Malpensa Airport yesterday to check on your flight, he followed me, and when there was no news, he said, "Papa didn't get there," and then to console me, he said, "Mamma, Papa won't crash." What a treasure! He thought of you all day, and I had him say the Hail Mary and Eternal Rest . . . often, his two favorite prayers that he knows by

---

5. As previously mentioned, Gianna was afraid of air travel. She nervously awaited news of her husband's arrival on the evening of April 7. Yet, because of the delay, confirmation came only the next morning. Hence, her anxiety.

heart. Mariolina runs to the front door crying, "Papa, Papa," every time she hears the doorbell. Gigi [Gigetto], like a big man, says to her, "No, little one, Papa's far away; he'll come back tomorrow." So you can see, dearest Pietro, that you are always with us, even when there is great distance between us. The little ones keep going to the phone to call Papa . . . and to make them happy, I dial a number and let them talk.

Try to stay well, Pedrin *d'oro*, and don't wear yourself out; use some of your free time to take naps. Don't worry about me—I have plenty of help and am not at all tired.[6]

Mr. Colombo[7] called today from the Milan office and wanted to know if he should sign your checks over to me. I told him not to, but to send me the envelope as usual. Is that okay?

Peppino Beretta's oldest daughter[8] is getting married on Saturday, May 2; the invitation came yesterday. I'm not sure what to give her. I think we gave her sister a crystal tray for her wedding; should I give her a set of ceramic pieces, to be different? I'll wait for your suggestions.

It's rainy and chilly here today. We turned on the heater again so the children won't be cold. They say on the radio that the bad weather is due to cold air and disturbances over the Atlantic—who knows what an awful flight you must have had! May the Lord be with you and protect you on all your other flights as well! I can only pray and give you to God's Divine Providence.

---

6. It is important to note the spontaneity with which Gianna passes from the love of her husband to the affection for their children, and to attention to relatives and friends. The Christian family is not closed in on itself, but is capable of opening up to others.

7. The accountant, Mr. Colombo, was the cashier of SAFFA.

8. Giuseppe Beretta, cousin of Gianna; the daughter getting married is named Zita.

Ciao, my dearest little husband, your dear *popi* kiss you with all their love.

Most affectionate big kisses from your

Gianna

Zita and Cecco[9] greet you and remember you with much affection.

BOSTON, APRIL 28, 1959
10:00 PM

Dearest Gianna,

Thanks to you and your fervent prayers, the Lord has allowed me to get here—after a quick flight—even though we had a ten-hour delay during which every moment "flew" by, both because I was constantly thinking of you and looking at your pictures, and because of the marvelous views (which changed constantly) of clouds, of the sea, of ice, of cities, and of the stars.

We arrived to the singing of "Ave, Ave Maria" sung by little polio victims and the Catholic sisters who cared for them, just coming back from a pilgrimage to Lourdes.

We were welcomed cordially. Our hotel is great; I'm on the fourteenth floor. The bed is long enough and very, very comfortable.

The rain that greeted us on our arrival yesterday evening has given way to beautiful sunshine.

Today was a full day of work, which went well. We got an order for SAFFA of machine parts to the tune of 3 million lire.

Breakfast and dinner were in excellent restaurants.

---

9. During her husband's long trip, Gianna had returned to live in the family home in Magenta, hosted by her sister Zita and her brother Francesco, who send greetings to her husband.

The people hosting me were full of admiration for our beautiful Pierluigi and Mariolina.

Tomorrow I hope to be able to send you an Actafone[10] tape with my voice.

Stay very, very well, my most beloved Gianna, and, with you, our *popi* too, and infinite best wishes. A great big kiss to you and our treasures.

Your

Pietro

Remember me to Mamma. Affectionate greetings to Cecco, Zita, and Liberata.

Sorry for the very hasty scribbling.

You begged me a lot to rest as much as possible.

APRIL 29, 1959
WEDNESDAY, 2:00 PM

My dearest Pietro,

I think of you as having already reached New York, though I haven't received your telegram yet. The little ones are already asleep, after hungrily eating their cereal, which was carefully prepared for them by Liberata. They are a little wild today, since it's raining and they can't go outside and run around in the garden. Magenta and Ponte Nuovo are full of the measles and chicken pox, but Pierluigi and Mariolina are very well. Hopefully, we won't catch anything. Rita[11] has a fever, so Nando is going to San Remo again today

---

10. Because of his profession, Pietro was constantly attentive to new technical developments. He sent his wife and children a taped message on an Actaphone machine, made by a company specializing in telecommunications.

11. Rita is the fourth child of Dr. Ferdinando Beretta and his wife, Laura Viola.

because he's afraid it's the incubation period for the measles. I lent him your car, because his doesn't run well and his in-laws' Fiat 1400 isn't working. Mr. Crotti[12] is driving Savina[13] to Milan tomorrow morning at 7:00; she asked me and I didn't want to say no. She'll be back May 15. As you know, Adelaide is leaving for Lourdes tomorrow. It's too bad it's raining, because the services at Lourdes are a little sad in the rain. Mamma[14] is fine, and she's thinking of you and sends her love.

There's nothing else new.

We are always thinking of you with great affection. Pierluigi recites a Hail Mary for his Papa every day and ends, "Papa, come back soon." Mariolina folds her little hands and blows kisses to the Blessed Mother. What treasures!

Ciao, my dearest Pietro, let me know how you're doing. Don't worry about us.

I kiss you with all my love, your

Gianna

APRIL 30, 1959
THURSDAY AFTERNOON

My dearest Pietro,

This morning I received the letter you wrote on Monday "up in the sky," as our Gigetto says. Were you really able to sleep? I'm so glad you woke up with the sun Monday morning. You would have thought there was a tempest here, with all the rain and wind we had, so we were all very anxious until we found out from TWA that your

---

12. Adolfo Crotti was Pietro's driver.
13. Savina Passeri was the domestic helper of Gianna and Pietro.
14. This is a reference to her mother-in-law, Pietro's mother.

plane had arrived safely in Boston. Gigetto is very happy because he got a letter from Papa, and he's keeping it safe in his little box along with the card from the plane.

He's as lively as ever, as is Mariolina. They couldn't sleep last night because of the storm—peals of thunder, torrents of rain, wind—it sounded like the end of the world.

They couldn't go outside today either, because of the bad weather. Patience.

I had to go to work yesterday evening and today, because I took Nando's place.[15] He's back with Rita now, who unfortunately has the measles. In isolation, of course, from our *popi*, and . . . we must hope for the best.

My Pietro, I think of you always, day and night, with so much affection, because I love you very much, you know. How nice it would be to always be together, but . . . let us offer everything to the Lord so that he will always help our dear and beautiful little family.[16]

A drug salesman at the office yesterday saw the photo of our two treasures and was so impressed he could not give them enough compliments, asking me what secret I had to make them grow so beautiful.

"It's no secret," I told him, "God gave them to me healthy, and let's hope they always remain so." Right, "paparino" of *d'or*?

Ciao, Papa, a thousand big kisses from your Gigetto and from your beautiful little girl.[17]

Pierluigi wouldn't leave me alone; he wanted to write to his Papa.

---

15. Dr. Ferdinando Beretta was the medical director of Magenta. It was he who, among other things, helped Gianna to begin her profession.

16. Faith gives us eyes to see God's gifts.

17. This line was written by Gigi.

Ciao, darling Pedrin, take care of yourself, and don't tire yourself too much. Many greetings from Zita, Cecco, and Liberata, and most affectionate big kisses from your

Gianna

MAY 1, 1959
FRIDAY AFTERNOON

My dearest Pietro,

A most loving greeting today, too, even though the mail won't go out because it's May Day.

The sun has finally returned and the children are outside enjoying it, playing in the garden and running through the grass in the vineyard. I went to the office in Mesero for a little while this morning, and I took Gigetto, Mariolina, and Zita with me so that Grandma[18] could enjoy their company for an hour or so. Flavio and Gianfranco[19] were also there, since they're on vacation with their Grandma while Adelaide is in Lourdes.

I'm still waiting for a letter from you from New York. All I know so far is that you arrived safe and sound in Boston. We always think of you, Pedrin *d'or,* and we wish it were already the end of the month so we could go and pick you up at Malpensa. Without you, the days seem much longer and pass more slowly. But don't worry, because I'm fine. The Lord certainly hears your prayers: our treasures are in the best of health. Pierluigi went to sleep last night at 9:00 and didn't wake up until 8:30 this morning; Mariolina, on the other hand, was awake at 5:30 this morning and just had to play, no matter what.

---

18. This refers to the paternal grandmother, Maria Salmoiraghi.

19. These are the sons of Adelaide. Gigetto and Mariolina were then able to play with their cousins.

Dear Pedrin, a big, big kiss from your treasures and a most affectionate embrace from your

Gianna

MAY 2, 1959
SATURDAY

My most beloved Pietro,[20]

I received your telegram from New York this morning, thanks be to God, and thank you for sending it to me.

The children are fine. And you? Do you still have that cough? And how are your teeth? Gigi always prays that Papa's hurts will go away.

Papa, *ciao*, come home soon.[21]

Satisfied with his masterpiece, he's leaving me alone now. He's always so mischievous, and he is never still; our little girl, on the other hand, is getting her first teeth, so she's a little cranky and doesn't sleep very much. But this disturbance will pass.

Mamma and Gina[22] had to go to Milan to pick up Teresina[23] this morning. She's been sent home because they think she might have whooping cough. The inconveniences of summer camp: two contagious sicknesses in such a short time! We're staying away from Mesero—I can't tell you how hard it is to make the children understand that they can't be together!

---

20. This is a postscript to the letter of the previous day that she could not send since it was May Day. So, Gianna sends additional news here.

21. A greeting from Pierluigi who was obviously learning to write.

22. Gina Galli Garacaglia, Gianna's collaborator at the hospital.

23. Teresina, the daughter of Rosetta, was Pietro's niece.

Ciao, Papa *d'or*. A big kiss from your beautiful treasures, and a big, big one from your always most affectionate

Gianna

NEW YORK, MAY 2, 1959

My dearest Gianna,

I have here before me your touching letter of Tuesday,[24] which I received today.

I'm so sorry for your hours of worry because of the more than six-hour delay right at the beginning of my trip. I want to reassure you that the flight was fine, without any strong turbulence. The whole way across the ocean, we were never advised to put on our seat belts. During the night I slept very well, without even noticing the strong contrary winds that forced our plane—which can fly more than 600 km per hour—to only go 300–350 km per hour.

The flight from Gander to Boston—I assure you—was very good, even though I had before me the chilling spectacle[25] of our little polio guests who had been on pilgrimage to Lourdes.

All our work in Boston went very well and profitably, and our work in this great city has also gone satisfactorily.

We have been welcomed very warmly. Pierluigi and Mariolina continue to bring in admiration, compliments, and kisses. "Beautiful! Beautiful! Very, very beautiful!" they exclaim, sending kisses: Mrs. Green, Mrs. Zweibach, Mrs. Lo Presti, and three other Venezuelan women, all from the two families who had us to dinner Friday night and Saturday night. Even the general director of [the company that manufactures] Formica was so impressed.

---

24. See the letter of Gianna of April 28, 1959.

25. In reality, Pietro was intending to express his deep sympathy with the little sufferers (see his letter of April 28, 1959).

No other children are as beautiful as ours!

Regarding the gift for Peppino Beretta's oldest daughter, the ceramic collection is a great idea.

But if you have a hard time finding a brand name and one that you like, we could always give her something made of silver.

As far as my paychecks, you wanted to wait till I come back. Thank you . . . but it wouldn't be right for you to use yours.

Don't worry about me. Best wishes and many kisses to you and the *popi*.

Your most loving

Pietro

Affectionate greetings to Cecco and Zita.

MAY 4, 1959
MONDAY

Dearest Pietro,

I just received the letter you wrote from Boston on the evening of the twenty-eighth. Thank you for letting me know how you are. We're all fine. The weather has calmed down and the little ones can go into the garden to enjoy the air and sun. I received the receipt for the 200 Sade shares from Belinzaghi Bank this morning. They came with a form to send back signed, along with another form from the same bank, on which is written: Pirelli Shares & Company.

Since they wanted a response by May 10, I decided to answer them myself.[26]

---

26. Questioned about Gianna's charity, Cicci Carones, her childhood companion, testified: "The Beretta family was known for its affluence. However, Gianna witnessed with an evangelical spirit to the detachment from inherited goods" (*Posizione sulle virtù*, op. cit., 259). This is an example that prudent management of family assets and charity need not be disconnected.

I've noticed that letters take eight days to get here. I had hoped they would come more quickly than that. Patience! A whole ocean is between us! Mamma and your family are fine. Teresina[27] is better; she doesn't have a fever. Don't get too tired, beautiful Pedrin, and stay cheerful.

Many big kisses from your treasures and a big hug from your

Gianna

NEW YORK, MAY 4, 1959
MONDAY, 11:00 PM

Most beloved Gianna,

I just got back from a walk with Mr. Corneo,[28] a very nice walk to help us digest our dinner and to enjoy a little cool air after the first really warm and sunny day. I also bought two nice records for Pierluigi and Mariolina.

You, Mariolina, and Pierluigi are smiling at me from your magnificent photos that I always keep with me in my room.

Today I joyfully opened and read and re-read your two most appreciated letters of Wednesday and Thursday. I am sorry to hear of our children's forced isolation on account of bad weather, chicken pox, and measles. It was good that you lent the 1100 [vehicle] to Nando. I hope Rita gets well soon.[29]

So far I haven't had any toothaches or headaches. The cough seemed to be instantly cured by the flight, and I haven't had a single cold. I hope things will continue this way in the coming weeks.

---

27. She is the niece Gianna spoke of in the previous letter.

28. Mr. Luigi Corneo was one of Pietro's closest collaborators. He was Pietro's technical secretary and accompanied him on his long trip to the United States.

29. See Gianna's letter of April 29.

Saturday morning—the first Saturday of the month of May—I knelt again, after twelve years, before the statue of the Immaculate Conception in the cathedral in New York. I prayed to our Lady to thank Jesus adequately for the infinite gift he gave me during those years, the gift of you, of Pierluigi, of Mariolina, and of the little one we are so eagerly awaiting. The distance between us makes me appreciate these gifts even more.

I rested on Sunday.

Today I worked till 6:45.

Gianna, together with you I offer the sacrifice of our being apart so that the Lord may continue to bless our dearest, beautiful family.

Give Gigetto and our beautiful little girl many, many big kisses in return for their big kisses, for their little folded hands, for their little angelic prayers, and for their anxiety and little sufferings because Papa is gone.

I kiss you with all my love and I wish you everything good.

Your affectionate

Pietro

Affectionate and grateful greetings to Zita and Cecco.

Grateful greetings to Liberata.

Remember me to Mamma and say hello to her for me.

NEW YORK, MAY 4, 1959[30]

MONDAY, 11:30 PM

Dearest Gianna,

Another good day of work and beautiful spring weather.

Today we were invited out for both breakfast and dinner. Dinner finished late.

---

30. Postcard.

More admiring compliments for Pierluigi and Mariolina and naturally for you from Mr. and Mrs. Watt who hosted us. Tomorrow we're off to Baltimore.

As I promised you, I'm going right to bed without working anymore.

You are always with me.

Many, many big kisses to you and to our treasures.

Best wishes,

Pietro

MAY 5, 1959
TUESDAY

My dearest Pietro,

Pierluigi and Mariolina received your postcard of April 29 from Boston. Gigetto showed it to everyone, explaining that "up there, up there, high up in that house, Papa was sleeping." At around 5:00 this morning, he half-woke up when he heard a plane passing over, and he called to me, "Mamma, Papa's airplane is passing by"; then he went back to sleep until 8:30. Every now and then he wants his Papa, and if I tell him that Papa is far away and can't come, he answers, "He should take an airplane and come home." What ideas he has! They're both just fine: they're eating well and their color is good.

I'm anxious to hear how you are doing, if you still have that cough, and whether you are suffering the heat a great deal.

There's nothing new here. Adelaide has come back [from Lourdes], but I haven't seen her yet. Mamma and Rosetta[31] are fine too, and they say hello.

Many big kisses from your treasures and from your

Gianna

---

31. This is Pietro's mother and his other sister.

Gianna, Pierluigi, and Pietro with his Rolleiflex camera,
in the garden of the house in Ponte Nuovo, spring 1958.

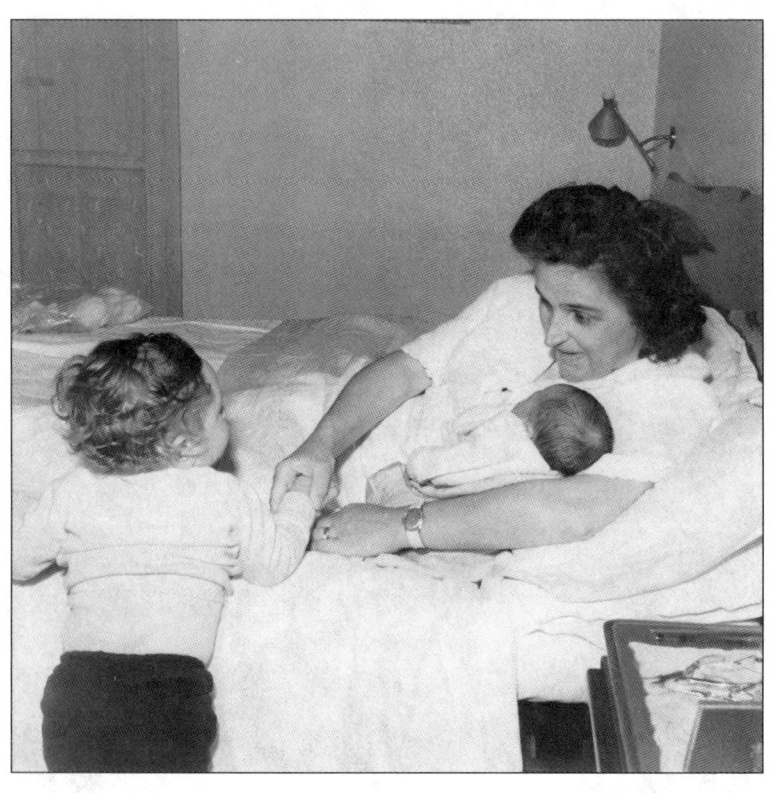

Gianna and the firstborn, Pierluigi, with the newborn, Mariolina,
Ponte Nuovo, December 1957.

MAY 6, 1959
WEDNESDAY

Pietro, my treasure,

I'm so happy right now because I received all the details of your trip to New York. I thank the Lord that he gave you a smooth journey. I can imagine how hard it must be to see the little polio victims. May God keep this terrible disease far from our treasures! I'm glad all your work is going well and that everyone is being so welcoming. Their kindness will make it easier to be so far from us. Is it true that everyone admires our little ones? How happy that makes me! They're so beautiful and sweet. Here in Magenta, too, people stop and look twice at them when we go out, and I do nothing but thank the Lord. I saw Adelaide this morning when I went to Ponte Nuovo to do laundry with the Bendix [washing machine].[32] She was all fervent and enthusiastic from her time in Lourdes; she asked me if I had gotten the tape[33] you recorded, but I told her no. Do you think it is being held in customs?

I saw Mr. Dotto,[34] who, as he promised, is looking after the plants and flowers in the garden. The Canossian Sisters always pray for you and they send you their greetings, so does Mother Virginia,[35] who came to Ponte Nuovo this morning to visit the children in the nursery school.

---

32. From Magenta, where she was a guest of her siblings, Gianna went to her house to use the washing machine and check up on the house.

33. To alleviate the suffering of his wife and children at the distance between him and them, Pietro thought to send them a tape recording of his voice.

34. Aldo Dotto, a friend of the family and a surveyor, lived in their home and took care of the garden in their absence.

35. The two sisters probably had an appointment to visit the Sisters so dear to them.

Angela Chiolerio's[36] father died suddenly the other night while he was writing in his study; his funeral is this afternoon. It's a relief for the family, but sorrowful because no one realized it and he died alone and without the sacraments.

Now I'm off to the office at the nursery school. I kiss you with much, much love. Take care and don't get too tired. Ten days have already gone by! Take care of yourself and don't get too tired.

Big kisses from your *popi*.

Your most affectionate

Gianna

Affectionate greetings from Cecco and Zita.

NEW YORK, MAY 7, 1959
THURSDAY, 11:30 PM

My most beloved Gianna,

I have here with me your dearest letters that I read, re-read, and kissed—the letters of Friday, May 1, Sunday, May 3, and Monday, May 4; I received them all this morning. Monday's letter only took three days to get here. I wish that meant that the distance between us was shrinking.

Thank you from my heart. You can imagine my joy and reassurance on getting good news of you and our dearest treasures—Mariolina's little problems will soon be things of the past.

Every day I pray that Jesus and our Heavenly Mother will preserve them from every illness. And your heartburn? Your headaches? I am sure you are keeping those from me, O my dearest little wife and incomparable little mother! I hope everything's okay!

---

36. Angela Chiolerio was a friend of Gianna. Her father's name was Carlo.

The cough hasn't come back. As for the toothaches, I only have them once in a while and just momentarily when some fruit or a drink touches my teeth. Here they don't serve water unless it is iced; ordinarily, it's not possible to have fruit that isn't cold [refrigerated]. I'm doing the orange juice, tomato juice, and grapefruit regimen.

I can't find the words to adequately thank you for your most attentive and appreciated daily letters. If you don't receive letters just as often from me, please forgive me. Some days, like yesterday and today, on top of work, we have what one might call "social" duties, supper invitations that unfortunately I can't refuse and that keep us from getting back to the hotel before 11:00 PM.

The weather is still nice—a passing storm cooled things off this afternoon.

What you told Belinzaghi Bank about the Pirelli shares is fine. Haven't they sent a confirmation of the 200 Sade shares yet?

Don't worry, my little wife d'oro, about my flights. We take the train whenever possible. Here they run over 100 km an hour. Yesterday we took the train to and from Baltimore, which is about 450 km from New York.

I'm happy to hear the good news about Teresina, and thank you from my heart for the news about Mamma.

These ten days that we've been apart seem like months to me. Right at this moment (about 5:00 AM Italian time) I picture all of you sleeping peacefully.

I wish I were there to kiss you lovingly—but very, very quietly so as not to wake you.

Kiss Pierluigi and Mariolina for me; I send you a most affection-ate hug and all my most fervent good wishes.

Your most loving

Pietro

Affectionate greetings to Zita and Cecco.

MAY 8, 1959
FRIDAY,

My dearest Pietro,

I received the long letter you sent from New York on May 4. A million thanks—even though you're tired from work and from the heat, you still manage to find time to keep me up-to-date every day on everything you're doing. We think about you all the time, Pedrin *d'or*, and you can imagine how happy we are reading your letters. What a hotel you're staying in! When Gigetto saw the card, he said that you are "way up high, up high, almost in Heaven."[37] I'm sorry it's so hot—it was sultry here yesterday, too. There's a breeze today though, and it feels better. Our treasures are well; they enjoy the sunshine in the vineyard almost all day long.

Angela[38] takes really good care of them, is very attentive, and knows how to help them play. If only Savina were like that! That will take some time and patience![39]

I took the *popi* to the cemetery in Mesero to visit their grandfather and their Aunt Teresina[40] yesterday morning. They prayed for you, with their little hands folded, that all would go well. The Lord cannot turn a deaf ear to our little angels. I am sure of this. Stay tranquil and be happy and cheerful, Pedrin *d'or*. Cecco took them to

---

37. It is evident that the skyscraper arouses the naïve child's admiration.

38. Angela Chiolerio, Gianna's friend.

39. Mrs. Passeri was constantly at work and left a beautiful testimony during the process. The divergence most likely had to do with the education of the children. Gianna tried to build up confidence, while Savina sometimes resorted to methods that got quicker results.

40. Paternal grandfather Luigi died in 1956, Aunt Teresina in 1950.

Lugano[41] in the afternoon. So many sweet memories! I saw the long lake where you took your first picture of me at the Felix Hotel. I wish you could have been there with me again, so I could embrace you and kiss you and thank you for your great love for me and all the joys you've brought me these past three years.

The little ones had a snack and then had a great time in the park at Lugano, with the little merry-go-rounds and swings and, as always, they entertained themselves by throwing stones into the lake.

Adelaide just called to tell me the tape you recorded has arrived; they were also waiting for it in Milan.

I had to call Mr. Roveda this morning because the switch burned out on the Bendix [washing machine]. He's going to get another one when he goes to Milan. I saw the house where your offices are. It's finished, and it looks really good—it doesn't seem like the same place as before. The workers' lunchroom has been torn down. When Gigetto saw this, he said, "Mamma, SAFFA fell down, you must write to Papa"—that's what he said!

Mrs. Valle[42] wrote to ask us to let her know when we will be arriving at the "Pinta," so she can fix it up a bit before we get there. I'll send her an answer today.

Ciao, my treasure, take care of yourself; your *popi* send you their most affectionate, big kisses.

I kiss and embrace you with all my love, your

Gianna

---

41. The Swiss town had been one of the first destinations that Gianna and Pietro visited when they first became acquainted.

42. Mrs. Valle was the owner of the house in Courmayeur where the Molla family spent their summer vacation. See the letter of the preceding chapter.

MAY 10, 1959
SUNDAY, 10:00 PM

My dearest Pietro,

I always imagine you well and working hard, here and there. It's too bad it's so hot; here, it's gray and a little bit rainy. Father Giuse[43] is with us, enjoying our little angels for a while. He celebrated Mass at Ponte Nuovo as usual and gave a special blessing with the asperges[44] to all his little nephews and nieces who were there. Mariolina was very good in church, but Pierluigi only stayed awake for about five minutes. After Mass, Father Giuse took them to the beach we go to in Turbigo[45] while I, quite willingly, stayed home to work on the little sweater I am knitting for Alberto or Emanuela.[46] By the way, have you thought of a name if we have a girl?

The children are asleep now. Pierluigi went to sleep at 7:00; I tried to wake him up to feed him some cereal, but he didn't want it, so he will sleep even better until tomorrow morning.

Now I'm going to bed, too, since there's nothing interesting on TV—just reruns!

Ciao, my treasure. Big kisses from your little ones and from your *popi* and from your most affectionate little wife.

---

43. Gianna's brother, Father Giuseppe, a priest of the diocese of Bergamo.

44. Gianna refers to the blessing that the priest gives by sprinkling the people with holy water.

45. Turbigo is a town on the Ticino River, between Milan and Novara.

46. As we know, Gianna was expecting their third child. The baby was a girl who was given the name Laura.

MAY 11, 1959

MONDAY

My dearest Pietro,

What a wonderful day this is: I received your letter from Thursday, May 7, the postcard with the cathedral like the Duomo of Milan, and Pierluigi's card with the long bridge. When he heard that you didn't have any stones to throw in the water, he took one from the garden and threw it at the postcard!

Thank you so much for letting me know how things are going. I'm sorry you get to bed even later in order to write to me. Do you have to get up early in the morning, or can you sleep in a little? I'm glad your cough is gone and your teeth are okay. Pedrin *d'or*, I wish you never had to suffer or that I could be with you when you're not feeling well.[47] Thank you for heeding my advice not to get too tired.

The bank sent the confirmation of the acquisition of the 200 Sade shares. There's nothing else new.

I'm going to start asking when you think you might be coming home. The mail does take three days, but it's already the eleventh.

"Papa pu [No more Papa]," says Mariolina.

"Papa will come back tomorrow," says Gigetto. In this way all of your Gigetto's other "tomorrows" will also pass until the real tomorrow comes, and we will finally be able to embrace you again.

Ciao, my dear treasure, I always give your *popi* big kisses for you. Take good, good care of yourself.

A most affectionate embrace, your

Gianna

Zita and Cecco return most cordial greetings.

---

47. It is beautiful to see this mutual attention to the suffering of the other. See the letter of Pietro of May 4, 1959.

WASHINGTON, MAY 11, 1959[48]

Dearest Gianna,

Today we had a six-hour train ride—to Baltimore till 1:00 PM and to Washington in the afternoon.

We did the tourist thing from 5:30 to 7:30 PM. It's a hot July. The White House is here, which I saw close up. Health good. At 11:00 PM I'll be on the way back to New York.

Many big kisses to you, Pierluigi, and Mariolina.

Your affectionate

Pietro

Affectionate greetings to Zita and Cecco.

MAY 12, 1959
TUESDAY

My dearest Pietro,

I'm sending you three color photos of our magnificent Mariolina, hoping they won't be too messed up by the time they reach you.

The children are fine; Gigetto plays all day long, and by 8:00 at night, he can hardly move, so he goes to sleep right away and sleeps until 8:00 in the morning. You should see what a brave little man he is when I give him a suppository or an enema for his cough. It's been a few days since he had one, so I'll give him one, but he's so good and doesn't say a word.

It's very hot here today—who knows what it must be like where you are!

I always feel the burning stomach pains, but I only have a headache every once in a while.[49] But all this will pass and within two months we'll have our newest little one [in our arms]!

---

48. Postcard.

49. Gianna minimizes the magnitude of her ailments that really were significant.

I also have a photo of your cousins here, which I'll send separately.

Take care of yourself, Pedrin d'or, and *arrivederci* soon.

Big, big kisses, and many, many of them from your *popi* too, your

Gianna

MAY 13, 1959
WEDNESDAY

My most beloved Pietro,

The last time I heard from you was May 8—you're working as hard as ever, are tired in the evening, but you still find time to write to me. Thank you so much.

The newspaper said that two planes crashed in the United States: one New York-Atlanta flight crashed in Baltimore, the other crashed as it was coming into Kanawha (West Virginia) airport, and both were Capital Airlines, four-engine planes. My Pietro, you can imagine how my thoughts are always with you as you travel, and how I wish that the day would come quickly when you're done flying. It's a good thing Gigetto has his little triple invocation whenever he prays: "Jesus, help my Papa *have a good trip*; Papa, *come home soon*; Papa, *don't crash*." But . . . distance is still distance.

I was watching Father Mariano[50] on TV last night talking about true love in marriage, and he said, "true love is the love which lasts not only a day but always." He also said that spouses who have always loved each other will find out in Heaven that the time they have loved on earth was short, and they will rejoice to

---

50. Father Mariano da Torino, formerly Paolo Roasenda (1906–1972), was a Capuchin priest who was well known for his television preaching.

know that they have all of eternity before them to continue to love each other.[51]

Pedrin *d'or*, you know how much I love you, how much I think of you and want to see you happy.

Come home soon, and many, many big kisses from your treasures.

A most affectionate embrace from your

Gianna

NEW YORK, MAY 13, 1959

WEDNESDAY EVENING, 10:00 PM

My dearest Gianna,

I'm imagining you sleeping peacefully right now,[52] and I wish you a restful sleep until our magnificent little Mariolina calls out, "Mamma! Mamma!"

I received your very welcome letter of Friday the eighth, which I received Monday evening when I got back from Baltimore and Washington. In spite of the 380 km that separate New York from the capital of the United States, we chose the train and enjoyed a very comfortable trip. The train and the stations were air-conditioned. In the space of just one week we've gone from *heated* trains to air-conditioned trains.

---

51. In this regard, Gianna made a most beautiful comment in one of her lectures to the youth of Catholic Action: "You cannot enter into the vocation of family life if you do not know how to love. To love is to desire to perfect oneself and the one loved, to overcome one's own selfishness, give one's self. . . . Love must be total, full, complete, governed by the law of God and the eternity of heaven."

52. In Italy it was 5:00 AM.

Today there was a heavy shower that restored a spring-like atmosphere after some rather warm days. I assure you that for our trips within the United States we go by train as much as possible, in sleeping cars.

Our work in Baltimore and Washington turned out well. We've had breakfast to the sound of *Io Sono Il Vento* and other Italian songs. Here you can't find a restaurant without either the owner or the waiters being Italian. Even in the factories you always come across Italians.

Yesterday afternoon, near New York, I visited an interesting plant that makes metal cabinets.[53] The owners are originally from Jerago (Gallarate) and have our same last name: Molla.

They gave me a hearty welcome at the factory and also at their home: a magnificent villa surrounded by a breathtaking garden of flowering azaleas. They want to have me over again and this time, to celebrate, they want to invite forty or so other people.

Sunday afternoon I visited Maria Maltagliati's family, relations of the Garavaglias on Via Monte Rosa and old friends of Mamma's.

Everywhere I go, I receive the most admiring compliments on our wonderful treasures and on your great beauty.

You can imagine my continual joy!

No cough, no headaches, no toothaches. So far I haven't needed to use that medicine.

I'm happy to hear of all the help Angela is giving you. Thank her from my heart and say hello to her from me. Thank Zita and Cecco so much for me. I thank you for your prayers and our treasures for their prayers for Grandpa and Teresina.

I share your joy and that of the children that you are in Lugano. Every time I take the train to Como (Brunate) and Lugano, it

---

53. La Molla Incorporated, Westbury, Long Island, New York.

reawakens in me the most wonderful, sweetest memories, and also gratitude to the Lord as well as prayers that I may always be able to make you happy in the most perfect way possible, as you truly deserve and as you know how to make me.

Reassure Gigetto that Papa will be home in time to "fix" the "fallen-down" SAFFA. His comments are so cute!

Don't worry about me.

Give great big kisses to Pierluigi and Mariolina for me.

I send you my most beautiful and dearest wishes and many big kisses, and a most affectionate hug.

Your most affectionate

Pietro

Give my greetings to Mamma, Zita, and Cecco.

MAY 14, 1959
THURSDAY

My dearest Pietro,

Today I received your letters of May 10 and 11. Thank you so much. Pierluigi was all ears when I read him your letter, and when he saw that I was moved, he said, "Mamma, don't cry, Papa will come soon." And yesterday, as I was putting him to bed, he said: "My beautiful big mamma" (who taught him this, I really don't know), "I'm your big darling." What ideas he has! He's growing up so fast.

I'm sorry it's so hot there and that you have to tire yourself by traveling for hours on the train in order to make me happy. Patience, Pedrin *d'or*, but I feel better knowing you're not "in the sky." You really are a wonderful Papa. Who knows what Pierluigi will think one day when he reads your beautiful letters! Papa prays so much for his little family. Thank you for the sweet words to their mother. I will do everything I can to stay this way, as you want me to be, as you see me.[54]

My Pietro, we're waiting anxiously to hear when you will be coming home so we can pick you up at Malpensa Airport. And then . . . we'll never let you go again!

Don't worry about us, we're fine. Cecco and Zita are always eager to help and like having us here with them.[55] They say thank you for your greetings and return heartfelt ones to you.

Mamma is doing well and sends you many greetings. She goes to the cemetery to pray for you often, for her dear Pietro. Teresina is doing better: she only coughs once in awhile. Adelaide and her family are fine, too. I saw her yesterday when she gave me some chocolates and a doily from Father Felice.[56] Now I'll write to Miss Maria to thank her.

The Sisters are very happy with their piano; it's more than an octave long and it has a beautiful sound.

The new dining hall is being built very quickly. Pierluigi would stay there forever, watching the cranes moving up and down. He says that he wants to be an "engineer" just like his Papa when he grows up.

"The beautiful little one," Mariolina, is a little lady. She is never still; she laughs, dances, makes faces, and throws a few temper tantrums.

---

54. In the correspondence of Gianna and Pietro allusion to the famous passage of Proverbs 31:10–12 is often found. Then, as now, the text was often read in the liturgy of the Mass.

55. We recall that in the absence of her husband, Gianna and the children are living in Magenta with Cecco and Zita.

56. Father Felice Dominioni had been the bishop's delegate at Ponte Nuovo di Magenta until 1951.

Ciao, my most beloved Pietro, take good care of yourself and *arrivederci* soon.

If you're tired, don't write every day.

Many kisses from your *popi*

and from your most affectionate

Gianna

NEW YORK, MAY 14, 1959[57]

THURSDAY, 11:00 PM

Dearest Gianna,

Tomorrow morning I have to get up at 6:30. I'll be leaving for Bridgeport, which is about 150 km from New York. I'll be back here in the evening.

Today it wasn't too hot.

I'm still doing well.

I give your photos a great big kiss and send my dearest wishes again.

Kiss Pierluigi and Mariolina for me.

A most affectionate hug from your

Pietro

Greetings to Mamma, Zita, and Cecco.

Papa will go up to the top of this skyscraper[58] to make a beautiful surprise and a nice gift for PIERLUIGI!

---

57. Postcard.

58. The Empire State Building, at the time the tallest building in the world.

MAY 16, 1959
SATURDAY

My dearest Pietro,

I'm taking advantage of the visit of Mr. Piovesana's[59] sister-in-law from New York to send you the latest news. We are fine, the children are very lively—they're a handful, and I'm always afraid they'll hurt themselves, so I watch them constantly. The last letter I got from you was from May 11. When the mailman comes, Gigetto runs to see if "Papa writed," and he brings the letter to me all happy and satisfied, because he knows it will make me happy. And you can't imagine how happy I am to read your affectionate letters.

Now, though, I'm waiting to hear when you think you'll be coming home. It is much cooler here now, after all the storms we've been having the last few days.

"Thunder doesn't come from the wall, but from the sky," the newest statement from your little man. "I'm 'fraid," Mariolina says. What precious treasures! They're at an age when they're a lot of work, but they are wonderful with their innocent declarations.

As I write, Pierluigi is spreading out all the postcards you've sent him. "*Ciao*, Papa," he says while looking at the ones with airplanes, "you're already almost home." Just think of their joy when they see you again!

Come home soon, Papa, *ciao*.[60]

And your trips? You must be exhausted. Will you really fly right over the North Pole on your way back? Are you sure?

---

59. Giuseppe Piovesana was an engineer and Central Director of SAFFA.
60. This phrase is written by the unsteady hand of Pierluigi.

Ciao, Pedrin *d'or*, take very good care of yourself; we're always thinking of you.

Big kisses from your *popi*, and many, many most affectionate ones from

Your

Gianna

NEW YORK, MAY 16, 1959
SATURDAY EVENING

My most beloved Gianna,

Thank you for your wonderful letters of Sunday the tenth, and Monday, Tuesday, and Wednesday.

The good news about our treasures gives me the greatest joy. I wish you could also tell me that you had no more heartburn or headaches. I know you are a very strong little mamma, strong in your will, in your soul, and in your sufferings.

I can't do more than pray to Our Lady of New York (and I am doing just that) to lighten your sufferings as much as possible.

The wonderful photos of Mariolina arrived in perfect shape. Thank you so much. They will increase the praises of the Americans for our marvelous children.

Thank you, too, for the photos of my cousins. Those also arrived in perfect shape.

Don't worry about me. My health is still good. The heat has abated quite a bit after some rainstorms, and there is almost always a breeze.

Today I rested more than I usually do, thanks to the Americans who don't work [on Saturdays] and don't let others work. Tomorrow I'll rest again. I'll be spending the day as a guest at the country house of Mr. Green, the lawyer who visited us in Magenta. Mrs. Green just loves our children.

By the time you receive this letter, next week's flights will already be behind me: we are only flying Monday, Tuesday, and Wednesday. Don't worry about me. Jesus always hears the prayers of the little ones. We can be at peace with Pierluigi's three-part prayer.

Sometime next week, I should be able to let you know, if not the exact day, at least the exact week of our return. I'm trying to finish as soon as possible. But only five work days a week and the frequent long trips from one city to another make the weeks slip by quickly.

This morning I served a Mass at the Blessed Sacrament altar in New York's cathedral, and I heard three other Masses: one for you, one for Gigetto, one for Mariolina, and one for the little one we are expecting with so much love and eagerness.

This evening at 9:30 (the churches are open until 10:00) I recited the Holy Rosary before the altar of the Immaculate Virgin of New York.

Father Mariano[61] is perfectly right. Our love is true love, and if it has no spatial limits right now, neither will it have a time limit in the future. While I am so far from you, I feel it growing even more and I feel an even greater duty and need to thank the good God morning and evening, and, more than at home, I dislike missing Mass even on weekdays and not saying the Rosary before our Lady's altar. This is because I have become more and more aware of the immensity of the graces the Lord has granted me in you, in Pierluigi, in Mariolina, and in the little one we are awaiting.

I still don't know what name to suggest for the baby. In the next few days, I'll send you a list of names, but the final choice is up to the little mamma.

---

61. This is the Capuchin Father Mariano da Torino. See the letter of Pietro of May 13, 1959.

Take very good care of yourself, little wife *d'oro*, kiss our treasures for me, and here is a most affectionate embrace from your

Pietro

who loves you very, very much.

Say hello to Mamma for me, and tell her again not to worry about me.

Greet Zita and Cecco for me.

This evening I also went right up to the top of the EMPIRE STATE BUILDING, the tallest skyscraper in New York (400 meters), to make a beautiful surprise for Gigetto.

NEW YORK, MAY 17, 1959
SUNDAY, 11:00 PM

Dearest Gianna,

Imagine a splendid villa (like the kind we dream of having) with a wonderful sitting room, couches, carpets, figurines, a kitchen with an automatic dishwasher, magnificent bathrooms, a children's room filled with toys. Imagine it being surrounded by a garden of roses, azaleas, evergreens; pretend you are on the seashore and you can see motorboats, sailboats, warships going by, and in the distance, about 50 km away, you can make out the tallest skyscraper and the tallest bridge in New York, and off to the side are the green hills of Connecticut—and all of this in lovely peace and quiet. This was the relaxing atmosphere in which I passed my Sunday. If only you and the children had been here—how they would have run and played, and how many stones they would have thrown into the ocean!

Mr. Green has invited us to stay at least a week in this villa when you come to America.

Tomorrow I have a two-and-a-half hour flight from New York to the Canadian border and back.

Today Mrs. Green, who had us over and who just loved the new pictures of Mariolina, told me that her father (who must be an expert on beauty because he married one of the most beautiful and famous movie actresses) declared that he had *never seen children more beautiful than ours.* Many thanks to their little mamma!

Thank you, my Gianna—with all my love, I kiss you and our treasures.

Your affectionate

Pietro

Affectionate greetings to Mamma, Zita, and Cecco.

NEW YORK, MAY 18, 1959
MONDAY, 11:30 PM

Dearest Gianna,

I just arrived back at the hotel after an 800-km flight to Utica. We had a great trip and perfect weather. I just found your wonderful letter of Thursday the fourteenth. It's like a balm of family joy to me.

Thank you, thank you for all the good news, and forgive me if I write to you only briefly tonight. Tomorrow I have to get up early.

Kiss our treasures for me and tell Pierluigi to . . . make sure the work on my lunchroom is done just right.[62]

I kiss you with all my love.

Your affectionate

Pietro

Say hello to Mamma, Zita, and Cecco for me.

---

62. A lunchroom being built for SAFFA's employees.

Thank Cecco for the news. Please tell him that the commune should provide the necessary little things *at least* for the display for the schools.[63]

I didn't make any commitment except to leave some parts of Casa Giacobbe[64] for the schools' display. Beyond that I can't "push" with SAFFA.[65]

MAY 19, 1959

My dearest Pietro,

I received your letters from May 13 and 14; I hope your trip to Bridgeport went well. What skyscrapers they have in New York! It looks like a fairy kingdom with all those lights. Pierluigi is excited about his surprise. As usual, we're fine. Mariolina has been cranky the past couple of days and she doesn't want to eat, but she doesn't have a fever. Savina is back, very calm and happy for now—let's hope she always remains this way! The children are calmer and voluntarily stay with her.[66] The weather has been nice, so they stay outside in the garden almost all day.

---

63. A display commemorating the centennial of the Battle of Magenta (June 4, 1859), when the Franco-Sardinian troops commanded by Napoleon defeated the Austrians. This was a significant step toward the unification of Italy.

64. Casa Giacobbe was a historic house that had played a part in the battle.

65. Probably Pietro, as the director of SAFFA, had given a contribution toward the house to help keep the memory of that historic event alive. However, he also had to carry out administrative procedures correctly.

66. With Savina Passeri, her domestic assistant, Gianna had some reservations about the education of the children. Nevertheless, Savina testified: "The servant of God was good with her neighbor. She had kind words for everyone." She was also good with Savina. "In six years it happened only once that she made a remark to me: it made me realize that I was wrong" (*Position on virtue*, op. cit., 212).

I'm glad to hear the factory owners you visit are so welcoming and cordial! You really deserve it, since you're always so polite and helpful to them when they come to Italy.

When I went to Ponte Nuovo this morning, I saw water dripping from the ceiling in the bathroom. The plumber said the water heater's gasket was leaking—and not only that, but the heating element was burned. He fixed everything, but I don't understand why the element burned so easily.[67]

I saw Adelaide, and I heard your baritone voice when she played the tape on her recorder. Thank you for the greetings and the kisses.[68]

The mayor of Milan, and most of the city council of Magenta, visited on Sunday: they toured the nursery school and visited the Sisters and the Ponte Nuovo schools.[69] Cecco said they were very pleased, but it was a shame you weren't here to show them around.[70]

Continue being well, my Pietro, and come back soon. Wait till you see how much progress Pierluigi has made in expressing himself: he discourses clearly and at length, and repeats everything he hears with all the right words.

With all my love I kiss and embrace you along with our treasures.

Your most affectionate

Gianna

---

67. From this we can see how attentive and concrete Gianna was.

68. Pietro had sent a tape recording to Adelaide, his sister.

69. Gianna was particularly interested in the event because for some years she had been doing free work for the school children and their mothers under the direction of the Canossian Sisters.

70. The engineer Molla was interested in the church and the outbuildings that were owned by SAFFA.

MAY 20, 1959
WEDNESDAY

My dearest Pietro,

Thank you, thank you, from your children too, for the wonderful surprise.[71]

You can imagine Pierluigi's happiness at having two recordings "where Papa is talking." He wouldn't listen to anything today except your recordings. When Mariolina heard you say, "a kiss for Mariolina," she said, "Papa, Papa . . ."—she recognized your voice and sent you many kisses with her cute little lips. They really are a couple of treasures! And how could your good and dear little wife not be moved hearing such affectionate statements in your own voice! Thank you, Pedrin *d'or*, what a joy and comfort[72] it is for me to know that you're thinking of me and love me so much!

THURSDAY AFTERNOON

My dearest Pietro,

This morning I received your long letter from Saturday the sixteenth; thank God it was filled with good news. Such a wonderful and loving letter, with so many prayers for your family!

You always find time to attend and to serve Holy Mass. Unfortunately, I can never get out to it. Mariolina was awake this morning at 5:00, and I had to get up and dress her at 6:00 so she could play in the living room, otherwise, she would have awakened

---

71. As you can see by the continuation of the letter, there were two tapes made by Pietro with greetings for the children and for Gianna.

72. A veiled hint about the heartburn and other disorders Gianna suffered during the third pregnancy.

Pierluigi with her shrill little voice. Gigetto, on the other hand, sleeps until 8:30, since he doesn't take a nap in the afternoon anymore.

I was really hoping you would tell me that you're coming home before the end of the month . . . but you still don't know. Patience. Do you still have many more flights to take? Are you going to San Francisco?

Your letter from Sunday arrived, too. I enjoyed reading about the kind family you stayed with who admired our treasures so much.[73] I'm glad you could spend your Sunday in pleasant company.

We're all fine. Your Mamma is fine, too, and every time she sees me she asks me to say hello for her. Cecco thanks you for the stamps, and he and Zita say hello.

Dear Papa thank you for the tapes.[74]

This picture means many kisses. He wanted to write all by himself. If Gigetto is here when your letters come, I can't read them in peace, because he always wants to see them and, all serious, he reads, "Many big kisses to Gigi. Papa is still far away," etc. But now it's almost time for you to come home . . . don't you think?

Ciao, Pedrin *d'or*, take care of yourself; I kiss you with all my affection.

Thank you for everything, your

Gianna

---

73. On Sunday, May 17, Pietro had been a guest at the country home of the attorney, Mr. Green, who entertained a working relationship with SAFFA.

74. Written, as on other occasions, by Pierluigi.

NEW YORK, MAY 21, 1959
THURSDAY EVENING

My dearest Gianna,

Please forgive me for not writing last night. I was rather tired. It was a record-breaking day. Woke up at 6:30; breakfast from 7:00 to 7:30; in the car from 7:00 to 8:00; in the air from 8:05 to 8:35.

From 9:00 to 11:30, visited the Diamond[75] Company in Springfield (CT) (the same city Ovidio worked in for two months). Airplane from Springfield to Palmer 11:40 to 12:40; visit to the Diamond Gardner plant in Palmer from 12:50 to 2:50, lunch at the plant; car ride from 2:50 to 3:00; plane from 3:00 to 4:00; visit to the Diamond factory in Plattsburgh (on the Canadian border) until 5:50. On the plane back to New York from 6:00 to 7:50. It was Diamond's private plane (two motors, four passengers). I was up front with the pilot. An enchanting trip, up in the blue skies and in and out of the clouds.

Today we stayed in New York, where we will remain for some other tasks and to spend our Sunday.

Monday we'll start traveling again. Unfortunately, dearest Gianna, it's impossible to get in all the visits I'd like in the five days of the week, so, as I already telegraphed to SAFFA, I can't be back before June 10. Let us offer this delay to the Lord, too.

Thank you so much for the letter you sent with Mr. Piovesana's sister-in-law. I'm so glad to hear the children are doing so well.

I won't be coming back by the polar route, since I have to go through New York.

Don't worry about me. How many times I thought of all of you during the flights yesterday. At the airport in Plattsburgh I seemed

---

75. The Diamond-Gardner Co. of New York, producer of plastic packing materials.

to see our little ones in the many children staring at our little airplane!

My most loving best wishes, my dearest Gianna; many big kisses to you and the *popi.*

Your affectionate

Pietro

Loving greetings to Mamma, Zita, and Cecco.

MAY 22, 1959
FRIDAY

My dearest Pietro,

I have here your little note from Monday the eighteenth at 11:30 PM—you must be so tired, and you had to leave right away again on Tuesday morning! I still haven't gotten a letter from you saying, "I've finished my work . . . I'll meet you on such-and-such a day, at such-and-such time." Sadly, you still don't know. It's been twenty-six days since you left, and it seems like you've been so far away for months and months. Gigetto always says, "Papa isn't coming back, he's far, far away," and you still have to take such long flights.

We're still staying with Zita, though tomorrow I'll have to spend the night at Ponte Nuovo because I'm having the mattresses redone on all the beds.

Two Englishmen conducted a detailed visit at the Laminated Plastics plant[76] for three days. A thousand rumors were flying, Zita

---

76. The company for the production of plastic laminates, Formica, used in the furniture and electronics industries, was founded in 1950 on the initiative of the engineer Pietro Molla. Participating partners were members of SAFFA, Count Gerli, and the English Formica company, Thomas de la Rue of London. The plant was in Magenta.

said. The only news so far is that the lawyer, Zaninoni,[77] no longer introduces himself as a lawyer, but as "Mr. Zaninoni." Mr. Notari,[78] the engineer, asked when you would be coming back—I don't know why.

Cecco said that Mr. Denotti,[79] the engineer, provided some panels for the school's open house; he must have asked the higher-ups about it before Cecco wrote you. Everyone is busy preparing for Magenta's June festival.[80] Almost all of the houses are being painted . . . you wouldn't believe the colors—the most common is yellow, in a variety of shades.

The front of the church[81] is finished, and the scaffolding is down; it's very beautiful and imposing. Monsignor [Luigi Crespi] is very satisfied with the result, and is often seen contemplating it.

Belinzaghi Bank sent us some letters about the Pirelli shares; there's no reply deadline, so I thought you might be back in time to answer them, because I honestly don't understand very much about it.

Gigetto is very happy today because his new record, "All the Mothers," has finally arrived. He loves his music passionately—watch out if he can't play his records[82] for some reason! He knows your tape messages by heart and repeats them even before you speak. Both of them are doing very well: no sign of the measles, thank God.

Teresina has recovered completely, but now Luigino[83] is sick with whooping cough.

---

77. Mr. Zaninoni was Director General of the Plastic Laminates.
78. Mr. Notari was an executive of SAFFA.
79. Paolo Denotti was an executive of the furniture sector of SAFFA.
80. This festival celebrated the Battle of Magenta (June 1859).
81. This is the Basilica of Saint Martin.
82. At this time the widespread diffusion of pop music began in Italy.
83. Teresina and Luigino were Pietro's niece and nephew, children of Rosetta.

Mamma is fine; she always asks me for news about you.

In the hope of seeing you again soon, with much, much love, I kiss and embrace you, with your treasures.

Your most affectionate

Gianna

NEW YORK, MAY 22, 1959
FRIDAY EVENING

My dearest Gianna,

Today something unexpected happened. After weeks without any pain at all, about four days ago I began to have terrible toothaches again—still, and only, the first premolar on the left (the lower one), the same one the dentist repaired for me many times, and which repeatedly broke again, and in the last few days it completely overwhelmed me. So I had no choice but to go to a wonderful dentist. He immediately x-rayed me, and when he looked at it he told me right away that, in his opinion, I *absolutely* had to have the tooth pulled, since it was no longer repairable.

He sent me to another big room (four doctors and at least fifteen or so nurses). There I had another x-ray. Then, in the American way, off with my jacket and tie: they took my blood pressure and asked me about any illnesses I ever had or have now.[84]

They put a plastic apron over me and tied white cloths around my neck and head (Mr. Corneo, who stayed with me, said I looked like an Indian with a turban). The other nurses, after giving me an

---

84. Pietro was intentionally making fun of American medical procedures in order to downplay the situation. At the same time, he was describing everything in detail, knowing his wife's interest in medical developments.

oral disinfectant, gave me an injection for general anesthesia (it lasted three minutes) and after the "operation" they carried me, holding me up by the arms because the anesthesia made me woozy, to a little room and laid me down on a cot for about twenty minutes. I was lying flat on my back. After they had given me some coffee, a penicillin pill, instructions for making a disinfectant solution, and a paper napkin in case I had to spit up, they . . . sent me off. It was thirty-one dollars total, about 20,000 lire. It took all morning to go to the dentist and get a tooth pulled.

At lunchtime and this evening I ate normally. I haven't felt a bit of pain since, and not even a single side effect from the anesthesia: just a little tiredness, which I took care of by staying in bed from 2:00 to 5:00 and then in my room after that.

Tomorrow I will have to process all the information gathered during the visit to the match factory in Springfield for a technical discussion I will be having tomorrow night with the head of that company.

Sunday I'll try to rest as much as possible.

This coming week we'll be leaving New York for fifteen days. Unfortunately, since we have to depend on many different groups we can't always group our visits together.

Today I received your dear letter of the nineteenth of this month. I hope dear Mariolina's little problems are already over. I'm glad Savina got back safely. Tell her hello from me.

Gigetto is right that SAFFA is broken . . . it's always broken, at least its roof which leaks water! I'm glad the prefect visited. I certainly would have liked to accompany him. You can imagine how I'm dying to hear and enjoy our little man's brilliant discourses!

I served Mass at the altar of Saint Elizabeth, our Lady's cousin, the mother of Saint John [the Baptist] and the "patroness of expectant mothers"! All my prayers there were for you. And so much love with the prayers.

Kiss our treasures for me. A most affectionate big kiss to you.

Your affectionate

Pietro

Remember me to Mamma.

Affectionate greetings to Zita and Cecco.

> NEW YORK, MAY 23, 1959[85]
> SATURDAY, AN HOUR AFTER MIDNIGHT

Dearest Gianna,

Mr. and Mrs. Kalbrenner had us over to their beautiful house in Stamford (60 km from New York) this afternoon.

We had plenty of technical conversations about matches. For dinner they drove us 40 km farther to this typical restaurant that you see in the photo. We just got back to the hotel a few minutes ago. Everything's fine. No more toothaches.

I'm thinking of the children who are just waking up now, and of you.

Big kisses to you and our treasures.

Your

Pietro

---

85. Postcard.

MAY 24, 1959
SUNDAY

My most beloved Pietro,

It's 3:00 PM, and our little angels have gone to Legnano[86] with their aunts, Angela, and Savina; Mr. and Mrs. Viola[87] invited them there to see the floats at the festival. I preferred to stay at home where it's quiet, since the ninth month starts today and I get tired easily.[88] All alone and with much emotion, I read and re-read the most affectionate letters you've sent me so faithfully every day from America. I am in your dear company, feeling better today . . . but yesterday, I will admit, I was a bit down. I wanted you here with me, and I missed you so much that I decided to write and tell you to come home right away. But the feeling passed. . . . Today I say, "Come home as soon as possible, Pedrin *d'or*, as soon as you can."[89]

Last night, before going to sleep, Gigetto said to me, "Mamma, I want to see my Papa. He's still so far away, he's never coming back!" What a darling, he loves you so much and misses you . . . "Papa has to fix my little red car . . . my tricycle . . . etc. I'm going up in the sky so I can see my Papa!" and so on; it's one statement after

---

86. This municipality in the province of Milan is 16 km north of Magenta. On May 29, 1176 a battle took place between the Emperor Frederick Barbarossa and the Lombard allies of Milan. The annual parade commemorates the victory by the municipalities.

87. Vittoria and Secondo Viola were the parents of Laura, the wife of Gianna's brother, Ferdinando.

88. Gianna, as Pietro, minimizes the notable difficulties with this pregnancy, in order not to alarm her husband.

89. Just a glimpse of this letter is particularly moving. There one can read in rapid sequence the anxiety of waiting for imminent motherhood, sorrow at the absence of her husband, joy at the affection evidenced by his letters, and the recollected solitude and serenity that come from faith and prayer.

another, as if he were already grown up. Mariolina is as wild as ever, and she does everything that Gigetto does, so they often end up quarreling. They are doing very well and, thanks to your prayers, there have been no "misfortunes."[90]

My cousin Piera[91] had her baby and they named her Simonetta. Piera is still in the hospital, though, because they had to do a C-section, I'm not sure why. But she's all right and hopes to go home within the week. What a thought, though . . . I trust in our Lady, and I'm sure that she will help me this time, just as she did before. The prayers of my dearest and most loving Pietro are too many for her not to. Thank you for everything, Pedrin *d'or*, for your great love for me and for our treasures, for your fatigue and all your hard work, and for all your sacrifices.

I hope it's not too hot where you are. It's been rainy and chilly here for the past few days, with a little bit of clearing in between. I'm glad it's been cool, because the heat would be too much for me.

Archbishop Montini[92] will be here on June 2 for the opening of the front of the Basilica; the schools will be closed and the preparations for the ceremony are underway.

I hope I'll receive word of the day of your return tomorrow.

---

90. The conversation moves naturally to their children. The result is a new sweetness that defuses the previous tension.

91. Pier Angela Beretta is a cousin of Gianna. She testified, "The first feature in Gianna's exercise of Christian virtue, in my opinion, was that it did not weigh on others. She had a natural spontaneity in the exercise of virtue" (*Posizione sulle virtù*, op. cit., 330).

92. This is Giovanni Battista Montini, the future Paul VI, then archbishop of Milan. At the death of Gianna, he became actively interested in the story of the woman who bravely offered her life.

I kiss you again and again with all my love, and your dear treasures kiss you with me.

Ciao, my Pietro, come back soon,

Your

Gianna

NEW YORK, MAY 25, 1959

Dearest Gianna,

Yesterday, which was Sunday, I had to work with Mr. Corneo to get our notes in order for the upcoming visits, as well as those from the visits we've already made, since we have to leave for Cincinnati.

I rested, too.

In the morning, we assisted at Spellman's[93] Pontifical Mass at the cathedral.

After Friday's procedure, I have no more toothache at all.

My health is very good, and so is my digestion.

I am so disappointed to have to prolong my absence. The things we have to do have multiplied, and it's a long way in between cities here. Often we have to visit the same place more than once for further discussions.

I recorded a tape for you and the children in my room—Room 617 at the Essex House.

Have someone bring you the tape player from my office. That way you can listen to it all together.

How much I want to see you all again and stay with you!

Kiss the *popi* at length for me.

---

93. Francis Joseph Cardinal Spellman (1889–1967) was archbishop of New York from 1939 (and cardinal from 1946) till his death in 1967.

A most loving kiss and infinite, affectionate best wishes to you.

Your

Pietro

Greet Mamma, Zita, Cecco, Adelaide, and Rosetta for me.
One tape is for Adelaide—SAFFA

MAY 25, 1959
MONDAY EVENING

My dearest Pietro,

Our dear little ones have been asleep for three hours already, like two little angels, tired out after running and playing in the vineyard. If you could only see Pierluigi's energetic somersaults! He's better at it than his cousins, and Mariolina follows him around and tries to do everything he does. So when nighttime comes, they're tired and fall asleep in two minutes.

I got your letter of Thursday the twenty-first this afternoon. I can't deny, Pedrin *d'or*, that when I read you wouldn't be back until June 10, I got very depressed. I had a good cry . . . then I offered this sacrifice to the Lord for you so that he might protect you during your continual flights, and for the baby we are expecting, so it will be born beautiful and healthy. And so, I resigned myself.[94] I gave Gigetto and Mariolina many kisses, pressed them to my heart, and with them, I felt you very close to me, as if you were already here with us.

Try not to get too tired, my Pietro; if all your days are as busy as Wednesday was, I can imagine how exhausted you must be every

---

94. Gianna is not exaggerating. Actually, in those days she wasn't doing well; however, she found strength and support in her faith.

night. Yet, you still manage to send me your loving words. I will always be grateful to you, my husband and Papa *d'or*!

Pierluigi came into our room in Ponte Nuovo this morning and, seeing our engagement photo, said, ". . . Papa, Papa, he's back, look, I saw Papa . . ." He didn't know how to show his joy at seeing you—he pressed the picture to his heart . . . what a beautiful child! One cannot help but be touched by his displays of affection!

Going back to your flights, are the two-engine planes safe? Excuse my ignorance, but it seems to me a four-engine plane could better handle the air pockets, etc. I was happy to hear that you had an enchanting trip, though, sitting close to the pilot, and close to Heaven! And since we are always close to you, it's almost as if we are also enjoying the beautiful things you tell us about.

I don't think the death of Foster Dulles will prevent you from working, but I hope the factories don't close, otherwise June 10 . . . might turn into June 20![95]

Ciao, my Pietro, don't worry about us, we're fine.

Big, big, big kisses, and many, many of them from your treasures and from your most affectionate

Gianna

MAY 26, 1959
TUESDAY

Dearest Pietro,

A loving little greeting today, too, from your wife and from your little ones, who, thanks be to God, are fine even though everywhere in Ponte Nuovo there are cases of measles and whooping cough,

---

95. John Foster Dulles (1888–1959) was Secretary of State for President Eisenhower and played a central role in the implementation of the Marshall Plan.

and scarlet fever in Magenta. I only take the children out in the car, and after all, they do like playing in the garden and in the vineyard just as much as going out. Zita and Cecco[96] want us to stay here, rather than going back to Ponte Nuovo because they say the children are already used to it here and it would be a shame to take them away. My Pietro, I hope June 10 comes quickly—very quickly! My longing to see and embrace you again is too much! Don't forget—June 14 is the feast of Ponte Nuovo and Bishop Pignedoli[97] will be visiting and administering Confirmation and Communion. You'll be here, right?

Mamma is fine, and so are your sisters and their families.

Ciao, beautiful Pedrin, take care of yourself and don't get too tired.

Big kisses from your little angels and a most affectionate embrace from your

Gianna

MAY 26, 1959[98]
TUESDAY, 9:10 PM
ON THE FLIGHT FROM NEW YORK TO CINCINNATI

Dearest Gianna,

Our flight took off at 7:39 and we'll be in Cincinnati within an hour. Today we will have flown 2,700 km: from 8:00 to 9:50; from 4:10 to 5:10; from 5:56 to 6:34 and now since 7:39: New York, Greenville, Washington, New York, Cincinnati. I'm safe on the wings of your prayers and those of our treasures.

---

96. This is a proof of the affection that united the Beretta siblings, who, as affirmed many times, sustained and helped one another.

97. Bishop Sergio Pignedoli was the auxiliary bishop of Milan at that time.

98. Postcard.

I'm thinking of you with boundless love, and I send you a great big kiss.

Your affectionate

Pietro

All our flights were just perfect, in a magnificent sky. I'm flying in Formica's[99] plane.

You'll relive this flight in my FILM.

Today makes a whole month that we have been apart!

MAY 26, 1959
TUESDAY, 10:00 PM
ON THE FLIGHT TO CINCINNATI

Dearest Gianna,

I've been flying since 7:39 from New York directly to the "homeland" of Formica:[100] Cincinnati.

And this is my fourth flight today.

Since 8:50 we've been flying in the dark; we have radar to guide us. I was just looking at it. Look, here is what I can see on it:

The two dark areas are two storms [drawing].

We are flying peacefully in between them. We are flying at an altitude of 3,000 meters and at 450 km an hour.

The flight's been wonderful, as were the other three. Splendid sunshine in a magnificent blue sky and a marvelous sunset.

10:10: We are starting our descent toward Cincinnati.

The hearty welcomes I get are really touching.

---

99. Private plane owned by the Formica Corporation of Cincinnati, Ohio.

100. The plastic laminate used to cover furniture and for electronics was invented in Cincinnati, Ohio in 1913 by Daniel O'Connor and Herbert Faber.

On this magnificent airplane, today at 9:00, the vice president of American Cyanamid[101] and Lederle Medicinals pronounced our children "marvelous" and "really beautiful."

Each day, my joy at the compliments our children receive diminishes the pain of being so far from you, which gets harder every day.

10:15 PM: We can see the countless lights of Cincinnati. We are circling the city, waiting for the airport to let us land. Here even airplanes get in line for takeoff and landing. In New York, there were a good six airplanes behind us waiting for their turn on the runway.

10:23: The plane just touched down. We've flown about 1,100 km in two hours and forty minutes.

I'm thinking of you all sleeping serenely and I send you a most loving kiss, but without waking you up.

Your

Pietro

Say hello to Mamma, Zita, and Cecco for me.

MAY 27, 1959
WEDNESDAY

My dearest Pietro,

I was so sorry to hear about your toothache; you did the right thing by having it pulled. I can't believe you had to have it done in America! If I even had to go to the dentist in Mesero—you can imagine.[102] Let's hope you won't have any more trouble with it.

---

101. The American Cyanamid Company of New York, a firm producing plastic laminates and wood paneling.

102. At this time medical specialization was not very widespread, so Gianna also pulled teeth.

When Pierluigi heard you had to have a tooth pulled, he immediately told everyone—his uncle, his aunt—"Poor Papa, he had a tooth pulled, he had to have a shot and they put a bandage around his head!" He just finished pretending to be Modugno,[103] with his arms opened wide, moving his legs just like Modugno does. He had another revelation last night: "Mamma, when I'm big, I'll go to school with Iucci and Toia:[104] then when I come home, I'll say, '*Ciao*, Mariolina, I'm back!'" He is already so big, very mischievous, and always on the move. Mariolina watches the other kids riding their bikes and tries as hard as she can to follow them on her tricycle—and she's only a year-and-a-half old!

I'm sorry that you won't be able to hear from us for two weeks[105] because of your traveling away from New York. But these wanderings of yours will end! And then you won't have to go away on other trips again, as you told me the evening of the concert, right? I put my foot down . . . no, just kidding, not I, but the third *popo*.

My Pietro, I can imagine how much you want to come back to us, but patience! The Lord asks us for this sacrifice. He is so good to us! We're all doing well, and the children become more beautiful every day.

The historical display[106] will be opened by the authorities in Milan tomorrow. The panels you ordered with the history of Milan

---

103. As mentioned previously, this was a time of great popularity for Italian musicians and children enjoyed imitating them. That year, among others, Domenico Modugno had triumphed at the San Remo Festival with *Volare*, one of his most famous songs.

104. Toia is a nickname of his cousin, Maria Vittoria, and Iucci, as we know, is Toia's sister, Amalia.

105. Just on the twenty-seventh, in fact, Pietro began a series of trips through the country from Cincinnati to Chicago and California, which prevented him from receiving regular letters from his wife.

106. Cf. Pietro's letter of May 22, 1959.

are at the plastics plant, but no one knows where to put them—not even Mr. Denotti, the engineer.

Ciao, Pedrin *d'or*, take good care of yourself; your little ones send you many kisses with their little lips and their little hands.

A most affectionate embrace from your little wife who always thinks of you and who loves you very, very much. *Arrivederci* soon,

Your

Gianna

Zita, Cecco, Liberata, Angela, and Savina return affectionate greetings.

CINCINNATI, MAY 27, 1959[107]

6:00 PM

Dearest Gianna,

I just now finished my visits to two huge, most interesting Formica plants. I had a warm welcome and they praised me for what I've done for the plant in Magenta.

Tonight I'm invited to dinner by the president of the company. I'm not in a huge hotel, but in a nice room in this Mayfair Motel.

Big kisses to you and to our treasures,

Pietro

Tomorrow afternoon we'll be in Chicago.

---

107. Postcard.

MAY 28, 1959
THURSDAY, 3:30 PM
ON THE FLIGHT FROM CINCINNATI TO CHICAGO

Dearest Gianna,

I've been on this flight since 2:30 local time.

Now we're already starting our descent into Chicago, where we'll arrive within fifteen minutes.

Great flight, clear skies, and bright sunshine.

3:45—We just touched down in Chicago: a perfect landing. Thank you again for your prayers.

4:30—I'm once again at the Morrison Hotel in Chicago where I stayed in 1947.[108] A very pleasant room. Tomorrow we'll be here in Chicago. Saturday and Sunday I will rest, with a stop in Lincoln (Nebraska) to visit my cousins, and I'll arrive in Los Angeles Sunday.

I'm feeling great and the weather is good.

Last night we spent the evening as the dinner guests at the home of the president of Formica. It was an ideal setting that I would dream of for our kids: a splendid villa in the middle of an estate; two horses for the girls (nineteen and fifteen years old), two ponies for the boys (nine and seven years old), fields, swings for the children, puppies, cows in the pasture. The O'Connors moved here, away from the city, ten years ago so the children could have an ideal atmosphere to grow up in. It's 35 km from the plant and from the schools.

We were given a most cordial welcome. They invited me to come back with you. Naturally, they loved our children!

Last night Mr. O'Connor told me that the greatest insurance we had on the American Cyanamid [Company] plane Wednesday was

---

108. On a previous business trip.

not the radar, but the fact that the pilot had *six* small children waiting for him at home!

Right now you're all asleep: it's already after midnight in Ponte Nuovo.

Good night, and many, many, many, many big kisses to you and to Pierluigi and Mariolina.

Best wishes from your affectionate

Pietro

Say hello to Mamma, Zita, and Cecco for me.

Tell Zita not to worry,[109] and tell her, *confidentially,* that Laminated Plastics has a very secure future. The praises the president gave me could not have been warmer, and he could not have been more welcoming.

Ciao! Tuesday, I will finally begin . . . with stops . . . the flight back toward all of you.

MAY 29, 1959
FRIDAY

My dearest Pietro,

The last letter I got from you was from May 24; I was hoping to receive something today, but I think the mail takes longer to get here since you're traveling. I trust in the Lord, however, and think of you as tired but in good health, without toothaches or headaches. We are just fine here.

I took the children to see the procession for the feast of Corpus Christi yesterday:[110] banners, little girls dressed in white—it was a

---

109. Zita, as we saw before, was employed by Laminated Plastics. See also Gianna's letter of May 22, 1959.

110. Before Vatican II, Corpus Christi, which falls on the Thursday after Trinity Sunday, was celebrated with great solemnity and participation of the people.

real treat for them. The historical display at the Giacobbe House was also opened yesterday, and the ceremony was broadcast on TV in the evening; two hundred important people from Milan[111] were there. Cecco said both the ceremony and the display came off very well, very interesting. Partly due to you, Pedrin *d'or.*[112]

In twelve days, we'll all be together again. You can imagine how I'm counting the days and the hours, along with Gigetto, who keeps asking me, "When is Papa coming home?" You've never been gone this long before.

Tomorrow afternoon, Mr. Crotti will take Zita, Gigetto, and me to Milan to buy a few little things for the children; Piera will be expecting us at 4:30 PM at Aunt Virginia's house for Simonetta's Baptism.

Piera is fine now, but she suffered a lot; she says she's forgotten all that, though, because Simonetta is such a wonderful baby. The Lord consoles mothers quickly, doesn't he? Mamma, Zita, and Cecco send you their affectionate greetings, and they think of you often.

Ciao, my little husband, how much I want you!

I kiss you and your treasures a great big kiss, and I embrace you most affectionately,

Your

Gianna

---

111. The display was accompanied by a conference of historians, coming mainly from Milan.

112. As Gianna said in previous letters, Pietro designed the exhibition panels and had them produced.

CHICAGO, MAY 29, 1959
FRIDAY, 11:00 PM

My dearest Gianna,

Monday, in California, I'll be able to read and kiss your affectionate and very appreciated letters that I had forwarded on to me from New York.

I asked Dr. Parten's[113] mother and sister to call you right away, as soon as they arrived in Italy, to let you know that I'm all right.

Today we finished the first part of our work in Chicago. Tomorrow and Sunday we'll rest, except for a few hours of travel.

This morning I heard Mass and received Holy Communion in the church of the Franciscan Fathers, which is very close to my hotel. I prayed especially for Father Alberto[114] and I wrote to him.

Is Gigetto . . . tired of the long, too-long absence of his papa? And how about his little mamma?

This evening I had supper on the forty-second floor of my hotel. The Italian songs, some of them the same as those on Gigetto's favorite records, made me miss you even more.

I have many other things to tell you, but I must remember your advice and rest.

You are smiling at me and you are close to me with our treasures in your wonderful image here on my night table.

Today someone asked me whether Gigetto and Mariolina are movie actors, since they are so beautiful.

---

113. Dr. Parten was a SAFFA official in New York.

114. Father Alberto, Gianna's brother, was a Franciscan who at the time had already labored many years as a medical missionary in Brazil.

No toothaches or headaches, and no cold. My digestion is good.
I kiss and embrace you and our treasures with all my love.

Your most affectionate

Pietro

Say hello to Mamma, Cecco, Zita, and my sisters for me.

OMAHA, MAY 30, 1959[115]

SATURDAY, 2:30 PM

Dearest Gianna,

I'm halfway between New York and Los Angeles.

I'll be staying here in Lincoln, Nebraska (about 100 km from
Omaha), tonight to say hello to my cousins (Mamma's nephews).[116]
Great flight.

All is well. Many, many best wishes and most affectionate
kisses,

Pietro

The flight from Chicago to Omaha was good. There were two
Sisters and a lot of children on my plane.

Dearest Gigetto and Mariolina,

Papa is here in the land of hunting grounds and Indians. I'll
bring you a nice cowboy outfit.

Up in the air with Papa, there are many children.

Papa kisses you very, very much, and you kiss Mamma for me.

---

115. Postcard.
116. The two sons of Enrico, brother of Pietro's mother.

LINCOLN-OMAHA (NEBRASKA)
MAY 31, 1959
SUNDAY, 9:30 AM

Dearest Gianna,

An hour ago, at the Lincoln airport, I said goodbye to my cousins, who came with me. I stayed at their house yesterday (Saturday) from around noon till this morning.

Both of my cousins (first cousins because they are the sons of my mother's brother Enrico), their wives and children were so excited to see me after twelve years. The one who was most moved was my uncle's widow, who is seventy-nine years old.

In forty-five minutes I'll board the plane for Los Angeles: an eight-hour flight. The flight will take off at 4:30 Italian time and land in California at 12:30 AM (Italian time); that will be 3:30 in the afternoon in California.

I'm feeling fine.

Today is the last day of our Lady's month, and our Heavenly Mother will surely grant me a safe flight.

I feel you and our treasures are especially near, more than ever, just now when I'm about to travel another 2,000 km farther away from you. In Los Angeles I'll be 11,000 km from you.

I can just hear Gigetto's touching prayers; I can see Mariolina's little folded hands, and I see your loving and anxious glance.

Forgive me for the worries I cause you.

When I'm back with you all, I'll repay you all with greater affection, greater care, and attention.

I embrace you and kiss you and our treasures with infinite affection.

Your

Pietro

NEW YORK, MAY 31, 1959
SUNDAY, 1:50 PM
(MOUNTAIN STANDARD TIME)
8:50 PM ITALIAN TIME

My most beloved Gianna,

I'm flying in a beautiful clear sky—at an altitude of 6,000 meters—above the Rocky Mountains and the Grand Canyon of Colorado and Utah. It's a sight I will never forget: eroded mountains, rising straight up from the rivers and valleys, rivers which wear the rock away and snake through it: green rivers and blue lakes; rocks which go from yellow-gold to scarlet red and to dark red and copper. It's a powerful sight that I never expected.

In this sky and above these rocks which at times break down into a desert of red sand and which speak more than ever of the power and the Providence of the Creator, I repeat the prayer I say when I fly. I begin at this moment when we are between the Heavens and the rocks, and I am looking at the marvelous pictures of you and our treasures, which I kiss up here in the Heavens:

Jesus, who created me and preserve me with graces and blessings without number: you who among the long flights of time and of today, up here in the Heavens, have given me the immense gift of a wife of gold, more marvelous than the dawn which can only be admired from up here, and of two treasures, who are as splendid as the sky in its full brightness, which one can only be embraced from on high: you who will soon give us again the divine gift of another treasure, listen to my prayer:

Bless Gianna and our treasures! Change into grace their anxiety and worry over my long absence and my flights.

Please hear, today and always, the prayers of Gianna, of my Gigetto, of my mother and of all those who love me! Look upon my Mariolina's little folded hands! Grant me the grace of a happy return!

And grant that I may advance in your ways at every moment, just as the plane flies right on course, safely, directed by radio.

May I always have a holy fear of you, the kind one can feel up here. May I be entrusted more than ever to your Divine Providence, sustained on the wings of the prayers of Gianna, of my treasures, of my mother and of all those who pray for me.

Grant that a serene and luminous atmosphere may always enfold our family, like the atmosphere in the sky through which I am flying, and the purity of the clear air I am breathing.

Grant that the clouds quickly disperse and leave us alone, like the little clouds up here.

Keep my family and my dear ones safe, happy, and peaceful in the way of your light, today and always until the day we will fly up, up, always higher, up to you. Amen.[117]

5:04 Los Angeles time (11:04 in Italy)

Great flight. We are in Los Angeles. Gigetto, you're so cute with your prayer: "Papa, don't crash!"

But this time Papa is really far, far, far away!

Many, many big kisses, Gianna!

Many, many big kisses, Pierluigi and Mariolina!

MAY 31, 1959

SUNDAY

My dearest Pietro,

Thank you for your greetings "in your own voice." I went to your office yesterday with Mariolina and Gigetto to listen to your tape.[118]

---

117. Rather than a prayer while flying this could be called "A Prayer for the Family."

118. This is the cassette recorded by Pietro with greetings for his wife and children.

It's too bad the machine makes your voice sound more baritone, so the children weren't really sure it was you. They loved how you made the tape with words and music, though; they'll understand even more when they're older. I also received your letter from Monday the twenty-fifth, the night before you left New York; it's a good thing these are the last ten days and that . . . they, too, will pass.

We're waiting to hear when we should come pick you up at Malpensa. Each evening, before he goes to sleep, Pierluigi sends you a kiss with his little hand and says, "Baby Jesus, take this kiss to my Papa." I bought him his first little suit jacket in Milan yesterday— you should see what a big boy he is! (He wears the size of a four-year-old.) Now, when he gets himself dressed, he looks at himself in the mirror and comments, "How nice, I look nice." I tell you! This morning, he just had to go to Mass, no matter what: "I'm big now. I'll be good." After Mass, we all went with Zita to visit Aunt Ginia.[119] She's a little tired, but her spirits are good. She's waiting for Father Alberto[120] so she can ask his advice. His companions are already arriving, but he is only flying as far as Lisbon, so that he can visit Fatima and Lourdes before returning in August. That's what one of the Franciscan brothers on Monfort Street[121] told Father Giuse. I sent a letter to Grajaú, and now I'm waiting for an answer.[122]

Another notice from Belinzaghi Bank arrived for the Edison shares. I have to respond by June 8. Every nine of the old shares yielded one of 2,000 lire. I will answer yes. What do you think? It's

---

119. Virginia De Micheli was the sister of Gianna's mother. At that time she was sixty-three.

120. Gianna's brother, a Franciscan priest and doctor in Grajaú, Brazil.

121. Monfort Street in Milan was the Franciscan community where Father Alberto was expected. Here Father Giuse had asked for and received news of his brother.

122. Another sign of the affection and bond that existed among the Berettas.

always better to buy them; the old shares are two hundred eighty-eight, so the new ones would be thirty-two.[123]

Ginia, Nando, and Aunt Piera[124] thank you for the greetings you sent them; they return them sincerely and they all hope everything is going well for you.

Darling Pedrin, don't worry about us, because we're fine. Have a good trip and don't get too tired—if you don't manage to do everything, don't worry, because you have already done so much that your bosses can't help but be pleased.

The Englishmen are still visiting the laminates plant: Dr. Bottoni[125] showed two of them around the other day, and the lawyer was with Count Gerli yesterday. The rumor is that the Englishmen want to do business with SAFFA and they want you as director.

Ciao, my Pietro, I give you a great big kiss and I, together with your treasures, embrace you with all my love,

Your

Gianna

JUNE 1, 1959
MONDAY

My dearest Pietro,

I just received your cards from last week and the letter that you wrote on the plane owned by Formica. You really are more in Heaven than on earth. How many journeys! And how much

---

123. Besides being a loving and charitable woman, Gianna was a careful and prudent administrator of the family's assets.

124. Aunt Piera was the younger sister of Gianna's mother.

125. Doctor Franco Bottoni was Central Director of SAFFA. Cf. the letter of Gianna of May 22, 1959.

distance you cover in just a few hours! We think of you constantly and accompany you with our prayers, hoping this really will be our last week away from each other. I'm glad everyone is welcoming you so courteously. Zita says nobody knows what's going on at the laminates plant.[126]

Two invitations came for you: one for tomorrow's inauguration of the basilica,[127] the other for Thursday, June 4.[128] I passed both of them on to SAFFA; Mr. Tarsi[129] will probably go.

Thanks to you, the historical display is extremely popular, for its content as well as its elegance. There are always crowds of people going to see it.

We're all fine here. I always have the burning stomach pains, but at least I have some suffering to offer the Lord for you, my treasure, so you come back safe and sound—and soon. Our marvelous children play and enjoy themselves in the garden all day long. They're eating well and sleeping. They send their hellos and kisses to any airplane that passes overhead.

Ciao, my Pietro, thank you for always giving me news of where you are and what you are doing; I anxiously and joyfully await your letters.

Big, big kisses, your

Gianna

---

126. At that time Zita worked in the laboratory at Laminate Plastics, a factory connected to SAFFA, which, as the letter stated, was taking on a new corporate set-up. In any case, in the letter of May 2, which apparently Gianna had not yet received, Pietro wrote, "Tell Zita not to worry, and tell her, *confidentially*, that Laminated Plastics has a very secure future."

127. The basilica was being newly opened after restoration work.

128. June 4 was the centenary of the Battle of Magenta.

129. The engineer, Pietro Tarsi, was Director of General Services at SAFFA.

JUNE 2, 1959
TUESDAY

My dearest Pietro,

It's 9:00 PM; our treasures have already been asleep for half an hour. They went to bed because they just couldn't keep their eyes open. They're so active,[130] and it's a good thing they have guardian angels[131]—what one [child] doesn't do the other dreams up. Let's hope that they'll calm down a little as they get older.

There was a big celebration to welcome Archbishop Montini[132] today. I didn't go, but Zita said there were a lot of people. Even now, I can hear people passing by on their way to the church, because there's a solemn procession with the urn of Saint Crescenzia, something that hasn't happened in a long time.

Tomorrow morning at 8:00, Mr. Crotti is going to take Mamma and Teresina to Monza to pick up Sister Luigia[133] and take her to Central Station. As usual, she came to bring back some children and pick up others. She told me on the phone that she's doing all right, though she's a little tired.

And you? Who knows where you might be right now.

I'm waiting for a postcard from San Francisco, the last, long leg of your trip.

---

130. Witnesses confirm that the children of Gianna and Pietro were very lively. The saint, however, always opposed any attempt to curb their natural exuberance.

131. Faith proves to be a valuable ally to establishing a good family training.

132. Giovanni Battista Montini, Archbishop of Milan, who would later become Pope Paul VI.

133. Sister Luigia Molla was Pietro's sister. She resided in Imperia-Porto Maurizio and was director of the boarding school "Smile of Italy" with elementary schools and summer camps. The mother and her granddaughter seized the opportunity to go to Monza, where Sister Luigia had spent the night in the house of the Sisters of the Most Precious Blood, and spend some time with her.

Everyone here is asking when you'll be back.

Ten more days, my Pedrin, and then . . . enough of your being away! You'll be all ours.

Big kisses from your treasures. Take care of yourself, don't get too tired.

A very big hug from your most affectionate

Gianna

JUNE 3, 1959
WEDNESDAY

My dearest little husband Pietro,

I just received your postcards and letters from Chicago. How can I thank you for not letting a day go by without sending me word? The children are pleased with their cards, and are very happy because Papa is coming home soon. I'm glad to hear that you'll begin your return trip on Tuesday, or at least start moving back in our direction.

Thanks be to God! May the Lord accompany you, as usual, in your travels.

We're all fine. After we do some housecleaning, we'll return to "home base"[134] next week, to wait for the return of our dearest and most beloved Papa.

It's not too hot right now, and we hope you're not suffering too much from the heat.

I'm glad you're well, with no toothaches, and that your stomach isn't giving you problems.

Many greetings from Cecco and Zita.

---

134. As you will recall, in the absence of her husband, the saint had been a guest of her siblings, Zita and Cecco, in Magenta. Now, in anticipation of her husband's arrival, the family was preparing for their return to Ponte Nuovo.

Big, big kisses from your treasures and from your most affectionate

Gianna

SAN FRANCISCO, JUNE 3, 1959
WEDNESDAY

Dearest Gianna,

I have in front of me, together with your marvelous pictures, your loving letters of Sunday, Monday, and Tuesday, May 24, 25, and 26, which I had forwarded to me from New York.

I found them at Red Bluff, a little place in the far north of California, and I read and re-read them in this place that is the most distant point of our trip: more than 11,000 km; nine hours' time difference, and at an angle of 90 degrees between our respective positions when we are standing.

Yesterday morning, in the little town of Red Bluff dedicated to the Sacred Heart—on the second day of the month consecrated to him—it was so special to me to be able to assist at Mass and receive Jesus for you and our treasures. I felt so close to all of you in that beautiful church with the same crucifix, the same Blessed Mother, Saint Joseph, and Saint Francis of Assisi we find in our churches.[135]

I prayed especially for Father Alberto, and I sent him a letter today from this very city, because its name—San Francisco—must be particularly dear to him.[136]

---

135. Pietro had a vivid sense of the unity and catholicity of the Church.

136. As we have already seen, Father Alberto, Gianna's brother, was a Franciscan medical missionary in Brazil. Thus, Pietro reasoned, the city bearing the name of the founder of the Franciscans must be especially dear to him.

In Red Bluff I got a little taste—though just a quick one—of Old California: horses and cowboys.

My work went very well, and I was warmly welcomed as usual.

Today I'll be flying from San Francisco to Chicago.

My health is perfect, in spite of big changes in temperature and humidity from one place to another. Yesterday it was real California heat in Red Bluff; today the cool spring air in San Francisco.

I'm so glad to hear that everything is fine with our treasures, all due to their little mamma of gold. Gigetto's loving little words are so touching! He's so sweet!

In these next few days I'll try to "fly through" the remaining visits and talks I have.

I can't wait to hug you all again and be with you.

Yesterday evening from 7:30 to 9:30 it took *two hours to fly* from Red Bluff to San Francisco, with four stops in between; it was a real stop-and-go flight, not a direct one. But it turned out fine just the same.

Kiss our little angels very, very much for me, and for you I send many big kisses and a most affectionate embrace.

Your

Pietro

Greet Mamma, Zita, and Cecco for me.

SAN FRANCISCO, JUNE 4, 1959[137]

Great flight. I found your dearest letters. Greatest distance trip adding up. Thank you. Very best wishes. Kisses to you and to our treasures.

Pietro

---

137. Telegram.

JUNE 4, 1959

THURSDAY

My dearest Pietro,

I received your telegram from San Francisco this week: you're still having a good trip, thanks be to God! I just can't stand it anymore—I can't wait for you to come home; only when you're here with us will I be happy and . . . calm. I'm glad you got our letters in San Francisco.

Dr. Parten's[138] sister called to give me news of you and convey your greetings. I can imagine how hot it must be in California. It's been hot here, too, for the last couple of days: it was eighty degrees here today! The children are sweating and drinking a lot, but they're fine.

They enjoyed seeing the parade[139] this morning, with all the bands and banners, etc. Now they're sleeping like two little angels.

Mamma was able to spend some time with Sister Luigia[140] yesterday; she's doing really well. She thanks you in the name of Sister Rosina[141] for calling her brother. Just think, when Sister Luigia read Sister Rosina the letter in which you told her that you spoke with him, Sister Rosina fainted with emotion and joy.

It's 11:00 PM now, and I can hear loud bangs from the sports field—it's the fireworks. I wanted to bring the children to see them, but it's very late for them. I don't think they've woken up yet!

---

138. See Pietro's letter of May 29, 1959.

139. The parade, as previously mentioned, was for the centenary of the Battle of Magenta.

140. Religious of the Congregation of the Most Precious Blood, sister of Pietro.

141. She was a sister of Sister Luigia's congregation.

Which route are you taking home? Are you stopping in Paris, too? My dearest Pietro, I can imagine how much you miss us and how anxious you are to come home. Can't you skip any stops?

I have to go to the children—they're waking up, frightened and calling to me.

There, now they're asleep again; the fireworks are over.

Friday

I received your postcards and the magnificent prayer you wrote on the flight to Los Angeles.[142] I love hearing about the wonders of nature; your descriptions remind me of those films we saw together at the Manzoni,[143] remember?

We remember you in our prayers and always think of you.

Ponte Nuovo is still full of the measles, so I'm waiting till next week to bring the children home. Your treasures kiss you with love.

Gigi is impatient—he wants to go mail the letter to his Papa. It's his "job": when he escorts Zita to the plant at 1:30 PM, he goes to the post office with Cecco to drop the letter off.

Many greetings from Mamma, Zita, and Cecco.

Big, big kisses, your

Gianna

You really are the dearest and most affectionate little husband, a saintly papa, not of gold but of diamond, the biggest and most precious one there is on earth! *Ciao*, my treasure, *arrivederci* soon.

---

142. See Pietro's letter of May 31, 1959.
143. The Manzoni Theater in Milan.

CHICAGO, JUNE 4, 1959
THURSDAY EVENING, 11:00 PM

Dearest Gianna,

This is how I *"celebrated"* the centennial of the Battle of Magenta:

From midnight till 8:00 in the morning (Italian time) I slept in San Francisco, recuperating from the flights of the day before;

From 8:00 till 2:00 (Magenta time) I was flying, a direct flight, more than 2,700 km from San Francisco to Chicago. It was a good flight, through the night: we left San Francisco at 11:30 PM (8:30 in the morning Italian time) and we reached Chicago at 8:00 in the morning their time (6:00 AM San Francisco time).

From 2:00 to 4:30 PM, a short rest, actually very short because we were traveling in the car and getting ready for another flight;

From 4:30 to 5:30 (still Italian time) a short flight of 300-km;

From 5:30 to 8:30 (Italian time), visit to a paper mill;

From 8:30 to 9:30, another short 300 km flight;

9:30, to bed.

The flight from San Francisco and today's flight were magnificent and relaxing because of the nice weather—not a trace of wind or clouds.

Tomorrow I'll visit a match factory, and Saturday and Sunday I'll rest.

On Thursday the eleventh, I should be back in New York.

I'll do everything possible to be home by Sunday the fourteenth, but I fear that some commitments I have in New York, which I can't get out of, will delay my return till Tuesday the sixteenth.

In the next few days I'll send you a telegram with the exact date.

My teeth are all right. I don't have a cold, in spite of changing in one day from very hot (Red Bluff, California) to an almost arctic wind that forced me back into my coat and hat (last night in San Francisco). Today in Chicago it's back to the heat.

On the plane from San Francisco to Chicago, there were about a dozen children who couldn't have been older than three. Two of them were only a few months old. Naturally there was some crying. When I saw the babies asleep next to their mothers, it seemed to me that you were all with me.

Good night, my dearest little wife. Kiss our treasures for me.

Very best wishes and kisses from your

Pietro

Say hello to Mamma, Zita, and Cecco for me.

JUNE 6, 1959
SATURDAY

My dearest Pietro,

You can't imagine how we're counting the days till you come home. I imagine you're already on your trip back to New York before you return to Italy.

"Papa is coming back soon," Gigi tells everyone, and he can't wait till we can go to pick you up at Malpensa. He wakes up every morning and asks, "Mamma, is Papa coming today?" Mariolina waves to you with her little hand when airplanes go by.

It is still pretty hot here; how is it there? I think we'll have to send [the children] to Courmayeur before the end of the month.[144]

Mrs. Valle[145] still hasn't answered the letter I wrote her a month ago, but that's how she does things.

We're all fine, and so is your family. Mamma was pleased to hear that you visited her relatives [in Lincoln, Nebraska].

---

144. With the approach of summer heat, Gianna thought of sending their children to Courmayeur for vacation.

145. Mrs. Valle is the owner of the house that the Molla family rented for some years now.

Ciao, Pedrin *d'or,* take care of yourself and *arrivederci* soon; big kisses from your *popi* and from your most affectionate

Gianna

ST. LOUIS, JUNE 7, 1959[146]

Dearest Gianna,

Since last night I've been the guest of my cousin Antonietta[147] and her relatives.

They welcomed me very kindly.

Every day I think more of you and our treasures.

Arrivederci very soon.

Big kisses to you, Pierluigi, and Mariolina.

Pietro

JUNE 7, 1959
SUNDAY

My dearest Pietro,

It's 4:00 PM and while our treasures are out playing in the garden, I can't deny that I'm feeling a little sad as I think about last Sunday at 4:00 PM.[148] Pietro, we're so far apart, and it takes so long for the mail to get here! Then I start thinking that my letters won't reach you at all, or if you do get them, the news will already be old. My thoughts are always with you, especially when you're flying; things are always happening, and we read about air disasters almost

---

146. Postcard.

147. Antonietta was the daughter of Carlo, one of the brothers of Pietro's mother.

148. The preceding Sunday Gianna had not felt very well.

every day. I won't say anything more; I'm praying and trusting in the Lord.

Zita and I brought the children to see Mother Virginia[149] in Milan this morning; she was able to visit with us for a couple of hours. The children put on quite a show: playing, dancing, singing. Rita[150] seems to be over the measles, and Nando thinks it must be an allergic kind, but we are still keeping the children separated, just in case.

Pierluigi loves talking about his Papa—today, he helped me clean the living room, since "his Papa" is supposed to arrive. Every time he hears a plane, he looks up at the sky and says to you, "*Ciao, Papa, come home soon,*" and Mariolina also waves her little hand, saying, "Papa, Papa!" Gigi wants the kisses his Papa sends him from far away in the evening: one on the forehead, one on the cheeks, and one on the lips—what an angel!

Beautiful Pedrin, now here are many, many big kisses from your Gianna who loves you very much, who thinks of you and wants you to always be happy.

With all my love, I embrace you,

Gianna

CHICAGO, JUNE 7, 1959[151]

EVENING

Dearest Gianna,

I arrived back here from St. Louis tonight, and here at the hotel I just found the wonderful surprise of your welcome letters from May 27, 29, 31, and June 1.

---

149. Virginia, younger sister of Gianna, was a Canossian Sister.
150. Rita is the daughter of Nando and niece of Gianna.
151. Postcard.

Thank you, thank you again and again. How happy I am to hear that everything's fine.

I have so much I want to tell you. But tomorrow morning again, I have to leave very early.

I am well, and now within eight days we'll be in each other's arms again. If you only knew how much I want to come back to you and our treasures, and be home again.

Yesterday I flew 1,300 km, today 500, tomorrow 1,500.

Big kisses to you and our treasures.

Affectionate greetings to Mamma, Zita, Cecco.

Greetings to Savina.

JUNE 8, 1959
MONDAY

My dearest Pietro,

I'm hoping that by the time this letter reaches New York, you will already be on your way home. Gigetto is here and he won't let me write in peace: "I want to write, too," he keeps saying. He had a high fever and sour breath on Saturday, but it passed quickly and by Sunday he was as lively and mischievous as ever. Because of the heat, they've been drinking a lot, and come to think of it, I think it was too much water that made him sick. He's waiting for his Papa, and he wants a big iron wagon, a little tricycle, and a big car like Alberto[152] for his name day.[153] What big dreams he has!

Yesterday was the Bersaglieri's holiday in Magenta, so they marched in formation down the street with fanfare. You can picture

---

152. Alberto was the son of Gianna's brother, Nando.

153. This refers to the party for their son's name day that is celebrated on June 21, the feast of Saint Aloysius.

the children at the window enjoying the spectacle; then, at 5:00 PM, the *Giro d'Italia* [Italian Bikers' Tour] passed by and the street was filled with bicycles, motorcycles, cars. A helicopter even landed near our vineyard. Gigetto thought it was your plane: "Papa's come, here in our garden."

Dearest Pietro, I don't know how to thank you for the wonderful and most affectionate letters that you had the goodness to send me every day. These letters, your words, tell of all your love for me and your dearest treasures, words that mirror your good, sweet soul, your great heart, your faith, your spirit of prayer.[154]

Thank you, thank you with all my heart for everything. Waiting to embrace you again, I kiss you with much, much love,

your

Gianna

Ciao, Papa; Gigi and the *popa* are waiting for you and give you a very big kiss![155]

ON THE FLIGHT TO MEMPHIS, JUNE 8, 1959

MONDAY, 6:20 PM

(12:30 AM TUESDAY, ITALIAN TIME)

Dearest Gianna,

Right now I'm flying along the Mississippi [River], from St. Louis to Memphis.

From 4:10 to 5:40 we covered the first part of today's flights, Chicago–St. Louis; from 6:00 to 7:20 the second, St. Louis–Memphis; and from 7:30 to 8:20 the final third, from Memphis to Greenville in the state of Mississippi.

---

154. A beautiful harmonic progression of human and supernatural virtues.
155. Written by Pierluigi.

There Mr. Collins will be waiting to pick us up, the same Mr. Collins who was in Magenta for about two months, getting the cellulose plant opened. So once again I'm among very hospitable friends. This morning in Chicago, the director of International Minerals and Chemicals[156] received me most courteously.

Today your prayers will keep me going another 1,500 km.

Tomorrow, toward evening, we have just a short flight of 300 km. Wednesday morning, another 300-km flight, and then a long one—all night—to New York.

My work is going very well. No cold, no headaches, even though sometimes the temperature jumps from 8 degrees to 33 degrees [Celsius] in one day.

All my flights lately have been just short ones. Each one is a little step bringing me closer to New York, and from there, to you. Finally I'll be able to embrace you all, kiss you, talk to you, *stay* with you, enjoy your company, your sleeping, your irreplaceable affection.

Just now, on the plane, I re-read your four last letters. Thank you with all my heart. Tell Gigetto that Papa is already enjoying the handsome jacket that Mamma chose for him. I too want to compliment him! When I come back, he really deserves to go to church with me on Sunday!

On the plane, there are two Sisters seated next to us who are praying the Rosary! The best company.

Now there are only five days separating us: on Sunday I should be arriving at Malpensa!

And you, little wife, so good, so wise and strong, keep loving me like this. You know how much I love you. You couldn't have helped me more or given me more affectionate company during my long absence than you have done with your loving letters.

---

156. A firm producing phosphorous and related chemicals.

Tell Pierluigi and Mariolina that Papa sends Mamma and them many, many, many big kisses from up in the sky, and I will see them Sunday.

I embrace you with all my love and many, many affectionate good wishes..

Your

Pietro

Say hello to Mamma, Zita, Cecco, and Savina for me.

7:20—We just touched down safely in Memphis.

JUNE 9, 1959
TUESDAY

My dearest Pietro,

I had been hoping to receive the telegram saying, "I will arrive Thursday the eleventh," but instead, you won't be coming until Tuesday.[157] Always *fiat!* Your Mamma told me yesterday that I shouldn't let you go, that I should forbid it. "It would be wasted breath," I told her. "It's part of his job." But I said to myself, "Enough, SAFFA, leave him alone for a while—he's already done enough!" And then today I received your letter of June 4, in which you tell me you won't be home till the fourteenth.

---

157. Pietro actually arrived Wednesday, June 17. Meanwhile, Gianna's health had suffered a complication that forced her to go to the hospital on June 15. This is most likely the reason why her letters to her husband ceased a few days before his arrival. Here is how Gianna related the incident to her friend, Mariuccia Parmigiani: "A month ago, on June 15, I had to be admitted to emergency for poisoning. I was experiencing very strong contractions, continual spasms, fever and vomiting. I ran the risk of losing my child. I was pretty frightened and obeyed Nando and let myself be brought to Monza at midnight. Waiting for me at the hospital was the obstetrician we know well. With oxygen, soothing and injections the whole thing passed and I was able, after two days, to be at the airport to meet Pietro who was returning from America, oblivious to everything" (letter of July 18, 1959 to her friend, Mariuccia Parmigiani).

Poor Pedrin, I'm sorry about the heat and temperature changes; they certainly can't be good for you.

Flavio[158] was waiting because he wanted you to be his sponsor. I'm thinking of giving him a watch as a gift—I'll go to see Mr. Pozzi.

We're all fine. Gigetto is all better after Saturday's indisposition. He's very thirsty all the time, but it's very hot (higher than 30° C sometimes); it feels like the sultry days of July.

I'm enclosing a newspaper clipping about Laminate Plastics from today's *Corriere della Sera.*

The Church of Ponte Nuovo[159] is refurbished externally, all stripes, and is quite nice.

Bishop Pignedoli[160] will arrive Sunday morning at 7:45 for the first Communion Mass at 8:00. At the end of Mass the sponsors for Confirmation will come forward. There will be a procession at 5:00, just like every year.

My Pietro, do you remember the feast of Ponte Nuovo in 1955? It was the first time I went to your house—how much we already loved each other! It's because our love is so great that this separation is such a great sacrifice.

May the Lord accompany you on the flights you still have to take.

Not a day passes when your treasures don't ask about you. Mamma always remembers you and greets you with great, great affection; she is really well and never tired.

---

158. Flavio was Pietro's nephew. It seems that he was to receive the sacrament of Confirmation.

159. The church is Our Lady of Good Counsel.

160. Sergio Pignedoli (1910–1980), a future cardinal, was at that time auxiliary bishop of Milan.

I kiss you with much, much love, waiting to embrace you again and press you hard, hard to my heart.

Your most affectionate

Gianna

MEMPHIS, JUNE 9, 1959
TUESDAY, 7:30 PM

Dearest Gianna,

I arrived here in Memphis at 5:15 after an hour-long flight from Crossett. I'll be staying here just for tonight. Tomorrow morning at 6:30 another hour's flight to Florence (Alabama); we'll visit a big phosphorus plant, and in the evening I'll be back in New York.

Most likely, since it's not possible to make an appointment with the vice president of American Cyanamid before Monday the sixteenth, I will have to leave for Italy on Tuesday instead of Saturday. How long these last days seem to me!

Since yesterday I was certain we would leave Saturday the fourteenth, this delay seems so long to me. Sigh! But at least we can count the days now.

I am in the southern states: huge cotton plantations, enormous forests; more black people than white; prohibition of alcohol, beer, and wine. I have to be satisfied with soda. I would never have imagined that so many poor black families live in such small, broken-down wooden houses, such little houses that really trouble me to see.[161]

Tonight I'll eat early and go right to bed. It's very hot and tomorrow morning I have to get up early.[162]

---

161. From these particulars we can see Pietro's sensitivity.

162. This illustrates another characteristic of Mr. Molla's: his discipline at work and in his life in general, in order to be able to meet his family's needs and the demands of his job.

I'm anxious to get back to New York to read and kiss the dear letters I'm sure to find there from you.

And you, dearest little wife, take good care of yourself! I'm sorry that my absence is the cause of delaying the trip of our treasures to Courmayeur.

With all my love, I kiss you and our treasures.

Your most affectionate

Pietro

Remember me to Mamma and say hello to her for me.

Say hello to Zita and Cecco and Liberata for me.

Greetings to Savina.

ATLANTA (GEORGIA), JUNE 10, 1959
11:00 PM
AT THE AIRPORT

Dearest Gianna,

I'm waiting here at the gate to re-board my flight to New York. This is the city of the author of *Uncle Tom's Cabin*.[163] This morning I flew from Memphis, Mississippi,[164] to Florence, Alabama. Till 4:00 PM I was visiting a huge phosphorous plant to gather technical information for our plant in Spoleto, and from 6:00 to 8:00 I was flying again from Florence to Atlanta, Georgia. All the flights went fine.

---

163. Harriet Beecher Stowe (1811–1896) was the daughter of a Congregationalist minister and was a fervent protagonist of the anti-slavery movement. (Ed. note: In fact, it seems HBS never was in Georgia. She is from Litchfield, CT, and lived in Ohio and Florida.)

164. This is a small town in Mississippi about sixteen miles from the airport in Memphis, TN.

I ate onboard. Why is it that at home I can't digest even a cappuccino in the morning, while here I can digest five or six of them, or even more, every day? I'm also doing the orange juice cure. My stomach is just fine.

Unfortunately, our appointments for tomorrow and Friday with the vice presidents of American Cyanamid and Diamond Gardner were switched to Monday, and I can't get out of them. So I've had to delay leaving from Saturday till Tuesday afternoon. As I'll let you know by telegraph, I will arrive at Malpensa Wednesday afternoon at 2:20 or 2:30 on Lufthansa Airlines (a German airline) since there are no seats available on TWA or Alitalia.

If you only knew *how much*[165] I want to get back, to embrace you all again and to stay with you and our treasures!

The Lord has helped me, thanks to your prayers!

My health, my flights, my work could not have gone better. With all the changes, even daily, in temperature and humidity, which I already wrote you about and which are still going on, I can't understand how I haven't had even the slightest cold, not even a slight sore throat!

Last night I was in Memphis, in the state of Mississippi. I was sure that at least there, there couldn't possibly be any Italians. Instead, restaurants, shops, offices with Italian last names. I wanted to eat—I found some good spaghetti for the first time in the U.S.A.— at a restaurant named *BERETTA*![166]

The owners are from Genoa!

---

165. Underlined seven times.

166. Pietro notes the similarity between the restaurant's and Gianna's maiden name.

Already looking forward to the great joy of seeing you all again, of embracing and kissing you all, I kiss you and our marvelous treasures with all my love.

Arrivederci! Little wife *d'oro*!

Your

Pietro

Greet Mamma, Zita, and Cecco for me.

Also greet Savina for me.

Tuesday evening I stayed at the Rose Inn in Crossett, Arkansas.

NEW YORK, JUNE 11, 1959
THURSDAY, 11:00 PM

My most beloved Gianna,

When I got back here in New York, I found the gift of your five loving letters: from June 2, 3, 4, 6, and 8. These, together with those you had already written me during this long (too long) absence, I will always keep, together with the sweet letters you wrote while we were engaged and during my short trips out of the country. When I re-read them again in the future, I'll remember all the joy they brought me. I will have a loving diary[167] of you and of our marvelous treasures, and they will always remind me of the great, sweet love with which you have always surrounded me and of how you sweetly and wisely helped our treasures to remember their Papa who was so far away.

Every day, you've let me share in what you are doing so I feel you all very close to me.

---

167. Pietro almost seems to give a pre-publication name to this volume: "An Affectionate Diary" of the Molla family that would become a model of joy and gratitude for family life in general.

Unfortunately, your precious letter of the eighth finds me still in New York. I will leave on Tuesday at 4:00 and after a non-stop flight will arrive in Frankfurt at 11:00, and a few minutes later, another flight will bring me to you.

The wings of your dear prayers will sustain me on this flight, too.

"Papa, come back, now, soon!"

I'm so happy that they never get hurt even though they are always growing livelier.

I'm sorry to miss the Confirmation at Ponte Nuovo.[168] It just wasn't possible.

Last night's flight couldn't have been better: I fell asleep about ten minutes after takeoff and woke up over the skyscrapers in New York.

Here it's still over 30° C. But I'm making it fine.

As soon as I get back, we'll take the kids to Courmayeur.

When I read "Gigetto had a high fever on Saturday," I held my breath, but I was immediately reassured by the ending. That was due to his little mamma's wisdom.

Now, my sweetest little wife, I too am going nighty-night.

I'm really sleepy tonight.

Many, many big kisses again and a big and most affectionate hug to you and our treasures, and a true *arrivederci* in five days!

Your

Pietro

Say hello to Mamma, Zita, Cecco, and also Liberata for me. Greet Savina for me.

---

168. See Gianna's letter of June 9, 1959.

NEW YORK, FRIDAY, JUNE 12, 1959
11:00 PM

My most beloved Gianna,

Tonight as I was having supper at my hotel, the pianist Zimoli (a native of Italy) started playing (in his usual quiet way) "Come prima, più di prima . . . t'amero!" ["I love you as I did once, and more than ever!"][169]

My thoughts and my heart sped to you. The piano's music was the music of my heart, and the words the piano did not speak came spontaneously to my lips, and I meant them with all my heart.

Yes, dearest little wife, when I return, I'll love you just as before, more than before because I had to be so far from you right when I wanted to have you with me more than ever, and because during this long time away from you, I was accompanied at every moment by the fullness of your sweetest love, which I felt ever present to me—in your dear letters which I received each day, in your prayers, and in my absolute and joyous assurance in having our children cared for in an incomparable way by their amazing little mother![170]

I can never thank you enough!

Just about one hundred more hours till I see you again and we can finally stay together.

With all my love, I kiss you and our marvelous treasures.

Your most affectionate

Pietro

Greet Mamma, Cecco, Zita for me.

---

169. The song (composed by Vincenzo Di Paola and Sandro Taccani, words by Mario Panzeri) was first sung by Tony Dallara and immediately became popular all over Italy and abroad.

170. The song's lyrics are elevated and ennobled by the love between Gianna and Pietro and their ability to be guided by faith, both in the suffering of being apart and in the joy of coming together again.

JUNE 16, 1959
TUESDAY
ON THE FLIGHT FROM
NEW YORK TO FRANKFURT/MILAN[171]

My dearest Gianna,

Here's my diary today:

8:30 AM in New York: I received Jesus at the Blessed Sacrament altar; I served a Mass at the altar of Saint Thérèse of the Child Jesus; I recited the Holy Rosary kneeling before the altar of the Immaculata.[172] All my prayers were for you and for our treasures. I gave thanks for all the blessings of these past weeks and I also prayed for a safe return to you.

Yesterday, almost like a final satisfaction at the end of this long technical mission, I had the pleasure of hearing the very president of Diamond Gardner, Mr. Fairburn, declare that "the best engineers in the world for match machines are Italians."

At 4:00 PM, I was onboard the Lufthansa plane, ready for the flight.

At 4:15 PM, a perfect take-off.

At 6:00 PM, I left behind the last sight of land in Canada.

At 6:15 PM, the flight attendant showed us how to help others in case of a crash (really a water landing). I gripped the armrest.

At 7:00 PM, we were served dinner.

From 8:00 to 10:00 I admired a very long-lasting sunset, one of the most beautiful I've ever seen in flight.

---

171. This letter, in an envelope, was personally handed to Gianna by Pietro. On the envelope are written these words: "On the plane from New York (Tuesday, June 16, 6:00 AM) to Milan (Wednesday, June 17, 2:15 PM). To my dearest Gianna." This shows the attention and importance Pietro and Gianna gave to their correspondence.

172. Once again we note Pietro's fidelity to the sacraments and devotions as soon as his work permitted.

From 11:00 to 11:30 (from 4:00 to 4:30 Wednesday morning Italian time): We were halfway across the ocean. I said the Rosary and thought of you. The air was calm and the flight was perfect.

At 2:50 New York time (7:50 Italian time): we saw the last glimpse of the Island. The plane was flying at 500 km an hour. We will arrive in Frankfurt at 9:55: exactly twelve hours and forty minutes.

Every now and then you can hear a baby crying. It reminds me of our treasures.

Last night over the Atlantic, at 10:00 PM the horizon was still red from the sunset, and at midnight dawn was already breaking.

At 3:50 we flew over London, and at 4:30 over Brussels. The sun is shining.

At 10:00 we landed in Frankfurt.

11:45, we took off for Monaco.

12:30, we landed in Monaco.

At 1:00 PM, we were finally on the last flight of the trip.

At 1:50 we are flying above the snows of the Saint Gotthard Pass.

Imagine, Gianna, what I am feeling after fifty-three days of being separated from you, to be able to embrace you again, kiss you and enjoy your smile, and your affectionate, loving, sweetest company within thirty minutes?

I can't find the words to express my joyful excitement. I can already feel your affectionate greeting and your kisses and those of our treasures.

We are flying at an altitude of 5,500 meters, and I'm racing toward you at 500 km an hour.

I embrace you and kiss you most lovingly along with our treasures.

Your most affectionate

Pietro

PART IV

"Your Watchful and Wise Presence Comforts and Quiets Me"

Letters of Maturity

PARIS, DECEMBER 14, 1959

My dearest Gianna,

It hasn't even been twenty-four hours since the loving, tender goodbye of my beloved little wife and our beautiful treasures, and already I'm missing you all so much—you all seem so far away.[1]

Luckily, this is a very quick trip and tomorrow night I'll be able to hug you and kiss you all again, and best of all, stay with you.

I had a good trip, although it was long and the temperature in our compartment kept changing dangerously from hot to cold and back again according to the tastes of the various passengers.[2]

I'm in a very nice hotel facing the Tuileries Gardens and close to the Opera. The weather is good, not too cold, and no rain, snow, or fog.

Last night by 10:00 PM I had already left my suitcases at the hotel. I went out for a short walk to the square by the Opera, where they were having a production of Bizet's *Carmen*. I browsed a bit in the shops of Paris—at least, some of the high fashion stores.

If you had been here, we certainly would have bought an evening gown.[3]

---

1. As can be seen from the context, Pietro had left on a brief trip to France. Thus, after six months, he resumed his habit of writing to his wife.

2. Pietro was taking the train again in deference to Gianna's fear of air travel.

3. Gianna loved to go out every now and then in the evenings, especially to attend classical music concerts at the Milan Conservatory.

If only it weren't so difficult for us men to understand feminine fashions!

I was picturing my sweetest little wife, with all her marvelous beauty, in a splendid evening dress! At the same time I thought I should take her, at least a little more often, to concerts and the opera.

I had a restful night. My work begins within an hour, and I hope it will turn out well. It's important to me because it has to do with SAFFA's patent in my name.[4]

And now, wishing and hoping I can return to Paris soon with you, I embrace you, Pierluigi, Mariolina, and Lauretta, very affectionately, and I kiss you with the most affectionate kisses.

Your

Pietro

Say hello to Mamma for me.
Greet Zita, Cecco, and Savina for me.

BERNE, FEBRUARY 26, 1960[5]

Most affectionate kisses to you and our treasures,

Pietro

Greetings to Savina.

---

4. SAFFA had patented match-producing machinery and other products both in Italy and abroad. Mr. Molla himself had invented the machine of which he speaks in this letter.

5. Here follows a series of postcards, testifying to the fact that, even on very short trips, Pietro was thinking of Gianna and the children.

MARTIGNY, MARCH 14, 1960[6]

Dearest Gianna,

After a very good night at Montreux, in a pleasant hotel on Lake Geneva, we had a nice sunny day at Martigny, in the part opposite the Gran San Bernardo.

I am thinking of you and our treasures with great affection.

I can almost hear Gigetto's prayers.

Big kisses to you, Pierluigi, Mariolina, and Lauretta.

Pietro

Greetings to Savina.

NAPLES, APRIL 3, 1960[7]
HOTEL ROYAL

Here in the same hotel we stayed at during our honeymoon, I am remembering you and I kiss you with all my love, and I kiss our marvelous treasures.

Pietro

LYONS, APRIL 7, 1960[8]

Most loving greetings and big kisses to you and the children.

Pietro

---

6. Postcard.
7. Postcard.
8. Postcard.

MAGENTA, JUNE 24, 1960[9]

ST. JOHN

With infinite, most affectionate good wishes, I kiss you together with our three marvelous treasures.

Your

Pietro

JUNE 27, 1960

MONDAY EVENING

My dearest Pietro,

We've arrived and are all settled into our "cute"[10] little house, as Mariolina called it. The weather is beautiful, so the children stay outside in the meadow all day long.

Lauretta[11] is already doing better: she has some color and is eating well. She didn't take a nap again today, so she was in bed this evening by 8:00; she's sharing a room with Mariolina, who is happy to have her little sister to keep her company. Gigetto, on the other hand, only just went to bed, and so everything is quiet. Dear Pietro, how beautiful it is to be able to stay with them day and night, to watch and enjoy them all of the time. I can imagine how disappointed you must be when you come home in the evening and they're already in bed. It doesn't seem real to them to have their Mamma all to themselves all of the time. Gigetto—maybe because

---

9. A note for Gianna's name day: Pietro was thinking of his wife and sent her a gift.

10. In the preceding years the Molla couple had rented a house from Mrs. Valle. In 1960, instead, they rented a new house from the Cortellis family of Courmayeur.

11. Laura was born July 15, 1959 and was now eleven months old.

he's going to preschool—does nothing but call to me, and he would like nothing better than to have me all to himself.[12]

They're really three treasures. What a pity I don't have my fourth big treasure, my most beloved and most affectionate Pedrin. I think of you many, many times and I'm close to you in my heart, with my prayers.[13] Don't get too tired, do you understand? Go to bed early—I go to bed by 10:00, if not earlier. Last night we were all asleep by 9:30.

Thank you for your phone calls; Pierluigi insists on staying up until you call, because, he says, "I must talk to my Papa."

Here is a list for you when you come: apples, oranges, bananas, 2 kg of meat (the kind I usually get in Mesero), a pillow for Gigetto, because the ones here are too high for him, old records in the red bag for Mariolina—33 rpm records, your overcoat, a feather pillow for you, and a high chair.

It might be good if you could drive the Fiat 600, if it's there, and come with Mr. Crotti in two cars, so that I can keep one here to take the children out.

That's all for now. Don't worry about us because we're doing fine. Gianfranco[14] is looking out for Gigetto like a guardian angel. Greetings to Mamma, to Adelaide from all of us. A big hug and a big, big kiss for you from your treasures and from your most affectionate

Gianna

---

12. There is a feeling of tension here between the demands of her work as a physician, attentive to her patients, and the desire of her son to have his mother all to himself.

13. This combination should always characterize the relationship of a Christian couple. In this way the marriage is simultaneously profoundly human and Christian, based on the love of Christ.

14. Gianfranco, Pietro's nephew, was twelve years older than Pierluigi.

JULY 4, 1960
MONDAY EVENING

My dearest Pietro,

Our treasures are asleep, peaceful and happy. Happy because of the magnificent little house their Papa found for their vacation. Pierluigi and Mariolina are two "big kids," sleeping by themselves. When they wake up in the morning, they talk and tell each other stories, happy in their little beds with the blue bedspreads. Pierluigi keeps his little glow-in-the-dark statue of Our Lady of Lourdes on his night table, and woe to his sisters if they dare to touch it! They play in the garden all day, sometimes with little stones, sometimes with their constructions; later in the day I take them to Verrand, with Savina, up where it's safe.[15] Laura and the children[16] arrived today; Pierluigi, Mariolina, and Lauretta enthusiastically showed them every corner of the house, inside and out. You should have seen them, the little treasures; it's so true that beautiful sunshine and a happy atmosphere make even the children more serene; they enjoy it so much. It's all because of you, Papa. Your treasures and I thank you over and over again.

I think of you every moment, in your travels and your work, and I am very close to you with all my affection and love.[17]

---

15. After the somewhat anxious letters of 1959 when the saint was expecting their third child and her husband was far away, the summer of 1960 is striking for its serenity. She hints at a rich and harmonious family life in a union of love for God, her husband, their children, relatives, friends, and life itself. This is also the period of maturity, the fullness of human and spiritual life of the saint.

16. Laura Viola, wife of Ferdinando, was the sister-in-law of the saint. They will relive the good company of previous years.

17. It had been five years now since the day of the wedding. Far from being weakened, Gianna's love has become more mature and intense.

We'll be waiting for you on Saturday—come early in the evening, not late.

Big kisses from your dearest *popi* and many, many most affectionate ones from your

Gianna

JULY 1960[18]

My dearest Pietro,

Thank you for your most loving greetings. I return them with all my heart, along with many kisses from your little ones. When Lauretta wakes up in the morning, she calls, "Papa, Papa!" What a treasure! The poor thing still has a little bit of a cough. Last night, Gigetto sounded like he was starting to get whooping cough, and today he coughed twice more. Patience, let's hope medicine and fresh mountain air will help avoid a really bad case.

The weather is terrible today—it's cold and cloudy, but we can still go higher in the mountains, since we have the car.[19]

We'll be waiting for you excitedly on Saturday afternoon; come as early as you can.

I'll need some *wine* and the two *salamis* that are still there, and *oranges and apples*; I'll buy the meat. Nothing else at the moment.

Thank you for the two wonderful photos: imagine how nice they would be if they were in color. The money is more than enough.

---

18. The date is not specified, however, it is from July 1960. Because of the content it is inserted between those dated July 4 and 12. It could be of Thursday, July 7 or Friday, July 8.

19. See the letter of June 27. Pietro had brought the car so that Gianna could visit nearby places with the children.

Ciao, Pedrin *d'or,* take care of yourself, don't work too much, and *arrivederci* on Saturday. Big kisses from all of us and greetings to Mamma.

Your most affectionate

Gianna

JULY 12, 1960
TUESDAY

Dearest Pietro,

I'm sending you some suppositories for Gigetto. Give him one in the morning when he wakes up and one in the evening before he goes to bed.[20] When he takes a nap at 2:00 PM, give him a Guajakirsch suppository.

I went to the nursery school this morning to tell the Sisters that I'm getting vaccinations for all the children;[21] unfortunately, many children have the same type of cough that Gigetto has. It's a good thing our children are already in the mountains, since they can get better more quickly there. I'm fine; after sleeping for ten hours last night, my headache is gone. I'm here, but my thoughts are always with you, my dearest treasures.

Hopefully, I'll arrive late on Saturday with Zita;[22] her new boss, an engineer from the Alcha Company (I think that's spelled right) is arriving Saturday, perhaps with a new manager for the firm, but nothing is certain yet.

I have re-sent you an express that arrived this morning; I'll bring a registered letter that came from Belinzaghi Bank when I come.

---

20. Gianna writes from Magenta where she returned because of work commitments. Her husband stayed at Courmayeur with the children.

21. Note the professional commitment of the saint. She is worried about her son, but at the same time extends her care to the kindergarten children.

22. As at other times, Gianna was the guest of Zita and Cecco in Magenta.

Kiss the children for me and let me know how they are; warm greetings to everyone and a big hug for you,

Your

Gianna

For the aerosol bottle, buy an injectable bottle of strepto-chem-icitine; dilute it with the little vial that's attached to the bottle, plus a vial from the red box that is on the buffet, and give it to him twice a day. If there's any liquid left in the aerosol bottle, change it and rinse it with water before using it again.

Thank you, Pietro; I don't want him to get whooping cough. Kisses to everyone, especially Lauretta on Friday morning.[23] Don't let the cousins come over; have a party[24] at home with cake and candles. I embrace you and *arrivederci* on Saturday.

COURMAYEUR, JULY 13, 1960[25]

WEDNESDAY

On our way back from the Val Veny Chalet, where we spent some wonderful hours running around in the sunshine and ate some wonderful polenta, our marvelous babies wanted to stop at the shrine[26] so Pierluigi and Mariolina could each light a candle and say a Hail Mary, with their little hands folded, for their far-away Mamma.

We remember you with boundless love and we kiss you,

Pietro

---

23. Friday, July 15 was Laura's first birthday.

24. Gianna feared Pierluigi would pass on his cough to his cousins. She also wanted to avoid increasing the work for her husband.

25. Postcard.

26. The Sanctuary of Notre Dame at Guerison (Our Lady of Healing).

COURMAYEUR, SUMMER 1960[27]

Dearest Pietro[28]

I expect you Saturday morning at 10:30 in Morgex, where I am going to pick up meat.

Arrivederci and have a good trip.

Big kisses from all of us

Gianna

LONDON, AUGUST 3, 1960[29]

Dearest Gianna,

You can imagine my joy on feeling you so close at least with your voice on the phone![30]

The trip was wonderful and interesting! Only an hour and forty minutes!

The hotel is great and the weather isn't cold.

Thinking of you with great love, I kiss you and our marvelous treasures!

Kisses to Grandma[31] and Gianfranco.

A big hug from

Your Pietro

---

27. Notecard.

28. In a new inversion, Gianna returns to the mountains and Pietro to work.

29. Postcard.

30. Pietro had talked to his wife and children by phone, but still felt the need to write.

31. Pietro's mother.

LONDON, AUGUST 4, 1960

My most beloved Gianna,

This morning, when I heard your sweet voice and Gigetto's precious little voice right here in my room, it seemed like there was no distance between us. For just a few moments, I no longer felt homesick.

The 800-km Caravalle flight that will bring me back to you in just an hour and 40 minutes makes the distance between us much easier to bear.

During this time I keep thinking of the marvelous, unforgettable days in Naples and Capri when we fully relived our honeymoon; and it comforts me to think of the smiles and joyous happiness of our babies and how secure I feel since you are with them.

I'm looking forward to the joy of being back here in London with you: everything will be more beautiful to me then.[32]

With the most affectionate remembrance, I embrace and kiss you with all my love. Kiss our treasures for me.

Your

Pietro

Remember me to Mamma and say hello to Gianfranco for me.

LUCERNE, SEPTEMBER 16, 1960[33]

A most affectionate remembrance and many, many big kisses to you and our treasures

Pietro

---

32. Pietro promised to bring Gianna on a trip to London. This took place in December of that same year.

33. Another series of postcards and notes, revealing his constant closeness to his family.

MAGENTA, SEPTEMBER 24, 1960[34]

To my dearest Gianna,[35]

On our fifth very happy anniversary, together with our marvelous treasures, and with all my love, your

Pietro

ROME, OCTOBER 5, 1960[36]

I remember you with all my love, and I kiss you and our treasures.

Pietro

HEIDENHEIM, NOVEMBER 8, 1960[37]

Thinking of you with all my love, I kiss you and our ineffable treasures.

Pietro

VIENNA, NOVEMBER 25, 1960[38]

With all my love,

Pietro

---

34. Note.
35. Written on the envelope.
36. Postcard.
37. Postcard.
38. Postcard.

L'AIA, JANUARY 25, 1961
WEDNESDAY, 11:30 PM

My most beloved Gianna,

I'm at the Hotel Des Indes, on the second floor, in a room just like the one we had in December for those wonderful nights of kisses and ineffable caresses and sweetest love.

You are truly my full and perfect joy, most beloved and my most loving little wife![39]

I think of you, at this moment sleeping so sweetly next to our marvelous treasures: such a diligent, caring, and untiring little mother.

And I thank the Lord once more for the incomparable gift he gave me and for the ineffable joys he grants to us and to our family.

Most lovingly, I kiss our children and I kiss and embrace you just as you kiss me and most sweetly press me to your heart.

Your

Pietro

COURMAYEUR, FEBRUARY 14, 1961

Dearest Papa,

Thank you for your card, your thoughts, and all your loving words. We are sorry you're not here with us to enjoy the warm sun and beautiful snow in Courmayeur! We are having so much fun.

---

39. This letter is a hymn to the fullness of joy of two spouses whose love is founded on Christ. This does not exclude the sacrifices and fatigue of the numerous tasks of daily life.

Thank you, Papa, for having brought us up here! Many big kisses from all of us, Mamma too, and *arrivederci* on Saturday!

Your three treasures

FROM COURMAYEUR

FEBRUARY 14, 1961

TUESDAY EVENING

My dearest Pietro,

Our three dearest treasures are asleep, after having walked, played, and skied all day—they were tired tonight. Afterward, Pierluigi didn't want to eat and just drank a little tea.

Tomorrow, I'll keep them in the yard so they won't get so tired.

I hope the weather stays as nice as it has been: it's calm and the sun is warmer than in July, and the mountains look bright and clean, even more beautiful than in the summer.[40]

All the women are sunbathing at Checrouit, while the children fly down the hills on their skis and sleds like perpetual motion machines.

Lauretta wouldn't leave me again today; she's still getting used to the new surroundings, to the snow and the sun. Mariolina, on the other hand, gracefully plows through the snow in her boots.

As I told you on the phone, this year Pierluigi is having a ball with his sled and isn't a bit afraid of going down the hill by himself; he trudges back up, pulling his sled, and after about an hour of doing this, he sits down and says, "I've played a lot today!"

Too bad it's [the sledding hill] twenty minutes away; it would be so much easier if it were right outside the house.

---

40. These brief descriptions give a sense of Gianna's passion for the mountains, and her love for life.

My Pietro, how often I think of you and how I wish you were here with us! Thank you for everything, Pedrin *d'or*: for your great love, your care, for all your goodness. Your treasures kiss you with much love, and together with them your most affectionate

Gianna

PERUGIA, APRIL 4, 1961[41]

A most loving remembrance and many big kisses to you and our treasures

Pietro

PARIS, MAY 8, 1961[42]

Full of joy as I remember the very quick visit with you, and with even more joy as I look forward to the coming visit, which will be much calmer, I send you and our treasures the most affectionate greetings and many, many big kisses.

Pietro

BOURNEMOUTH, MAY 15, 1961[43]

This seaside city—50 km southwest of London—reminds me of the unforgettable trip with you last year to Great Yarmouth on the North Sea.

Many, many loving kisses to you and our treasures.

Pietro

---

41. Postcard. SAFFA had a plant in Perugia.
42. Postcard.
43. Postcard.

LONDON, MAY 15, 1961
MONDAY, 11:30 PM

Dearest Gianna,

I just got back from a splendid concert at the Royal Festival Hall, at my hotel facing the Savoy.

At . . . our Savoy. Just a few moments ago we got something to drink.

What memories of our unforgettable time here! Everything speaks to me of you!

How different the trips are when I don't have your loving company!

How it saddened me and continues to weigh on me, your quiet crying on Sunday during breakfast! Really, the rhythm of my work[44] and one trip after another is too much. Something has to change.

Tomorrow I will be in Sheffield. I'll be back in London Wednesday evening.

Thursday morning I have another technical meeting that wasn't planned when I left Milan.

I'll be flying back to Milan in the afternoon.

I am always thinking of you with immense affection — adorable, affectionate, and caring little wife, wise mamma of our treasures; I think about our babies. And with this thought I kiss and embrace you with all my love.

I send you many, many big London kisses again!

Pietro

---

44. Gianna had already raised this question in early 1955 when she realized how heavy Pietro's work schedule was (see her letter of March 25, 1955). On more than one occasion Pietro had promised to reduce his work hours, but evidently he found this difficult (see also his last letter to his wife on December 13, 1961). This also shows that balance in family life is never definitively in place, but must be sought constantly, day by day. This is the only way to establish harmony, guaranteeing serenity for both parents and children.

*Pietro with Pierluigi and Mariolina on the steps of the Sanctuary of
the Madonna of Guérison, Val Veny, summer 1958.*

Gianna, Pietro, Pierluigi, Mariolina, and Laura, Courmayeur, summer 1960.

COLOGNE, MAY 26, 1961
FRIDAY, 11:30 PM

Dearest Gianna,

I still seem to hear your sweet voice as I did last night, when you were so close to me.

If you only knew how painful it is to me to be continually far from you and our treasures, even if it's limited to just a few days. How much better it would be if, at least when I'm home, I could be back among our children no later than 7:00 or 7:30![45]

This is my second night in Cologne, and it brings me joy to remember our passing through here in October '55, at the end of our honeymoon. Since that time, how many joys we've had, and how much I have to thank Heaven for you and our ineffable treasures!

I remember you, I embrace you and kiss you with all my love.

Your

Pietro

Kiss our treasures for me.

HAMBURG, JUNE 1, 1961[46]
MIDNIGHT

I'm just getting back to the hotel. If you only knew how much I hated to miss Lauretta's party.

With all my love, I kiss and embrace you and our treasures who are always seeing me leaving,

Pietro

---

45. See preceding footnote.

46. Postcard. The first of June was the feast of Saint Laura and thus the name day of the couple's third child.

STUTTGART, JULY 3, 1961[47]

So glad to hear your own dear voice telling me everything's fine. I send you and our marvelous children many, many big kisses and a most affectionate hug.

Pietro

JULY 5, 1961
WEDNESDAY EVENING

My dearest Pietro,

I'm glad your trip[48] went well, and it was good to hear from you, but you seemed very tired. You really need a few weeks of complete relaxation. How can you go on like this?

It's so beautiful to spend the entire day with our treasures. They are calmer these days, but I have to watch them and keep them from quarreling.

We walked down to Pré-Saint-Didier to get the coupons,[49] but the Cortellis[50] had not notified the office, so we couldn't get any. I called Mrs. Cortelli and she assured me that her husband would take care of it when he goes to the municipality tomorrow. If you pass by Pré-Saint-Didier on Saturday and feel like stopping in the municipality, you can pick them up yourself.

You should see how Lauretta is walking without any help at all. Today, I bought all three of them a pair of tennis shoes because they needed them.

---

47. Postcard.

48. Pietro had been in Stuttgart, Germany for a few days.

49. These were the coupons for gasoline. The government was giving them out in these years to encourage tourism.

50. The Cortellis were the owners of the house of Verrand (Courmayeur) that the saint and her husband had rented for the 1960–1961 season.

Today was a beautiful day, and there is a serene, star-filled sky this evening.

Here is a list of what we need:

1. an iron, the light one we always use;
2. the orange juicer;
3. the big oval skillet (shallow) for steaks—the stainless steel one;
4. salad servers;
5. ask Adelaide for one skein of white yarn to finish the baby's sweater;
6. one kitchen calendar (to keep track of how much milk we buy every day);
7. 3 kg. oranges, 3 kg. apples, 1 kg. bananas from the fruit vendor in Boffalora.[51]

Please put everything in a suitcase, since I'll need one for going home.[52]

Ciao, Pedrin, I'm sorry if the list is a little long; I hope it doesn't take up too much of your time.

We'll be waiting for you—you can imagine how excitedly.

Warm greetings to Mamma, Adelaide, and the big nephews.

A big kiss from your *popi* who are sound asleep; thank you for your ever most affectionate greetings from Stuttgart.

A big hug from your

Gianna[53]

---

51. Boffalora Sopra Ticino is just a few km from Ponte Nuovo.

52. In fact, in the following days, Gianna had to return to Magenta most likely for professional duties while Pietro remained in Courmayeur.

53. This is the last letter from Gianna to her husband. Subsequently, the times they were apart became less frequent. In addition, they now resorted to the phone for communication.

COURMAYEUR, JULY 6, 1961

Dear Papa,[54]

Now we, your children, are sending you many big kisses and many thanks for the beautiful house that you have given us.

Gigi, Popa,[55] Lauretta, and Mamma

MAGENTA, SUMMER 1961

MONDAY EVENING, 11:30 PM

My dearest Gianna,

I just got back from the council meeting for the Magenta hospital.[56]

I think of you all sleeping peacefully, and while I enjoy the marvelous smiles of Gigetto on his little bicycle and of Lauretta in the home movie we made in the field behind our garden in Ponte Nuovo, how I hope that their coughs will get better instead of worse. Your watchful and wise presence comforts me and quiets me, as do your prompt remedies. What a sacrifice it is that I have to be so far from you and can't help you take care of our children.

And you, Gianna, rest a bit more. May my many affectionate thoughts be your companions.

Many, many big kisses to you, Pierluigi, Mariolina, and Lauretta

From your Pietro

Affectionate greetings and kisses from Mamma.

Greetings to Gianfranco and Savina.

---

54. A postcard written by Gianna to Pietro in the name of the children.

55. Mariolina was affectionately called Popa.

56. Pietro was appointed a member of the administrative council of the Giuseppe Fornaroli Hospital of Magenta in December 1956 and held that position until May 1961. At the time, the council was made up of "Cornerstone Friends" of the new hospital.

I'm enclosing 30,000 lire; it's better to have a little extra. I'll bring more Saturday.

MAGENTA, SEPTEMBER 24, 1961[57]

With all my infinite love, I rejoice with you on our very happy anniversary and also in the ineffable thought of the little angel[58] growing within you.

Together with our marvelous treasures, I pray and offer most loving petitions for your health, and I kiss you with infinite tenderness,

Pietro

SPOLETO, OCTOBER 6, 1961[59]

Remembering that wonderful trip to Spoleto, I kiss you affectionately and send you warm wishes.

Pietro

PARIS, OCTOBER 17, 1961[60]

Loving thoughts and big kisses to you and our treasures.

Pietro

LONDON, NOVEMBER 22, 1961

Most beloved Gianna,

This evening I heard our children's voices on the phone, seemingly so close and so loving, and in their voices I also heard yours.

---

57. Note for their sixth wedding anniversary.
58. Gianna was expecting Gianna Emanuela.
59. Postcard.
60. Postcard.

How much I regret having to leave you so often and being a cause of worry and anxiety to you.

I am reminded of the unforgettable days we spent together in London, and from the same city I send you my most loving thoughts and wishes.

Take good, good care of yourself, O my dearest little wife.

Kiss our children for me, and here is a big, strong hug with many big kisses for you.

Your Pietro

LONDON, DECEMBER 13, 1961
WEDNESDAY, 11:45 PM LONDON TIME
12:45 AM ITALIAN TIME

My most beloved Gianna,

What a joy it was this evening to hear you and our treasures so close to me, almost as if you were in London. Your sweet and affectionate voices seemed to bring you so near that you all seemed to be right here with me. And you say you're doing "all right."

How anxious your suffering and your own nearly daily anxiety make me, especially when I'm so far away!

I know you are a woman of strength in suffering and that you know well how to hide your worries. I also know that you don't want me to worry about you, but I hardly ever manage not to worry. Be calm, dearest Gianna; you will see that your fourth pregnancy will be blessed and happy like the previous ones![61]

---

61. Anxiety and trust in Providence alternate in the husband and wife who are trying to encourage each other while expecting their fourth child. It would appear that the Lord does not hear their prayers, but who can comprehend God's plans? Job says at the end of his book: "I know that you can do all things, and that no

At this time our precious treasures must be sleeping soundly, after having prayed for their papa who is far away, and how I hope you too are sleeping soundly and peacefully!

Please forgive me if, despite my promises, I haven't managed to limit my working hours better.

I remember our unforgettable trip to London, and I embrace you and kiss you with all my love.

Kiss our treasures for me.

Your Pietro

---

purpose of yours can be thwarted. 'Who is this that hides counsel without knowledge?' . . . I had heard of you by the hearing of the ear, but now my eye sees you" (Job 42:2ff., NRSV). In his presence-absence, God was close to Gianna and Pietro, just as he is present to us through these authentic witnesses to Christian family life.

Chronology

Important Dates in Gianna Beretta's Life

October 4, 1922 Gianna is born in Magenta (near Milan), to Alberto Beretta and Maria de Micheli, at the country home of her paternal grandparents. She is the tenth of thirteen children. Both parents are Franciscan tertiaries.

October 11, 1922 At Saint Martin's Basilica in Magenta, the child is baptized and given the name Gianna Francesca.

October 1922–1924 Gianna lives in Milan at 10 Risorgimento Square. Her parents attend the Capuchin church on Viale Piave.

1925 Her family moves to Bergamo in Borgo Canale.

April 4, 1928 At the age of five and a half, Gianna receives her first Communion in Santa Grata Parish.

1928 Gianna begins school. She attends first and second grade at the Scuola Elementare di Colle Aperto; third grade with the Sisters of Wisdom; fourth and fifth grade at the Canossian Institute on Via Sudorno.

June 9, 1930 Gianna is confirmed at the cathedral in Bergamo.

1933 She starts her first year of middle school at the Liceo Classico Statale Paolo Sarpi in Bergamo.

January 22, 1937 Gianna's older sister Amalia dies at twenty-seven.

1937 The Berettas move to Genoa Quinto al Mare, and Gianna attends her fifth year of middle/upper school at the Dorothean Institute.

March 16–18, 1938   She attends the Spiritual Exercises preached by Jesuit Father Michele Avedano at the Dorothean Institute.

1938–1939   At her parents' decision, Gianna takes a year off from school.

October 1939   Gianna begins her classical studies at the Dorothean Institute in Lido d'Albaro (Genoa).

October 1941   With her family, Gianna moves back to Bergamo, to the maternal grandparents' house in San Vigilio. Her mother, Maria, had already been suffering from heart trouble that was worsened by the bombings in Genoa.

November 1941   Gianna returns to Genoa to finish her studies.

April 29, 1942   Her mother dies at the age of fifty-four.

June 1942   Gianna receives her classical studies diploma.

July 1942   She rejoins her family in Bergamo.

September 10, 1942   Her father dies at the age of sixty.

October 1942   Gianna and her siblings return to Magenta, to the country home of their paternal grandparents. Gianna takes part in Catholic Action, the Saint Vincent de Paul Society, and parish work.

November 1942   Gianna enrolls in medical school at the University of Milan.

1945   She continues her university studies at Pavia.

November 30, 1949   She receives her diploma in medicine and surgery at Pavia.

June 20, 1950   Gianna is inscribed on the official roster of the Professional Medical Association of Milan.

July 1, 1950   Gianna opens a medical office in Mesero (Milan).

July 7, 1952   She obtains a license as a pediatric specialist from the University of Milan.

April 11, 1955   Engaged to Pietro Molla.

September 24, 1955   Gianna and Pietro are married at the Basilica of Saint Martin in Magenta. They move to Ponte Nuovo di Magenta, into the small house built for the director of the SAFFA plant.

November 19, 1956   Pierluigi is born.

December 11, 1957   Maria Zita (Mariolina) is born.

July 15, 1959   Laura is born.

April 20, 1962   Gianna is admitted to the maternity ward at Saint Gerard Hospital in Monza.

April 21, 1962   Gianna Emanuela is born.

April 28, 1962   Gianna dies at home in Ponte Nuovo.

April 30, 1962   Gianna's funeral takes place in Ponte Nuovo, and she is buried in Mesero, Pietro's birthplace.

February 12, 1964   Mariolina dies at age six.

1965   Gianna's remains, together with those of Mariolina, are transferred to the family chapel in Mesero's cemetery, where they remain to this day.

November 6, 1972   Cardinal Giovanni Colombo, the archbishop of Milan, promotes the beatification cause of the Servant of God Gianna Beretta Molla and asks that documents and information be gathered.

April 28, 1980   Cardinal Carlo Maria Martini, the new archbishop of Milan, signs the decree introducing the cause and begins the investigational process regarding the life and virtues of the Servant of God.

April 24, 1994   John Paul II proclaims her Blessed Gianna Beretta Molla.

May 16, 2004   John Paul II proclaims her Saint Gianna Beretta Molla.

Important Dates in Pietro Molla's Life

July 1, 1912   Pietro is born in Mesero, a little village near Magenta, west of Milan, to Luigi Molla and Maria Salmoiraghi, the fourth of eight children.

July 3, 1912   In the parish church at Mesero he is baptized and named Pietro Mario.

1918   Pietro begins elementary school. He attends the first four years at Mesero's elementary school, and has a private tutor for the fifth year.

April 8, 1919   Pietro is confirmed in the parish church in Mesero.

July 31, 1919   Pietro receives his first Communion in the parish church.

1923–1928   He attends Saint Joseph College (middle school-high school) in Monza.

1928–1931   Pietro attends the three years of classical studies at the Liceo Statale Bartolomeo Zucchi in Monza, where he earns his diploma.

During these years he continues to board at Saint Joseph College where he serves as prefect.

1931 He moves back with his family in Mesero. He begins his engineering studies at the Politecnico in Milan.

1933 Pietro joins the Italian Catholic Action Youth, with whom he will be associated until 1943. He offers to help the parish priest, teaching catechism to adults on Sunday afternoons.

November 7, 1936 Pietro receives his diploma in industrial and mechanical engineering from the Politec o.

December 1936 He passes the state   enabling him to practice as an engineer.

December 9, 1936 Pietro is hired by SAFFA (Società per Azioni Fabbriche Fiammiferi ed Affini, a company producing matches) as technical advisor to the plant director in Ponte Nuovo di Magenta.

1938 Pietro is named vice director of the plant.

Early 1940s He moves to Ponte Nuovo.

1950 Pietro becomes central director of the Ponte Nuovo plant and is put in charge of expansion, planning, and establishing new plants for SAFFA and its affiliates.

April 21, 1950 Pietro's younger sister, Teresina, dies at the age of twenty-three.

April 11, 1955 Engagement to Doctor Gianna Beretta.

September 24, 1955 Pietro and Gianna are married at Saint Martin's Basilica in Magenta. They move to the house built for the director of SAFFA's plants.

March 21, 1956 Pietro's father dies at the age of seventy-two.

November 19, 1956 Pierluigi is born.

December 1956 Pietro is elected a member of the administrative council for Giuseppe Fornaroli Hospital in Magenta. He retains this position until May 1961.

December 11, 1957 Maria Zita (Mariolina) is born.

July 15, 1959 Laura is born.

1961 Pietro becomes vice general director of SAFFA.

1961 Pietro is an associate founder and first president of Magenta's Rotary Club.

April 21, 1962 Gianna Emanuela is born.

April 28, 1962 Pietro's wife Gianna dies at age thirty-nine.

February 12, 1964 Mariolina dies at the age of six.

1966 Pietro is appointed general director of SAFFA, with specific responsibilities in the technical section.

1970 He joins the Lombard regional group of UCID *(Unione Cristiana Impreditori e Dirigenti: Union of Christian Businessmen and Directors)*, of which he became a very active member.

1972 He joins SAFFA's administrative council.

December 13, 1978 Pietro's mother dies at the age of ninety-two.

July 31, 1979 For age-related reasons, Pietro retires from his position as general director of SAFFA.

1980 He moves to Milan with his children.

1986 Pietro is president of Seatek—Advanced Marine Propulsion Technology.

1988 He retires from SAFFA's administrative council.

April 24, 1994 He attends the beatification of his wife, Gianna Beretta.

1998 Pietro ends his service as president of Seatek.

May 19, 1999 Together with his brother-in-law, Father Giuseppe Beretta, Pietro founds the Blessed Gianna Beretta Molla Foundation.

Autumn 1999 Pietro moves to Mesero with his daughter, Gianna Emanuela.

May 16, 2004 Pietro attends the solemn canonization of his wife.

September 24, 2005 In Saint Martin's Basilica in Magenta, Pietro attends a celebration in honor of his fiftieth wedding anniversary.

April 3, 2010 Pietro dies at home in Mesero.

April 6, 2010 Pietro's funeral takes place in Mesero. He is buried in the family chapel alongside his wife, daughter, parents, and sister.

BOOKS & MEDIA

The Daughters of St. Paul operate book and media centers at the following addresses. Visit, call, or write the one nearest you today, or find us at www.paulinestore.org.

CALIFORNIA

| 3908 Sepulveda Blvd, Culver City, CA 90230 | 310-397-8676 |
| 3250 Middlefield Road, Menlo Park, CA 94025 | 650-369-4230 |

FLORIDA

| 145 S.W. 107th Avenue, Miami, FL 33174 | 305-559-6715 |

HAWAII

| 1143 Bishop Street, Honolulu, HI 96813 | 808-521-2731 |

ILLINOIS

| 172 North Michigan Avenue, Chicago, IL 60601 | 312-346-4228 |

LOUISIANA

| 4403 Veterans Memorial Blvd, Metairie, LA 70006 | 504-887-7631 |

MASSACHUSETTS

| 885 Providence Hwy, Dedham, MA 02026 | 781-326-5385 |

MISSOURI

| 9804 Watson Road, St. Louis, MO 63126 | 314-965-3512 |

NEW YORK

| 115 E. 29th Street, New York City, NY 10016 | 212-754-1110 |

SOUTH CAROLINA

| 243 King Street, Charleston, SC 29401 | 843-577-0175 |

TEXAS

No book center; for parish exhibits or outreach evangelization, contact: 210-569-0500, or SanAntonio@paulinemedia.com, or P.O. Box 761416, San Antonio, TX 78245

VIRGINIA

| 1025 King Street, Alexandria, VA 22314 | 703-549-3806 |

CANADA

| 3022 Dufferin Street, Toronto, ON M6B 3T5 | 416-781-9131 |

¡También somos su fuente para libros,
videos y música en español!